Forbidden Fruit

Forbidden Fruit

Fruit
The Ethics
of Humanism

by

Paul Kurtz

91 90 89 88   4 3 2

Library of Congress Cataloging-in-Publication Data

Kurtz, Paul W., 1925-
    Forbidden fruit: the ethics of humanism/by Paul Kurtz.
        p.   cm.
    Includes bibliographies.
    ISBN 0-87975-454-0: $19.95   ISBN 0-87975-455-9 (pbk.): $11.95
    1. Humanistic ethics.   I. Title.
BJ1360.K79   1988
171'.2—dc19   87-37461
                                                                    CIP

Contents

Part III

Forbidden Fruit
The Ethics of Humanism

by
Paul Kurtz

Acknowledgment

I wish to thank the John Dewey Foundation for providing me with a Senior Fellowship, which enabled me to complete this book. This work is written in the general tenor of the philosophy of John Dewey— to whom I will be forever grateful.

Introduction:
Living
Outside
Eden

The Knowledge of Good and Evil

If God is dead, does anything go? If a person rejects belief in a divine creator, is everything permitted? Without faith and religion, would morality collapse?

In Feodor Dostoyevsky's novel *Crime and Punishment,* Raskolnikov robs and murders two elderly women, for he finds no moral structure to limit his passions. The rule of self-interest runs unbridled; the young believer is transformed into the nihilist. Without God, cries Dostoyevsky, life and the world have no meaning. Without a doctrine of divine retribution and salvation, Dostoyevsky can find no basis for moral obligation, no sense of duty or responsibility toward others. There are no moral values beyond subjective caprice or desire. Human existence becomes a mere flicker between two oblivions. Everything is permissible, and hedonistic pleasure and self-aggrandizement dominate us. There are no standards of good and evil, right and wrong, nor any moral purposes behind human reality.

This bleak picture is an untrustworthy appraisal of the human condition. On the contrary, if we affirm that God does not exist, perhaps only then can we begin to recognize fully that human beings are autonomous and that we are responsible for our own destinies and those of our fellow human beings. Perhaps only then can we summon the courage and wisdom to develop a rational ethics based on a realistic appraisal of nature and an awareness of the centrality of the common moral decencies. Perhaps only then will it be possible for us to create an authentic secular society and live by humanistic principles and values.

Theists deny the possibility of morality without God. According to the biblical myth, Adam and Eve fell from God's grace because they disobeyed him. God had allowed them the right to eat of every tree in the Garden of Eden but the tree of knowledge of good and evil, thereby forbidding any autonomous human quest for ethical knowledge. He said, "But of the fruit of the tree which is in the midst of the garden, . . . you shall not eat of it, neither shall you touch it, lest you die." (Gen. 3:3).[1] Eve saw that the tree had good fruit, that it was pleasant to the eye, and that it was a tree to be desired for the wisdom it conferred. And so she ate of the tree and persuaded Adam to do the same. This so provoked the wrath of God that he drove them out of the Garden and cursed them: Eve would henceforth suffer the pangs of childbirth and would be ruled by her husband. Adam would toil in sorrow to produce his bread by the sweat of his brow. Adam and Eve and their successors would die, and immortality would elude them. The moral appeared to be that God did not want humans to judge what was good and evil for themselves apart from divine commandment.

Yet countless numbers of enlightened men and women have abandoned the illusions of theistic religion, and have nonetheless led ethical lives. They have been inspired by noble ideals and moral values. Using their knowledge of good and evil, they have cultivated a deep appreciation for the good life, including a sense of community with other human beings, and they have been devoted to social service, benevolence, and justice. They have forsaken neither their plans and projects nor the will to live. Science and technology, philosophy and poetry, the arts of civilization and high culture have all been created by human ingenuity and endeavor. Generation after generation of unsung secular heroes have discovered that life is rich with opportunities and hence is meaningful. Although not religious, they have not given up concern for the good of others, nor have they denied moral values and principles in the living of their lives.

Yet today, as of old, a familiar litany is heard from the disciples of supernatural religion: Without belief in God all is lost; without fidelity to divinely inspired commandments, corruption and sin will overtake us.

The religious message is beguiling; belief in a transcendent God is *the* dominating myth of human history. The poets and prophets have fashioned out of human imagination a divine being who reflects their image of man and who was invented to fufill their deepest longings: God created the universe. All morality must emanate from him. There is a divine plan for us, they affirm, even though the transcendent God is clothed in mystery, and the veil can be penetrated only faintly by the metaphors and symbols used to depict him. Our ultimate moral duty is to accept God as the only source of morality.

Central to theism is the doctrine of salvation; that is, God will save man from sin and death and confer eternal happiness upon him. In order for a person to earn this reward, it is essential that there be faith in God. Some theologians believe that faith alone is sufficient for salvation; others maintain that by doing good works one can earn salvation. Christians, Jews, and Muslims have different paths to salvation, but the end is similar.

Are those who reject theism evil and without any redeeming moral virtues? Surely, to believe in God is no guarantee of moral virtue, for there have been innumerable individuals who have professed religious faith and yet pursued immoral lives. The corridors of history resound with their infamies. Evil deeds clearly have been perpetrated by believers and nonbelievers alike, Christians and atheists, Jews and Hindus, Muslims and absolutists, theists and secularists. Immorality has no boundaries. From Cain, who slew his brother Abel, to Caligula, Attila the Hun, Genghis Khan, Torquemada, Cesare Borgia, Hitler, and Stalin, immoralists have soaked the earth with blood. It is false to maintain that the only saints in history are those who have been wedded to churches and temples and that the only sinners are those who lived outside them.

According to the Bible, the greatest evil and the cause of man's fall from grace is to eat of the tree of knowledge of good and evil, to engage in ethical inquiry, and to ground principles and values in autonomous reason. There is a historic tradition in civilization, however, of ethical persons who have eaten of the forbidden fruit of this bountiful tree. Living outside of Eden, they have discovered significant ethical values and truths that guide both self-reliant and other-regarding conduct.

Ethics Without God

For those who live outside of Eden and view the Eden story as mythological, the universe is without any divine plan or purpose. They believe that our primary need is to *cultivate* the tree of knowledge of good and evil rather than to shun it. It is apparent that if we remove the threat or fear of divine retribution, people will not necessarily rob, rape, and kill; without divine sanctions, individuals can be honest, truthful, sincere, and just, and they can and do develop a sense of responsibility toward others. In their own inner lives, they do not despair, nor do they become nihilists. Nor will they necessarily flout the standards of civility and decency, degenerate into fleshpots, or take part in orgies. There is a high humanistic motivation for ethical conduct. If religious foundations are removed, morality does not collapse; nor does hedonic self-interest become the rule of the day.

The ethical and secular humanism that I will explicate in this book is based on a scientific and naturalistic theory of nature and human nature and is grounded in the rational knowledge of good and evil. The orthodox religions that are fixated upon the Old and New Testaments, the Koran, and other so-called sacred documents involve circular reasoning. These religions implicitly presuppose a set of moral values, which they then seek to justify by reference to a transcendent source. But this mysterious entity, under critical scrutiny, is shown to be a giver of values that are already cherished. It is hardly necessary for man to invent a God who then gives man the moral prescriptions that have grown in his own mind and conscience.

Human beings who refer to the Bible or Koran to justify their belief in a set of commandments or ethical principles are deceiving themselves, for theistic religions are simply spun out of human imagination; they have no independent reality. The great deception is to consider an act good or evil, right or wrong, in the name of God when the act is actually judged within a historical cultural tradition and only later is sanctified or condemned by ecclesiastical doctrines and institutions. The idea of God is synonymous with our own deepest moral ideals. Our conception of Him is the standard by which we measure our pain and project our hope. We invoke him to compel us to obedience. Men and women themselves see the immorality or harm of stealing or killing, so they reinforce sanctions against these acts by calling them divine edicts: "Thou shalt not steal" and "Thou shalt not kill" they attribute to God.

But the divine sanctions are simply proxies for a deep-seated moral revulsion against these acts. All ethical systems are woven out of the materials of human desires and purposes. The theist persists in his conviction that his moral ideals are divinely inspired and hence beyond modification. This masks a deep self-deception. There is no evidence that Moses received the Ten Commandments from on high, that the moral parables of the Sermon on the Mount were enunciated by God appearing as Jesus, or that Gabriel delivered the Koranic moral code to Mohammed—although believers persist in their convictions that these miraculous events occurred.

In an earlier book, *The Transcendental Temptation: A Critique of Religion and the Paranormal*,[2] I have shown that these claims of revelation are totally uncorroborated. In my judgment, they are products of human contrivance and express a hunger within the human breast that seeks ultimate meaning as a response to the tragedies encountered in life. They are myths of solace and magic that enable us to escape the finitude of the human condition, the mortality of life, and the finality of death. And they are reinforced by religious moral systems that prescribe propitiatory prayer and strict moral codes, celebrate rites of passage, and provide a sanctuary for shared huddling.

A genuine question often raised is this: If *all* moral systems are products of human culture and if we remove the self-deceptive faith systems that sanctify them, is it still possible to lead an authentic ethical life in which a responsible morality can be developed? Can we build new secular ethical communities?

The purpose of this book is to show that *there can be an objective and positive humanist basis for ethical conduct.* Indeed, the full dimensions of the ethical life can perhaps only be realized when we break the bonds of theistic illusion and move on to a new stage of creative development. An authentic morality relevant to the emerging civilizations of the future can be developed when we cast off the tribal limitations of our ancient past—retaining the best but discarding the inessential and the false—and move ahead to create a genuine appreciation for high ethical values and principles.

Unfortunately, the moral systems of the past, the pre-existing mores, social customs, and traditions that developed, were fixed and sanctified by religious authorities and traditions. Every culture needs an established set of moral principles and values to live by. They govern conduct and define the parameters of legitimacy and illegitimacy. Only given such a system could social life proceed. Those moral rules that are considered most important are encoded into legislation and enforced by law. In the long history of humankind, morality has been indissolubly wedded to religion, and values and norms have been given priestly support and theological justification.

The pace of social and technological change is so rapid that today we cannot look backward to the primitive nomadic and agricultural civilizations of the past and the venerated religions that grew out of them in order to derive our moral principles, even though humans constantly long for an ancient shore where they can rest and feel secure. The orthodox religions place obstacles in the way of social progress and impede creative innovations in post-modern technological societies. They express the tragic Faustian theme that the quest for knowledge is limited, that man can never be fully satisfied in and of himself, and that his queries will lead ultimately to his own destruction. Many fearful individuals thus wish to restrain the genie of modern science and technology and return it to the bottle; they yearn for the absolute moral certitudes of yesteryear. Rooted in habit, anprehensive of change, these followers of authoritarian structures distrust any experimental revisions in morality.

Theistic moral systems that seek to preserve the archaic formulas of the past are rooted in arbitrary and fallacious ground. Roman Catholicism, Orthodox Judaism, fundamentalist Protestantism, and absolutistic Islam, held with intense fervor by disciples, clash with each other about basics. Moreover, they impede the revision of moral codes that have been outdistanced by modern science, parts of which are irrelevant to current needs. The old religions have often opposed sexual autonomy, the liberation of women, the emancipation of disadvantaged minorities, the toleration of alternative lifestyles, and the building of a world community. They seek to solidify ancient dogmas in unchanging absolutes. They shield their children from the expanding horizons of education, and they abhor exposure to new ideas and values. But we need to overcome such intransigent moral systems based upon the transcendental temptation and occult pictures of reality. "No deity will save us," we should again affirm, "we must save ourselves"[3]—especially from the folly and errors of our forebears.

We, not God, are responsible for our destiny. Accordingly we must create our own ethical universes. We should seek to transform a blind and conscious morality into a rationally based one, retaining the best wisdom of the past but devising new ethical principles and judging them by their consequences and testing them in the context of lived experience. Humanistic ethics, insofar as it abandons mythological fantasies and confronts the human condition for what it is, is more honest and responsible than transcendental moralities.

We are thus challenged: Is it possible to build a genuine system of ethics devoid of transcendental faith? Can we fashion autonomous ethical principles and values that will provide individuals with meaningful goals in their lives? Can secularists and humanists develop a mature sense of responsibility toward others? The task of this book is to set forth and analyze the main features of the ethics of humanism.

Jesus, Moses, and Mohammed Versus Socrates

There are two opposing approaches to morality and ethics that have been in constant conflict in human culture. The first is best exemplified by Jesus, Moses, and Mohammed, who declared that moral principles are divinely inspired and who enunciated them without any effort at rational definition or justification. The second is typified by Socrates, who sought to use reason to define and justify his ethical ideals and continually subjected them to critical scrutiny.

The first, *transcendental theistic morality,* is the belief that morality must originate in a divine source. This is rooted in a belief in divine revelation, and it is supported by a tradition of faith grounded in authority. In Western civilization, it is the Judeo-Christian basis for morality. In the Islamic world it is rooted in the Koran. Other traditions find solace in still other sacred texts handed down from a dim past or even created— "revealed," their adherents say—in recent historic times.

The second, *humanist ethics,* is based primarily on man's own perception of good and evil, though, like theistic morality, it is as ancient as Western civilization itself. It finds its initial inspiration in Greco-Roman texts, particularly in the philosophy of the Sophists, Plato, Aristotle, Epicurus, and Epictetus; it is the effort to provide some rational basis for ethical conduct. The quest for a rational ground for morality continues throughout the history of ethics and can be found in the writings of Spinoza, Kant, Bentham, Mill, Moore, Russell, and Dewey. Nonetheless, the humanist must be tempered by his confidence in the power of rational ethics in human affairs. For men and women have built cathedrals, temples, and mosques to sanctify the messages of Jesus, Moses, and Mohammed, and have adored them as divinely inspired. There are few temples erected to honor reason; neither Socrates nor his successors have been apotheosized by later generations. We have, however, built colleges and universities, research institutes and scientific organizations, hospitals and museums, and we have used the secular, social, and political institutions of modern society to help create a better life for all. Yet, for all too many in the modern world, morality is still mired in divine revelation—and they cannot comprehend how men and women can be moral and not believe in God.

Have we not finally reached a moment in human history where we can definitively divorce the historic marriage of religion and morality? Is it not time for the moral life to be transformed fundamentally by critical ethical inquiry? This transformation began in the so-called pagan world, but it was almost destroyed during the Dark Ages. Ever since the Renaissance, the dawn of modern science, and the Enlightenment, the secularizing influences of the modern world have attempted to dissociate religion from morality. Is it not time that we help quicken the growth of an autonomous and independent ethics based upon critical intelligence and secure its influence by creating new institutions for the future?

Interestingly, today's vociferous critics of the ethics of humanism seem totally unaware of the rich intellectual heritage bequeathed by philosophers who have deliberated about the meaning of *good, value, right,* and *justice,* and about questions concerning obligation and duty, subjectivity and objectivity. What is at stake is the viability of reflective ethics, for the philosophers have demonstrated that we can make reasonable ethical choices independently of theological guidance, and that ethics can be an autonomous field of inquiry. Metaethics—that is, discourse about the meaning of moral concepts and the epistemology of ethical judgments—is one step removed from *normative* ethics. In my view, it is not sufficient in itself to understand the general foundation of ethics; we must derive concrete values and principles of action. We need to offer practical guidelines for reflective, ethically concerned persons.

Transcendental theistic morality proclaims absolute commandments derived from God, but these more often than not mirror the prevailing moral traditions of a people. Philosophical ethics, on the contrary, is an effort to find some rational basis for conduct. There is a marked difference between these two approaches to morality: the first presents a set of unquestionable absolutes to guide conduct, the second takes these as data for reflection, analysis, and modification.

When philosophers engage in ethical inquiry and deliberate about moral values, moral absolutists become uneasy; when skeptics point out that in moral deliberation there is often a conflict between rights and duties and goods and values, and that what should be done can only be determined by reference to concrete situations, their critics rail against "situation ethics." They invoke their fixed moral standards and insist that without eternal verities, ethics is betrayed. Instead of "thou shalt" or "thou shalt not," theists complain, we hear from ethicists only about rational qualifications, extenuating circumstances, and the subtle nuances implicit in ethical deliberation. "Insufficient!" is the verdict the theist passes on humanist ethics, for he hungers for certitudes.

Ethical inquiry is an essential human activity, and all human agents are compelled to engage in it more or less, even though absolutists resist it because of fear that it will subvert their convictions. But it is abundantly clear that it is possible to lead a virtuous life and cooperate peaceably with one's fellows without recourse to transcendental absolutes or theistic injunctions. Indeed, the latter are always in danger of being translated into self-righteous fanaticism, which can become a source of intense conflict, particularly in a pluralistic world, where there are competing value systems.

I don't mean to condemn everything about religious systems of morality. At best, theistic morality has inspired devotion to others, an appreciation for the brotherhood of man, and a commitment to charity; though theists have often been censorious and divisive in proclaiming their gospels and have counterposed differing theologies of virtue against one another. There is no guarantee that belief in the fatherhood of God leads to an ethical reality of the brotherhood of man. On the contrary, strict conformity to religious systems can engender fratricidal warfare. There is a difference, of course, between fundamentalist religions, which insist upon the inflexibility of the law, and reflective religious moralities, which have been influenced by humanist values and principles such as tolerance, which interpret their religious needs as metaphorical guides, and which draw upon philosophical inquiry in the framing of moral choices. Needless to say, it is the former forms of religion, not the latter, that I am objecting to most strenuously in this book.

These forms of transcendentally based ethical systems are at a lower stage of moral evolution, especially when they exalt obedience to commandments and inflexible adherence to rules instead of autonomous ethical choice. The ethics of humanism, by contrast, seek to develop mature individuals capable of ethical deliberation. Insofar as an individual is willing to assume some responsibility for his own choices, may we not say that he or she has reached a more mature stage of moral development?

His or her choices are not based on unquestioning obedience to a code, but on an affirmative, responsible process of ethical inquiry.

Does humanism lead to moral turpitude, as its critics allege? Does it unleash rapacious and grasping demons within the human breast? Is it insensitive to decent human conduct, unaware of the needs of others? Humanists can rightly disclaim paternity for these forms of immorality. It does not follow that without belief in a divine order all meaning in life would dissipate, nor does it follow that if there is no stamp of God on the universe nothing is ethically significant. Nihilism is not the only alternative to theism, nor is it the case that only a higher theistic empire of commandments can restrain the brute passions of man. Many transcendental theists are unaware of or insensitive to the deeper nuances of the ethical life. They bask in sublime ignorance of the complex nature of ethical choice.

The salient point is that *all moral and ethical systems are human* in origin, content, and function. The religionist is only deceiving himself if he believes that his morality is divinely ordained. And he is mistaken if he maintains that only God-intoxicated Christians, orthodox Jews, devout Muslims, or zealous Hindus can be moral. Since religious systems of morality are creations of human culture, invented and sustained by men, this belies the claim that human beings cannot, by their own effort, create a moral code or behave morally.

There is, of course, an alternative to both theistic and humanistic ethics. That is the amoral life, in which one is gravely undeveloped, insensitive to the needs of others, egoistic in the quest for pleasure, or interested in power for its own sake. This is the life of the undisciplined individual, whom Thrasymachus in the *Republic* heralds and Plato indicts. This life is one of profound disorder which, if allowed unlimited reign, leads to tyranny, unhappiness, and misfortune. Philosophers and humanists have always pointed out the self-defeating character of unbridled hedonism and self-aggrandizement.

But the alternative to a theistic ethic need *not* be amorality. Granted, theistic systems of ethics take a significant step beyond moral barbarism by imposing some degree of order on human conduct, restraining man's wild and selfish impulses and civilizing him. One might argue that at the very least religious moralities have tempered rapacious passions. But they have at the same time failed. For these systems are one or more steps removed from a still higher stage of intellectual and ethical development. I submit that it is the rational humanist approach to ethics that needs to be defined and vindicated if we are to outgrow the structures imposed in the moral infancy of our race. Indeed, humanistic ethics can provide a secure basis for the moral decencies, ethical excellence, and human responsibility; and it can inspire an abiding concern for human rights and the well-being of humanity as a whole.

Notes

1. All biblical quotations are based on the King James Version unless otherwise noted.

2. Paul Kurtz, *The Transcendental Temptation: A Critique of Religion and the Paranormal* (Buffalo, N.Y.: Prometheus Books, 1986).

3. Paul Kurtz, ed., *Humanist Manifestos I and II* (Buffalo, N.Y.: Prometheus Books, 1973).

Part I

1
The Failure
of Theistic
Morality

Transcendental Ethics

Theists maintain that only a moral code rooted in a transcendental realm can provide the basis for moral conduct. Unable to envision any other ground for morality, they vehemently oppose any efforts to modify their received doctrines. But the foundation of their system rests on shaky ground.

What is *transcendental* ethics? It has taken many different forms historically, for although people talk about the "transcendent," they disagree as to what it is. A purely transcendental ethics, unrelated to any human content, would be meaningless, since it would be empty of any empirical referent and irrelevant to human interests or needs.

Platonism

Plato is doubtless the main inspiration in Western thought for a philosophically based transcendental ethics, if not a theistic morality. Plato thought that there were universal moral ideas or forms. Presumably, a moral inquirer could use these as guides to conduct and seek to exemplify them in the empirical world.

Plato was inspired by Socrates' quest for truth and his devotion to the life of the mind. In various dialogues, Socrates attempts to define *justice, piety, truth, beauty, virtue,* and the *good.* He is not interested in extensional definition by reference to specific illustrations of any of these, but in an intensional definition whereby one is able to apprehend the real meaning of a moral concept; that is, its essential differentiating characteristic.

Plato postulates a realm of subsistent ideal essences in terms of which anything in the world of matter receives its existence. The concrete is what it is only because it participates in the universal class that defines it. All particular things would seem to have their counterparts in the realm of essences. Plato is primarily interested in mathematical concepts—which seem ideal and which provide the formal structure for nature—but he is also interested in moral ideals, of which the ideal of the *good* is the most fundamental. Plato thus attempts to provide an ontological basis for morality, rooted in some transcendent order.

The best critic of this theory is Aristotle, who asks: Of what help are such universal concepts to the ordinary man? They don't provide much aid for the carpenter or physician, who is concerned with achieving the good in his own field of specialty and must deal with the *good* in concrete terms and as the end of action.

The philosophical critique of Plato's position is well known: Platonic realism simply *assumes* its ontological postulate. There is no supporting evidence for the claim that there are ideal forms subsisting at large in the universe. Even if ideal essences subsist, they have no empirical content, and they do not tell us what we ought to do in concrete situations. Thus Plato's theory does not help us to resolve moral quandaries— if that is what is intended—and there are serious objections to both his theory of knowledge and his metaphysics. It does not succeed in providing a basis for morality, because its epistemological grounds are questionable. It is not at all clear that by means of the dialectical process of reason we can at some point apprehend these essences. Plato has reified the process of definition by objectifying elements in discourse and giving them ontological status. But terms and concepts have meanings only within the context of language, which is developed by human beings. Words cannot be abstracted from human communication or read into the universe. Justice, for example, is not a non-natural entity floating in ideal space separate and distinct from the world of men and women; it is a notion applied to human institutions that we have chosen to designate by language.

In spite of his transcendental theory, Plato was himself a strong critic of any attempt to derive ethics from religion. In the *Euthyphro,*

Plato asks if it is possible to deduce virtue from the sayings and examples of the gods. The prevailing religious mythology had been spun out by the poets, and Plato found the Homeric myths unreliable.

A day laborer has killed someone on the estate of Euthyphro's father. The latter has the offender bound and thrown into a ditch, and sends for a priest to tell him what to do. The offender dies before the priest arrives; Euthyphro blames his father and is so incensed that he demands he be prosecuted for murder. Socrates is surprised that Euthyphro has turned against his father, since to honor one's parents is a fairly widespread moral prescription. He asks Euthyphro for his reasons. Euthyphro replies that the gods dictate that a murderer should be punished for his crimes. But did not Zeus kill his own father Kronos, and Kronos, his father? Socrates is uncertain whether Euthyphro's father has committed premeditated murder and wonders what the gods themselves would do in such a situation. What is piety? he asks. Euthyphro replies with a statement of conventional morality: Pay heed to the gods, follow their dictates, and engage in religious ceremonies.

But, for Socrates, virtue is more basic than conventional piety supported by religiosity. A man should follow the dictates of his conscience, live by the light of reason, and attempt to do good, which is more important than blindly following customs. Thus ethics precedes conventional religiosity, and is not to be deduced from what the gods may or may not have said.

A similar criticism of conventional religious conformity appears in Book II of the *Republic,* where Plato has Adeimantus attack its hypocrisy and double standard. One can do evil and yet confess or atone for one's sins and thus propitiate and pray to the gods for help and forgiveness. Ethical devotion to righteousness based on reason must precede any such religious complicity. Nonetheless, Socrates does have intimations of immortality. If there is an afterlife, he has nothing to worry about, since he has been righteous. If there is no afterlife, death is like an extended sleep. In any case, he has no fear of death, and believes that a person must follow his reason and fulfill intrinsic justice aside from any considerations of instrumental rewards. This is the argument that Socrates proposes even as he awaits death, as dramatized in the *Apology, Crito,* and *Phaedo.*

Plato's postulation of an ideal realm as the source of ultimate moral ideas is followed by a long line of philosophical theorists, the neo-Platonists, who also divide the universe into the two realms of appearances and reality. The first contains material objects in space and time, coming into being and passing away, interacting on the level of sense observation. The second refers to another realm of ultimate reality, which we do not directly observe, but indirectly infer or intuit. For Plato, the unseen realm is intelligible only to reason; but for others, not even to that; they speak of a mystical presence, of which we may get only a glimmer.

There is a deep-seated conviction that some unseen realm transcends the natural world and is the basis for a moral order in which there is some deeper structure and purpose. Moreover, this provides an ontological basis not only for value but also for obligation. Even Kant, who believed in the autonomy of ethics and did not think that ethical imperatives could be deduced from religion but rather from independent rational grounds, said that by turning within to our moral conscience, we have some glimpse of a noumenal world and some intimation of a moral order. He is only one of many philosophers who have believed that there is an ideal and universal basis for moral conduct that transcends cultural relativity.

Theistic Morality

I do not wish to elaborate on and critique these philosophical theories here, but rather I shall focus on only one form of transcendental ethics: theistic morality. Belief in a transcendent moral order takes on special meaning to the person who believes that ethics must be given a divine basis. The Christian maintains, for example, that the universe is fulfilling some eternal plan. Although this plan is enveloped in mystery, God has nonetheless made known to us his moral principles (with Christ as exemplar), which it is our duty to obey. Salvation depends on whether we accept the reality of the power of God and are obedient to his moral dictates.

There is a strong and a weak form of theistic ethics; and there is within the theistic camp a sharp difference as to whether we should take the moral commandments as they are put forth in the Scriptures as absolute and explicit guidelines for conduct, or whether they should be interpreted in the most general metaphorical sense. Orthodox Jews, for example, believe the Ten Commandments and the minute rules for conduct outlined in the Torah to be of divine origin, to be followed to the letter of the law. Fundamentalist Protestants and conservative Roman Catholics accept the Old Testament (except of course for the prescriptions binding on Orthodox Jews), and look upon the normative moral principles of the New Testament as binding on *their* conduct. Similarly, devout Muslims accept largely and without qualification the moral and behavioral code enunciated in the Koran and the sayings attributed to Mohammed.

There are great problems in arguing for a literal interpretation of ancient documents. This is aside from the questions of whether God exists and whether these documents have been divinely inspired or are simply the inventions of human culture. My own view is that there is insufficient evidence for the existence of God and that therefore the religious texts cannot have been revealed by a god but rather are simply the expressions of human beings. Nonetheless, even if we were to grant these premises for purposes of argument, many difficulties follow.

First, it is apparent that from the fatherhood of God, contradictory moral commandments and prescriptions have been drawn by believers. The books of the Old Testament were written over the course of several hundred years and express the ethical thinking and social conventions of various periods. We see a transition in doctrines, and thus there are many contradictory injunctions. On the one hand, God says in the Ten Commandments (Exod. 20:13), "Thou shalt not kill." Yet only twelve chapters later (Exod. 32:27), a bloody-minded God commands the Israelites: "Put every man his sword by his side, and go in and out from gate to gate throughout the camp and slay every man his brother, and every man his companion, and every man his neighbor." Or again, in the Ten Commandments (Exod. 20:14), God says, "Thou shalt not commit adultery." Yet, after commanding the Hebrew conquering army to kill all Midianite captives, including innocent women and children, God permits the army (including married men) to seize and keep the young virgins for themselves: "But all the women children, that have not known a man by lying with him, keep alive for yourselves" (Num. 31:18).

The moral contradictions between the Old and the New Testament are legion. In the Old Testament, the retributive justice of "an eye for an eye and a tooth for a tooth" plays a prominent role. This is supplanted in the Sermon on the Mount of the New Testament by a "turn the other cheek" philosophy: "Resist not evil," says Jesus, "but whosoever shall smite thee on thy right cheek, turn to him the other also" (Matt. 5:39). The Old Testament condones polygamy, concubinage, and other practices that no doubt were widespread at the times different parts of it were written.

In the Old Testament, divorce is permitted if a wife no longer suits her husband: "When a man hath taken a wife, and married her, and it come to pass that she find no favor in his eyes . . . then let him write her a bill of divorcement, and give it in her hand, and send her out of his house" (Deut. 24:1). But in the New Testament, divorce is severely restricted. Jesus says, "Whosoever shall put away his wife, saving for the cause of fornication, causeth her to commit adultery" (Matt. 5:32).

Many Christians attempt to resolve the contradictions between the Old and New Testaments by saying that the latter succeeds the former and that a Christian morality of love and forgiveness replaces the early doctrines of a vengeful and narrowly conceived Jehovah. Jewish scholars and scribes have spent centuries writing and analyzing the Talmud in an attempt to interpret the Torah in reasonable terms. If one accepts a literal interpretation of both the Old and the New Testaments, then one must conclude that God has changed his mind.

Christians have interpreted the moral precepts and doctrines of the New Testament in radically contradictory ways, and have disputed endlessly about its meaning. For example, some have condoned and even justified slavery on the ground that the Old Testament permits the taking of human captives as slaves and the New Testament admonishes that servants should obey their masters. We are told, "Servants, obey in all things your masters according to the flesh. . . . And whatsoever you do, do it heartily, as to the Lord" (Col. 3:22-23). Or again, "Servants, be subject to your masters with all fear" (I Pet. 2:18). For a long time the Bible was used to justify the divine right of kings. As Christ is the ruler of the universe, so a king was considered the ruler of a temporal realm; this was used to demand obedience to the political authority of the king. Only in modern times, and largely because of the critique of liberal humanists, have Christians and Jews come to defend liberal democracy and argue for individual human rights. But it is difficult to find democratic moral principles in the ancient texts.

A theist presumably could argue that although people have historically used the Bible to defend a particular political and social system, they are not justified in doing so, and further, that there is no connection between the God of the Bible and slavery, or monarchy, or any other such system. But, by the same token, is there a *necessary logical connection* between the fatherhood of God, let us say, and moral principles that many or most modern people would accept? Can we deduce a doctrine of human rights from the idea of the fatherhood of God? Some believers think that we not only can but must, for without a transcendent being, such a doctrine must collapse.

Here we come to a nonliteralist interpretation, a weak form of transcendental ethics. For when we seek to be explicit, we run into contradictions. For example, what should be the role of women in society; should they have equality with men? The Old Testament constantly demeans women and gives them a lesser place in the social and moral order and in the marriage relationship, as in Genesis: "And thy desire shall be to thy husband, and he shall rule over thee" (3:16). The New Testament does the same. Paul reflects the primitive morality of his day when he maintains that a woman's relationship to her husband should be one of obedience. Women are to "keep silence in the churches;" if they wish to learn anything, they should "ask their husbands at home" (I Cor. 14:34-35). Paul says, "The husband is the head of the wife. . . . Therefore as the church is subject unto Christ, so let the wives be to their own husbands in every thing" (Ephes. 5:23-24).

It is impossible—and unnecessary—to take the moral insights, practices, and attendant limitations of the nomadic and agricultural societies of two to four thousand years ago and seek to apply them to modern society *in toto* and without qualification. It is true that much in the Old and New Testaments expresses profound moral insights— in particular, the Golden Rule, the need to be kind, considerate, and just toward one's fellow creatures. But there is much that is primitive and retrogressive. Since biblical times there has been an evolution of moral practices and new situations alien to ancient peoples and thus requiring recognition of new moral principles. Yet much of this is conveniently ignored by many theologians today.

But one logical point should not be fudged: Does one need the fatherhood of God as the foundation of morality? If so, how does one explain alternative moral systems, all rooted in belief in one—presumably the same—God? An illustration is the Islamic religion, based on the Koran. Although every word of the Koran was allegedly received by Mohammed through revelation, Islam justifies practices that Christians and Jews find abhorrent, such as polygamy (for men only), and the fact that a man (but not a woman) may divorce if he does not find his wife to his liking.

Is it the empirical issue or the logical issue that is at stake? It is clear that belief in God does not guarantee either universal moral conduct or even agreement about what is right or wrong, good or bad; there continues to be widespread cultural diversity and relativity. It is the existing social, political, and economic mores that more often determine the morality of an act, and not the converse. Men and women are apt to read into the universe their own cherished moral beliefs and practices. Muslims, like Jews and Christians, have called their own practices divinely ordained, even though their moral commandments were clearly brought by reformers—which Moses, Jesus, and Mohammed undoubtedly were.

It is not the case that through belief in one God, people will infer the same moral commandments. As we have seen, they have drawn contradictory ones, and have fought the bloodiest wars to promulgate their own notions of what God commands. Does one God condone mutually exclusive practices? It is difficult to find a necessary logical relationship between God and morality. Thus, though Muslims believe in God, they have not, in the past 1,400 years, defended democratic human rights or freedom of conscience, moral values that have recently come to be precious in many Western countries. Improved social conditions no doubt foster these ideals and hopefully, in time, democratic revolutions may sweep away archaic antidemocratic beliefs and practices. But if this happens, it will be because Muslims recognize moral precepts whose rationale is not based in the Koran but rather arise from secular considerations.

Given the long history of religious warfare and persecution among Catholics, Protestants, Muslims, Christians, and Jews, it is difficult to see how belief in one God is a sufficient guarantee that there will be a concomitant concern for fellow human beings of other religious persuasions, which is generally an accident of birth. Regretfully, the basis of religious morality is not discussed in terms of self-evident premises but rests on doctrines of faith and revelation and on religious traditions developed by church institutions, all claiming to be divinely inspired but obviously created by specific groups of men. Roman Catholicism, for example, has a long legislative tradition of papal pronouncements based on the premise that Christ commissioned Peter (the first pope) to build his church and that therefore all succeeding popes are infallible in their interpretations of God's will. Whether or not one accepts any system of faith usually depends more on social customs than on rational grounds. A moral code, then, is relative to historical traditions, as to both ancient roots and later interpretive traditions. It is easy to see that it is *not* rooted in unchanging transcendental concepts.

The idea that belief in God and/or a specific religious tradition is necessary for moral conduct is thus highly questionable. Even if one accepts faith in God and a specific religious tradition as a legitimate interpretation of God's word revealed in history, this itself is open to various interpretations. For example, the hundreds of different Protestant sects have reached different conclusions about any number of moral practices. It is similarly true for orthodox, conservative, reform, or humanistic Judaism, for conservative or liberal Roman Catholics, and for Sunni and Shia Muslims.

Many military dictators of Latin America have postured as devout Roman Catholics and attend Mass every Sunday; but so do the staunch priests of liberation theology who are in opposition. It is notoriously difficult to derive a simple set of absolute rules from any religious tradition and hope that these will serve to resolve every moral issue or moral dilemma that may arise in human experience. How do the ancient doctrines enable us to decide between capitalism and socialism as economic systems? Believers end up on different sides of political questions. In the 1930s, Generalissimo Franco of Spain and the dictator Salazar of Portugal, both pious Roman Catholics, defended an authoritarian society and were sympathetic to fascism, whereas the French Catholic, Jacques Maritain, defended a commitment to democracy. In the late twentieth century in the United States, much of the Roman Catholic hierarchy has been converted from conservative to liberal political positions. Indeed, in the 1980s, the Catholic bishops of America opposed nuclear arms and called for disarmament, whereas conservative Catholic laymen and some Protestants disagreed with them and insisted on a strong nuclear defense. The Catholic bishops have endorsed a liberal, socially conscious economic and political platform, whereas conservative Catholic laymen like Michael Novak, William Simon, and William Buckley have strongly dissented.

In some moral doctrines, Vatican theologians remain intransigent. They are opposed to divorce, birth control, and abortion, whereas many Protestant ministers, Jewish rabbis, and even many Catholics favor one or more of these. Similarly, for virtually every social issue with moral ramifications, such as homosexuality, euthanasia, or capital punishment, there are wide differences of opinion, and religious people divide on these issues just as often as secularists do. The difference is that the religious call their own moral doctrines the word of God—as specially interpreted by them, of course.

Absolute Morality Versus Situation Ethics

All of this demonstrates that even if there are moral commandments, rules, and principles that are widely accepted within a religious tradition, and even if these are commonly shared between traditions, the question of how to interpret or apply these rules often raises moral quandaries and produces differences of opinion. For example, the Sixth Commandment states, "Thou shalt not kill," or, as better translated in the New English Bible, "You shall not commit murder." Should this be taken as an absolute commandment without any exceptions? If so, what does one do in times of war when one's country is being invaded by an implacable aggressor? Depending on the context, one might reply, engage in battle. Can we engage in a preemptive strike when we know that an enemy is prepared to invade, or take part only in defensive military action? Is one permitted to kill the enemy? This is not murder, we are told, for it is done on behalf of a people defending itself.

In World War II, leaders bombed the industrial cities of their enemies—London and Rotterdam were nearly destroyed by the Germans, and Berlin, Tokyo, and other German and Japanese cities by the Allies. In the process many innocent people were killed. Were they murdered? One might argue that this was evil even though a strategic case had been made for such military bombing of so-called "open" cities. I remember being in London in 1944 at the height of World War II, visiting the bombed-out sections behind St. Paul's Cathedral and witnessing the buzz-bomb attacks on civilian populations, all designed to break the will of the British people. And then during the war as a member of the invading American army, I saw the bombed-out ruins of cities like Munich, Bremen, and Hamburg, and learned about the millions who died in such raids. After the defeat of Germany, the United States dropped atomic bombs on Hiroshima and Nagasaki. I was stunned at the massacre, though most of my fellow soldiers cheered, for they thought that this would end the war sooner.

I am not arguing here for or against the moral principle of prohibiting all killing, only questioning how one interprets the Sixth Commandment. Is it a universal moral absolute? If so, how we apply it depends on the context. Does one condemn all forms of terrorism? Can one use retaliatory violence as a response to it? Presumably if one kills for a "just cause," many people (including Muslims, Christians, and Jews) believe the act is vindicated even when it involves innocent civilians. For a long time I was opposed to capital punishment, since I did not think it was effective in deterring crime. I have since modified my views somewhat, and might under limited conditions apply it to heinous crimes like wanton murder. But I am puzzled by Bible-believers who say they accept the commandment against killing and yet are willing to condone virtually any kind of killing in time of war and applaud capital punishment as just, often quoting the Bible to do so.

"Thou shalt not kill" takes on special meaning in regard to euthanasia, for one can make a case for it on moral grounds: If someone is dying of an incurable disease, is suffering dreadfully, and asks to have the dying process hastened, then we may have a moral obligation to assist that person to die more quickly. The moral justification for that is beneficence or kindness.

It is now apparent that *absolutist* moral principles are difficult to locate. They are more likely *general prima facie* guides for conduct. How they apply depends on the context. This is particularly true where there is a conflict of duties. It is our moral duty, for example, not to lie, yet to do so on occasion may be morally justifiable. If your aunt labored all day to prepare a dessert you hate, you may believe that sparing her feelings and telling her you like it is a greater obligation than telling her the truth.

The moral life is often full of tragedies. It is not simply choosing between good and evil or right and wrong, for there is often a conflict between two goods or two rights, both of which we cannot have, or between two evils, and we choose the lesser. We often have a political choice between two candidates, neither of whom is to our liking, but we may decide after deliberation to support the least offensive. What does a young person do who has to choose between pursuing his education in order to develop a career and become self-sustaining and independent, or dropping out of school to care for and support an aging parent? We should honor our father and mother, but we also have an obligation to develop our talents to their fullest. We ought to keep our promises, yet we may have made a bad promise and when it comes time to fulfill it we may believe that the consequences could be disastrous. Socrates illustrates this dilemma in the *Republic:* A friend asks you to keep his weapon and return it to him when he requests it. You agree to do so, yet one day he comes to you in a fit of anger demanding it immediately, and you know that if you give it to him, he will injure or kill someone. Should you break your promise? Weighing the consequences of doing so may be more compelling than keeping your promise in this situation, and so you decide not to return the weapon.

"Thou shalt not commit adultery," says the Seventh Commandment. In D. H. Lawrence's novel *Lady Chatterley's Lover,* Lady Chatterley's husband is rendered impotent in wartime and cannot have sexual relations with his wife. Lady Chatterley has the option of having a love affair with her gamekeeper and thus satisfying her normal sexual desires, or divorcing her husband, for whom she still has some compassionate affection and regard. Should she practice chastity for the rest of her life, or break her marriage vows? She decides to engage in an adulterous affair, though she eventually divorces her husband and marries the gamekeeper.

My purpose here is not to resolve these dilemmas but simply to point out that any moral code needs to be interpreted and applied, and that only ethical reflection may assist us in such situations. Many people fail to understand the true complexity of moral choices. In debating fundamentalist critics of secular humanism, I am often amused by their railing against "situation ethics" without comprehending what it means.

One illustration sometimes used by college philosophy professors in elementary ethics courses is the so-called "lifeboat dilemma." The lifeboat dilemma illustrates a real problem, though we are warned by fundamentalists that in discussing it, we are undermining the morality of the young. A ship sinks in heavy seas and some passengers and crew manage to make it to a lifeboat. Unfortunately, there are more people aboard the small boat than can be sustained. It becomes apparent that if the lifeboat is not to be swamped, some passengers will have to go overboard into icy or shark-infested waters. To do so, however, will mean certain death. The moral dilemma raised is: What ought to be done?

"You are teaching young people to throw people overboard," a distraught mother once shrieked at me.

I asked her, "Madam, if you were in such a situation, what would you do?"

She answered, "We would huddle together and pray to Jesus."

I replied, "In that case, you might all go down together, instead of perhaps saving some of the passengers. You could ask for volunteers, perhaps draw straws. There are a number of alternative choices, all horrible, no doubt, but it may be that the lesser evil is the most suitable course to adopt in this situation."

To thus engage in ethical reflection, sensitive to the nuances and difficulties of moral choice, is not necessarily immoral, as critics believe, and it can help to enlarge a student's understanding of the complexities of ethical reasoning. It vividly demonstrates that moral principles need to be weighed in balance, and we may not always be able to fulfill them all at the same time. There is no substitute for developing some measure of ethical reflection, for it is a sign of ethical maturity.

God and Obligation

Conservatives who defend theistic ethics insist that without belief in God and a strong religious tradition, moral responsibility will not follow and people will do whatever they want. It is no good, we are told, to refer to an intellectual, historical, moral elite—Socrates, Aristotle, Epicurus, Epictetus, Spinoza, Kant, Mill—who did not accept traditional religion and yet behaved morally. The question is whether rational grounds for ethics are sufficient for the bulk of humankind. Napoleon and Metternich, although skeptical of theistic claims, nonetheless believed that strong religious institutions were necessary as bulwarks of morality for the general masses. Religious beliefs tend to reinforce specific virtues so essential for maintaining an ordered political community. Edmund Burke thought that there was a kind of wisdom of the race embedded in social institutions and that certain historical practices embodied the residue of moral insights of earlier generations of men and women who, facing the burdens of choice, developed general rules, supported them by both custom and law, and sanctified them by religious dogma and ritual.

There is in my judgment some point to this argument. It may indeed provide the strongest justification on behalf of religious morality. Some set of established social rules and regulations defining permissible conduct and providing some expectations and parameters for behavior seems to play an important functional role. "Why ought I not to steal from another?" asks the potential offender. He is told that this violates social custom. Moreover, he will be considered a scoundrel by the community. Moral disapprobation provides strong motivation for conformity. But not everyone is so moved: thus a system of clearly defined laws is enacted. Stealing is wrong because it is against the law, and one may be caught and punished for breaking the law. This deters a good deal of otherwise socially destructive acts. The fear of the consequences is a powerful inducement not to rob.

But what if an individual is able to avoid detection by the community and the legal authorities? Should he commit a crime if he can get away with it? If he calculates risks and benefits, long- and short-range goods and values, and the consequences of violating the customs or laws, he may conclude that the sum of his enjoyments and pleasures and of his power and ambition will be expanded by committing immoralities and crimes—if he can escape condemnation or punishment—rather than obeying the law. Here the religious response interjects itself. For if earthly authorities are unable to detect, apprehend, and punish violators, God in His infinite judgment will do so. Thus, there is an eternal lawgiver who knows what you do and why, and nothing can be concealed from Him. After your death, on judgment day, you will be brought to the docket and the supreme lawgiver will judge you, punish you for your sins, and reward you for your virtues. Social customs and legally enacted laws are transformed into divine laws given by God. Social approval or disapproval and legally sanctioned punishment are thus replaced or reinforced by divine sanctions. The ultimate answer to the question, "Why ought I to be moral?" is that God has legislated and commanded it, that it is your duty to obey His will, and that if you do not, you will be punished. Calculating long-term consequences, one thereby concludes that it is in his own self-interest not to break the law, for it has not merely temporal but divine force. Thus, out of fear of committing a sin, and in calculating the long-range negative results to a future afterlife, or even out of love of God and willingness to do His bidding in order to achieve salvation, one may conclude that one ought to obey the law simply because we are commanded by God to do so.

The key question is whether this argument is sufficient to solve the so-called riddle of obligation. Would one's sense of duty collapse if God, as the ground of morality, were absent? Is a person moral if he does something or refrains from doing it simply because God wills it and for no other reason? Is this the ultimate basis for moral responsibility? My answer to all of these questions is *No*.

A particularly striking illustration of this point is the biblical story of Abraham and Isaac (Gen. 22:1-19). There came a time when God put Abraham's obedience to Him to the test. God commanded Abraham to take his only son, Isaac, whom he dearly loved, to the land of Moriah to sacrifice him. Abraham was fully prepared to obey. Early one morning he gathered some wood, saddled up his ass, and embarked on his journey, taking Isaac and two servants with him. Abraham went into the woods alone with Isaac and constructed an altar. He bound Isaac, laid him on the altar, and then took a knife to kill his son, following the dictates of the Lord. At that point, the angel of God appeared and commanded him, "Lay not your hand upon the lad, neither do you any thing unto him: for now I know that you fearest God, seeing you hast not withheld your son, your only son from me" (Gen. 22:12).

Two questions come to mind. Was it right for Abraham to sacrifice his son by killing him? No, we strongly dissent. But what if God had indeed commanded him to complete this act? Would that make it right? *No!* again we say, for if the son were truly innocent (as Isaac was), then God had no right to command, and Abraham had no obligation to obey this immoral command. God would truly have been wrong to request it (even though according to the Christian legend, God killed Jesus, His only begotten son—one might say that was a morally reprehensible deed!). But when God tells Abraham *not* to kill Isaac, we breathe a sigh of relief. If we reflect upon the situation, we cannot help but be dismayed that God would so cruelly test Abraham and that Abraham would consider killing Isaac. We think that it is clearly morally wrong for a father to sacrifice his son. But again, is it wrong simply *because* God defines or dictates it as such, or is it wrong on independent grounds, whether or not God says it is so?

Any morally developed person would recognize that a father killing his innocent son (who had not betrayed him, had not committed an act of murder or treason, and was not dying of an incurable disease) is unjustifiable, whether or not God dictates it. I will argue later, in Chapter Three, that there is a body of common moral decencies that a developed person comes to recognize. These have some moral force, both intrinsically, since they are basic to the human community, and instrumentally, as a regulative principle guiding our living and working together. We do not need some outside being—real or imagined—to enunciate them for us.

I do not wish to defend such ethical principles simply on intuitive grounds or as self-evident; they are built into the very nature of the human animal as a social being. There are objective ethical insights and truths, I submit, that emerge upon reflection and that a morally developed human being will come to recognize.

Let me attempt to elaborate by embellishing on the Abraham-Isaac story. Let us imagine that a man agrees that it is wrong to kill his only son, but if you ask him why, he replies, "Because God commands us not to do so."

"Is that the *only* reason or even the *primary* reason for your statement?" I might ask him. If he were to answer *Yes*, we would wonder about his moral character, and whether there was not something morally deficient in him for not seeing it as wrong himself.

Living in a social community with others and in the family, we come to recognize that we need other human beings and that they need us, and that parents have special obligations and duties to preserve the health and lives of their children. Moreover, some empathy can or should develop between parents and children, sisters and brothers, husbands and wives, friends and relatives, and even among strangers and other members of our community or beyond it. We come to see that there are basic human decencies that we have an obligation to fulfill—for example, to avoid inflicting unnecessary suffering on others, to try to be honest, sincere, and just. There is a whole catalogue of such moral decencies.

That parents should not kill their children is one of our highest moral precepts. For someone to do so would violate all of the norms of human conduct necessary for living together in a community. We do not need God to tell us *that*. Indeed, the very idea that Abraham would have been willing to kill Isaac is reprehensible. He should have dissented and remonstrated with God. He should have attempted to change God's mind. And if God refused, Abraham should have refused to obey. Disobedience to divine commandments that are patently immoral is not sinful, for we learn by experience that moral principles have a kind of autonomy of their own, quite independent of God.

In Abraham's time, the injunction against child sacrifice must have been an advance over a more primitive morality that condoned and practiced it. Overwhelmed by contingent evil in the universe, perhaps out of desperation, some tribes practiced human sacrifice in order to appease the gods. This was wrong, said the Old Testament, but its wrongness appeals to the moral conscience on its own terms.

Interestingly, the biblical story allows animal sacrifice as a substitute for human sacrifice. Abraham sees a ram caught by its horns in the thicket, and offers it up to God as a sacrifice in place of Isaac. This is stated approvingly in the text. One might likewise dissent on moral grounds to this gratuitous act of sacrifice—animals have some rights too, we might say. They should not be killed or tortured indiscriminately. Thus, it is wrong to kill an innocent ram simply for a religious ritual— and indeed animal sacrifice has also gone out of favor in most parts of the world. Yet the essential message of the story is that Abraham is morally virtuous because he is willing to obey God no matter what. Simple and unquestioned obedience to divine commandments is considered the highest religious duty and moral virtue. This is the cornerstone of religious morality; we have an obligation to obey simply because God has commanded it. A mature adult surely should ask for reason or justification. If there is none, it would be unethical to perform a morally repugnant act.

In many years of teaching ethics courses at the university, I have often presented the Abraham-Isaac dilemma to my students and asked them whether they thought Abraham was right or wrong. Virtually all have agreed that it would have been wrong for Abraham to sacrifice Isaac. I can recall one notable exception: One outspoken student insisted that *whatever* God commanded was to be taken as right, and if God had indeed insisted that Abraham sacrifice Isaac, or that fathers kill their sons as a test of fidelity, it would have been right to do so. When questioned, he could give no reason, other than his belief that the commitment to God transcended all other considerations. But no one came forward to agree with his argument. He seemed, in this claim, to display his own undeveloped moral conscience; certainly his view that the highest virtue is obedience to moral law as defined by religious tradition is questionable. But there is a further test of the issue: If God commanded us, for example, to rape, steal, or murder, would that make those acts right? Or conversely, if God said do *not* rape, steal, or murder, does that in itself make the acts wrong? Surely not! There are a number of moral principles and values that we as civilized human beings recognize and cherish and that we are not prepared to abandon. One cannot be asked to give up what it means to be a developed moral human being. Thus a sense of obligation and responsibility has a basis and an appeal independent of theological foundations. And those who do not see this are displaying their own moral deficiencies. What is this ground? If God is dead or absent, what is the foundation of our devotion to morality? It is to these questions that we must now turn.

2
Ethical
Inquiry

Two Kinds of Morality

Two kinds of morality have emerged from our discussion: first, a morality
of obedience to commandments allegedly derived from a transcendental
theistic source; and second, an ethics based on the development of critical
rational inquiry and insight.

Although theological moral systems no doubt serve important
psychological and sociological functions by instilling individuals with
moral virtues and maintaining a social order, morality fixated at this
stage is primitive and underdeveloped. We need to move on to another
level of ethical development. Here we may draw upon the entire history
of critical ethical inquiry to see what ethical development entails. We
can also learn much from the work of psychological theorists who have
identified stages of moral development, especially in children.[1] Given
their findings, those who insist upon obedience to inflexible moral rules
as the be-all and end-all of morality may themselves be said to be morally
handicapped.

The term *morality* was originally derived from the Latin *mores*,
the plural of *mos*, which refered to customs, habits, and manners. These
were the traditional rules of conduct, the customary usages, and the
unwritten laws that governed a community of people living together.
Every society deems certain forms of behavior as good, right, just, or
virtuous, and other forms as bad, evil, wrong, or wicked. These moral
attitudes are deep-seated. They are carefully instilled in the young. The
ultimate transmission of morality is from parents and teachers, who

seek to inculcate the received moral code. Conduct regarded as good is positively reinforced by the contigencies of reward. Immoral conduct is punished. Conditioned responses build up habits of expectation, belief, and practice in one generation, which are then passed on to the next. It is the earliest formative years that are most crucial in establishing the basis of morality; but the process of social acculturation is a continuing one. Virtually the entire institutional framework is built around a set of values and rules that a society seeks to express, fulfill, and maintain. For example, historic Christianity condemned certain forms of sexual conduct as "sinful" and others as "virtuous," and an entire social order developed by sustaining these attitudes. Similarly, Judaism, Islam, and Buddhism have their principles of right and wrong. The approved moral principles and values are thus glorified and sanctified; the abhorred taboos are prohibited by the use of sanctions: ostracism, punishment, excommunication, exile, or death. Both religion and law support the moral code and are interpenetrated and influenced by it. To consider one's basic moral values sacred or divinely inspired—as religionists do—and to support fundamental concepts of appropriate moral conduct by enforcing the rule of law contributes to the stability of the social group.

Anthropologists and sociologists have pointed out the cultural relativity of social customs and the wide divergence of practices in different parts of the world. The primitive African Azande people believe that certain members of the community are witches, able to exercise a malignant occult influence over their compatriots. They partake of various rites in order to counteract the evil forces of witchcraft through the use of magical medicines.[2] Western Christian societies reject these beliefs as preposterous, though they themselves are willing to engage in magical rites at the Mass, by eating the flesh and drinking the blood of Christ— whether symbolically or by transubstantiation. Religious beliefs and practices thus vary widely, as do dress, speech, and other manners. In some societies, it is thought indecent for a man to wear a beard; in others, to go unshaven. Women in strict Islamic societies are sinful if they show their faces in public; in Western societies, they are prudish if they do not reveal the dimples in their knees! In some societies, homosexuality is rejected as repugnant and is severely punished; in others, it is more or less tolerated. In some societies it is wicked to kiss in public; in others, it is accepted as an appropriate sign of affection and romance.

In a relatively close-knit and isolated social group, it is possible to maintain a set of clearly defined and even rather rigid social norms.

It is possible to force nonconformity behind closed doors and to punish offenders severely. But it is clear that it is also difficult to completely do so. Social change is ongoing; populations die off, decimated by famine, war, pestilence, and disease. The morality of the elderly, though passed on to the young, never has precisely the same meaning or force. Moreover, interaction between social groups occurs; travelers from far-off lands, in meeting strangers, are struck by their oddities. Gradually new ideas and novel, useful, or pleasing practices are imported and exported along with goods and services in the process of commerce. Thus it is difficult for a social group to maintain unchanging fidelity to its moral beliefs. This is particularly the case when groups clash in warfare and seek to conquer or destroy other peoples. Widespread intermarriage may occur, and one culture may assimilate and absorb another. There is inevitable interpenetration and borrowing of beliefs and practices; in the process even stable moral codes may give way and be revised. There are continual efforts, however, to fix a moral code, particularly by religious and ideological propagandists who maintain an opposition to rapid change and admonish that there must be a return to the old ways. The Roman Catholic church attempts to solidify a tradition of ancient doctrines and many powerful church leaders resist efforts to modernize it. In modern-day Islamic nations, fundamentalists overthrow modernistic regimes, which they maintain have betrayed the Koran. In any case, it is when the old morality is challenged or begins to break down that ethical inquiry can begin. The older customary values and moral verities don't seem to be able to cope with new conditions. When confronted with alternative systems, there may be a sudden call for transformation, reformation, or even revolution.

One of the most dramatic illustrations of this phenomenon was seen in the dialogues of Plato. In them, the great Sophists, among them Protagoras, Callicles, and Thrasymachus, clashed with Socrates. The Sophists, itinerant teachers who traveled about the Mediterranean world, noted the wide diversity in cultural and moral beliefs and practices and the fact that each city-state—Sparta, Crete, Troy, Athens, Syracuse—considered its own traditions sanctified by the gods and superior to all others. Were they all equally valid? If so, contradictory moral principles and values would be both true and false at the same time. Is man "the measure of all things" as Protagoras taught? And if so, is morality relative simply to what individuals or societies prefer? The great debate in Plato's dialogues is between convention and nature. Is morality simply conventional, as the Sophists maintained, or did it have some basis in the nature of things, as Socrates and Plato argued? We have already seen that Plato postulated a realm of ideal essences in an effort to resolve the quandary.

But far more important, in my view, is the fact that here we find the dawn of critical ethical inquiry. It was initiated by Socrates, and also by the Sophists, who challenged the sacred cows of Hellenic culture. Socrates was condemned to death by the Athenians, for he challenged the reigning orthodoxy. The key point is that here we can see a crucial transformation from conventional morality to critical ethical inquiry— and the *Dialogues* of Plato are a reflection of what was happening in Hellenic civilization itself. What was unique was that the customary codes (including the received religious doctrines) were no longer accepted as the primary sources of moral guidance. The Greeks were coming to feel that their convictions about the "good" or the "just" needed to be examined rationally.

It was in the next generation that Aristotle defined ethics and elaborated on it as an autonomous field of inquiry. Aristotle defined the good as an end achievable by men. This he designated as well-being, *eudaemonia,* or happiness, and he proceeded to describe its main characteristics and indicate how and in what sense it could be attained. For Aristotle, the realization of human nature and the achievement of the rational life is the chief source of *eudaemonia;* practical and contemplative wisdom needs to be cultivated if we are to lead a life of nobility, excellence, and virtue.

I have placed these two kinds of morality in some historical perspective. The first is based on habit, passion, faith, and authority; it seeks to inculcate its universal principles of virtue in the members of a society. Although the second begins here, with the preexisting standards of society, it moves on to another stage, that of reflective choice. Moreover, theologians have in the past borrowed extensively from the ethical philosophers and have sought to interpret their religion in the light of their teachings. Clearly these two dimensions are not sharply divided, and there are differences in degree. Every group draws upon preexisting moral rules to guide conduct; rational ethical discourse presupposes them. It is not necessary for every generation to rediscover the elementary moral decencies, but no society can possibly cope with its ethical or moral problems, without some use of reflective inquiry; there is a continuous process of interaction between custom and reason.

John Dewey, the twentieth-century American philosopher, marked this contrast by distinguishing between prizings and appraisals.[3] "Prizings" refers to our antecedent values, the things we cherish and hold dear. These usually are motor-affective behavioral states, which spill out into action. The products of habit, they have a strong emotive component and are usually accepted unless a moral problem or quandary emerges. At that point, critical ethical inquiry is initiated, and we seek to evaluate our prizings and appraise their worth. "Appraisals," thus, refers to more developed processes in which a cognitive element intervenes, weighing and judging our values, validating and verifying them.

Ethical Dilemmas

The pre-existing values of customary morality by and large suffice to guide conduct until there is some challenge to them, some conflict of duties or values, or some perceived inability of the old morality to cope with new problems that may emerge. It is generally at this point that inquiry is initiated, either to reestablish and vindicate our habits of acting and believing, or to bring into being some new departures in thought and action. Although one can speculate in general about ethical theory on the meta- level—and this is an important kind of ethical inquiry— in the last analysis, it is in relation to the concrete contexts of lived experience that normative ethical reflection begins and is ultimately tested. And in particular, it is by reference to moral dilemmas, as they have been called, that the most intense kind of ethical deliberation ensues. Life is full of difficulties and we are rudely confronted by the tragic character of some of our choices. Alas, the received rules do not always help to guide us, and sometimes we become enmeshed in such an overwhelming moral dilemma that we are forced to plumb the inner depths of our souls for resolution, and even then we may not find a satisfactory answer.

The great poets, novelists, and dramatists have rendered eloquent the intensity and profundity of such moral deliberation. In Shakespeare's *Othello,* the central character is overcome by a corroding suspicion that Desdemona, his beloved wife, is unfaithful to him. The fires of jealousy and anger are stoked by his enemy, Iago, and Othello eventually kills

Desdemona, which in turn destroys him.

How poignant is the burden of choice, how often we are weighed down by it! Many would rather flee from certain situations than have to assume the responsibility of choice. Moral freedom is often found to be intolerable, and many defer to custom or authority so that others can decide for them. The escape from freedom and reason is a common symptom of the fearful soul unwilling or unable to choose. How deceptively warm and comfortable are the certainties of moral absolutes!

I should point out that most of our moral choices are not tragic, nor are they insuperable or beyond resolution. Perhaps some philosophers have highlighted the ultimate tragedies of life in order to dramatize the fact that some reflective process is essential to living. Since the crux of morality is an ethical dilemma, and the test of our principles and values are in relation to it, it would be well for me to characterize and define its nature now.

What Constitutes an Ethical Dilemma?

First, in an ethical dilemma there is some *problem* or question that needs to be resolved. It may involve some conflict between existing values, norms, rules, or principles. In our customary mode of acting we may encounter some difficulty or obstacle, or we may be challenged by others who disagree with our way of acting or with the things we consider right or wrong. Our usual way of acting, which might otherwise proceed without too much reflection, is thus put into question. We are thrown into a quandary. Should we continue to do what we have always done, or adopt a new procedure and embark upon a new course? We have to make a choice, and then justify it to ourselves and/or others. Some situations may be entirely novel, as, for example, the problems newly encountered in medical ethics and biogenetic engineering. None of the old guidelines seem adequate to the task of telling us what to do, for the problem may be unique and unsettling. Of course, we may refuse to choose or to act, but that is itself a kind of choice.

Second, at the very least, an ethical dilemma involves a person (or persons) called upon to make a choice or choices. This presupposes that we *can choose,* and that we have some measure of freedom to do so. The classical doctrine of determinism is often invoked to demonstrate that choice is an illusion, and that whatever we do is determined by antecedent causes. If this were the case, it is said, ethics would be impossible, for if our choices were caused by antecedent events, we would have no control over our lives, nor could we be blamed or praised for what we do. It is not necessary to resolve the classical problem of free will versus determinism to show the irrelevance of this argument. There is no contradiction in maintaining (1) that choice is a fact of the ethical life and (2) that our choices are caused or influenced by ancillary factual conditions. This is especially the case if we consider "cause" not as a compelling force (as David Hume pointed out), but simply as a concomitant conditional operative in behavior.[4] If there were no ordered regularities in human conduct, we could not count on anything; nor could we make reasonable choices based upon expectations of what is likely to occur. Our choices would be capricious, without rhyme or reason. No one could count on anybody or make reliable inferences as to how any person would be likely to behave. The freedom to choose thus presupposes some regularity in human conduct on the basis of which responsible expectations are possible.

The third feature of an ethical dilemma is that there are *alternative* courses of action to consider. If there were no genuine options and we were faced with only one possible course, then the notion of choice would make no sense. Such dead-end situations do occur in real life, as, for example, when a person is in a prison and is not allowed any freedom of movement or of exit, or when a person is dying and his or her death cannot be prevented. An ethical dilemma, therefore, must have two or more possible avenues of resolution. These alternatives may be givens, occuring within the situation through social or natural circumstances, or they may be a product of creative invention on the part of the inquirer. The following dilemma, although not ethical, illustrates the point: If a person is faced with the problem of crossing a river, he can wade across if it is not too deep, or swim across if the current is not too strong, or mount a horse to get across. But he may also build a raft or boat, construct a bridge, or burrow underneath the river by means of a tunnel. Perhaps he can even rent a helicopter. The latter methods are results of human invention, and they are a function of the level of technology and the social forces of production.

Thus the alternatives at our disposal are not necessarily given but may depend upon our own creative ability. The ends we wish to achieve depend upon our know-how and the techniques available to us. The seemingly insoluable ethical dilemmas of one day may be transformed by the expansion of alternative solutions the next. The power of human beings to act is a function of discovery and invention (art and technique). This reveals the revisionary character of much ethical reasoning and the difficulty of holding inflexible moral principles that will persist forever, unchangeable and unmodifiable.

To illustrate the ethical point: The care of the helpless aged is a perennial human problem, as old as civilization itself. There have been many solutions. The elderly can wander off to die so as not to be a burden to the young, as was the case in hunting-gathering Inuit (Eskimo) societies. In civilizations with different resources, sons, daughters, and other members of the family have considered it their duty to provide financial and moral support for their aging parents who are no longer able to work. Historically, the extended family would find a place for grandparents and aged aunts and uncles. In a culture where self-reliance and independence are valued highly, individuals have considered it their duty to make provisions for their old age through hard work and thrift. A person who was concerned about his retirement years was considered to be morally virtuous.

These methods have been replaced or supplemented by other social inventions. Social Security, financed by employee and employer contributions and overseen by governments, has made the problem of old age less onerous. There are annuities and other investment insurance plans, whereby funds appreciate by compounding. Moreover, medical science has achieved significant advances in combating the debilitating illnesses of old age, and people are able to lead productive and enjoyable lives far beyond the age of retirement. There are new moral dilemmas engendered by the healthy elderly. With many more productive people willing to continue working, there is competition for jobs. Hence there exists a tension between younger workers, who must support those living on Social Security, and older, unretired workers competing with them in the marketplace for jobs. With each new advance come new moral quandaries.

The problems encountered in medical ethics today especially illustrate the changing character of ethical norms. With the enormous expansion of medical technology many problems that were not present before dramatically confront us now. We can keep dying patients or gravely handicapped infants alive far longer than we ever thought possible. This raises questions of euthanasia or infanticide: Should we use such technological powers or allow people to die with dignity if they so wish? The character of ethical dilemmas is often a direct function of the availability of alternative means and the amount of power we have to choose and decide our own futures. A pluralistic and free society geared to progressive social change will always permit a greater range of innovative options for individuals than will an authoritarian, closed, and slowly changing one.

Fourth, in ethical dilemmas, we are able to reflectively evaluate and appraise alternative courses of action. This implies that some kind of *deliberate cognitive* process is present. There is a marked difference between moral norms, standards, and values that are accepted on the basis of custom and habit and supported by feeling and emotion on the one hand, and those which are supported or modified by some degree of reasoning process on the other. One does not have to naively insist that ethics is simply rational, nor deny that an attitudinal element is present in morality. We can feel strongly about the things we approve or disapprove of and still recognize that some cognitive element of choice can enter into the process. The reflective aspect is central to critical ethics, as distinct from customary ethics, for it is by means of reason that blind rules are transformed into conscious choices.

To passively obey the Ten Commandments or the injunctions of Jesus without being able to define or evaluate such prescriptions is hardly to have attained ethical awareness. To be able to transfer such moral rules into self-governing principles is possible for intelligent human beings, however, who are reflective about their values and principles. The emergence of some capacity for ethical reasoning, I submit, represents a higher stage of moral development.

A fifth ingredient in an ethical dilemma is that our choices are acted upon in the real world and thus have results. They are not merely expressions of idle speculative fancy. They inevitably have some effect upon the social and natural world. Thus choice is related to *praxis,* that is, to practice or conduct. It is causative in function, for it is able to change the course of events. Men and women can thus enter into nature and society to modify and restructure them. We are not simply passive meditators, contemplating the universe. Insofar as we act ethically, we are active doers, able to add to the world or change its direction. Hence our practical choices have empirical results that we can observe. The choices we act upon have *consequences;* this enables us to judge the nature of a choice and its effectiveness. Thus consequential, utilitarian, or pragmatic criteria are rather fundamental; for it is one thing to approve or disapprove of an act in purely hypothetical terms; it is another to see how a choice turns out, and to evaluate its results. We constantly bring consequentialist tests to human affairs.

Clearly it is not what we say but what we do that counts. In the last analysis, it is not our conceptions or intentions (important as they may be) but our actions that matter most in regard to other human beings. We may fantasize about what we wish to do, yet never quite do it. Our impulses and desires may far outstrip our capacity—or even desire—to act, but it is only the act that can create a fact. A man may imagine a dozen times disrobing and making love to a beautiful woman or inflicting sweet revenge upon an enemy. But unless or until he performs the deed, he is not culpable. It is the concrete display of behavior as a product of choice that is the nexus of ethics.

Sixth, insofar as an action follows from a choice that a person clearly makes (whether after a process of deliberation or not), and consequences flow from that, then the individual can be held *accountable,* in some sense, for his actions. This means that we can praise him if we approve or blame him if we disapprove. The issue of responsibility is relevant here, for, as Aristotle pointed out in the *Nichomachean Ethics,*[5] a person is responsible for an action if what occurred was what he intended, if he was consciously aware of the circumstances under which he acted, and if the choice was not made in ignorance of them.

I should note in passing that this differs from many theistic moralities, which hold people guilty for their thoughts. ("He who lusts after a woman in his heart commits adultery.") Unless or until an idea is expressed in action, one cannot judge its moral worth. Moreover, to condemn people for their inner reveries would no doubt condemn us all. The real test of a choice is its actual implementation in the world, and it is for that, that one is held accountable.

If a person driving a car on an icy road slams on the brakes and the car strikes someone, this may be purely accidental, especially if he did not intend it and shows remorse afterward. He is responsible in some sense because he is the driver. He is to be blamed, even if he did not intend harm, but was negligent or under the influence of drugs or alcohol. Of course, if it were proved that he had knowingly and with full intent and malice planned to kill the person, he would be declared guilty of first-degree murder and not second-degree manslaughter. In some cases, motive and intent may be difficult to establish.

In any case, a central lesson of critical ethics is that people can learn from their mistakes and modify their conduct in the future—even though it sometimes may be difficult or virtually impossible to do so. We constantly say to ourselves of actions we regret, "I made a mistake" or "I failed, I should have acted otherwise." Or, of effective action we approve, "I must do the same thing in the future, how brilliant of me." And we constantly attempt to instruct our children in the moral precepts that we have learned. We try to cultivate virtue and to inform and modify character. Certain behaviors (sloppiness, laziness, indifference to the needs of others), we hold deplorable, while others (neatness, kindness, consideration) are commendable. Related to ethical choice and actions, then, is the process of learning. Moral behavior is corrigible, capable of amelioration and improvement. Our systems of education and law recognize this, and we apply various forms of punishment to those whose behavior is deemed harmful or reprehensible; here the full force of the law is brought to bear in defining and punishing behavior viewed as criminal.

The Beginnings of Ethical Inquiry

Ethical inquiry can begin at different stages of life. Some people, hidebound by their religious codes, resist this. They are opposed to ethical inquiry because they fear change. It is threatening to them, and they seek to block it; yet no one can resist inquiry entirely. To live and function is to be challenged in one's moral beliefs and in how to apply them to concrete situations. The task of critical philosophical ethics is to engage in such inquiry directly and consciously. Virtually the entire history of philosophical ethics has been devoted to the effort to establish ethics on rational grounds. It is the quest for knowledge of good and evil. Where shall we begin this inquiry, we may ask?

Some important distinctions need to be made between normative ethics and metaethics. Normative ethics is concerned with issuing prescriptive recommendations of how we ought to live and with assisting us in framing value judgments. The normative ethicist will tell us what is good, bad, right, or wrong, and what is the just society. Philosophers from Plato and Aristotle to Spinoza and Mill have made an effort to provide practical wisdom to guide conduct.

Metaethics is one step removed from the actual decisions that people make. It is an effort to understand *how* people make ethical choices, and how they go about justifying them. There are two central problems to metaethics. The first concerns the definition of moral terms and concepts: Can we define *good, bad, value, right, wrong*? The second is concerned with the methods or criteria for establishing ethical truths; what do these moral concepts refer to, if anything? The problem of definition has been a complex one for philosophers. As we have seen, Platonists consider such concepts objectively real, and have postulated an ideal realm that may represent them. Such theories are tied to general theories of the nature of language. G. E. Moore considered the term *good* to refer to a non-natural property known by direct inspection but not capable of identification with any empirical or natural property, and hence, indefinable. Any effort to define it, he said, committed the "naturalistic fallacy."[6]

Other philosophers, such as A. J. Ayer and Charles L. Stevenson, believed that such terms have no objective reference at all. They are emotive and imperative, simply expressions of our attitudes that are used to influence the behavior of others.[7] This form of ethical skepticism has been hotly debated in the twentieth century. Critics maintain that its interpretation is too narrow, since value terms have many functions other than the expressive and imperative. There are many nuances governing their uses, and they make sense not simply as descriptives but are used to perform many functions.

Some philosophers have nevertheless attempted to provide naturalistic definitions of terms by reference to behavior; the task here is to seek to understand the phenomena. Values emerge where there is life, and in human affairs, where there are conscious processes of selection. Values thus refer to forms of preferential behavior; to say that something has value for an individual or society means that it is esteemed and has positive worth. This applies conversely for disvalue. Values are therefore the object of any interest or need.[8] Given the wide diversities in behavior, however, certain questions have been raised: whether all values are equal in worth—this would mean a kind of subjectivism—or whether it is possible to offer some kind of critical standards by which to judge them. Although values are relative to the valuer, there are degrees of objectivity concerning their moral worth.[9]

I submit that to say something has value need not mire us in subjectivity. In simply describing the behavior of humans, we find a wide range of preferential activity: People value everything from chocolate ice cream to ice hockey, from sexual pleasure to the Mona Lisa, from cricket to moral sympathy. The question is whether normative standards can be used to evaluate the diversity of likes and wants on a comparative scale of values. Here the ethical ingredient intervenes not only for the individual in terms of his personal life, but for the society, where values either come into conflict or harmony.

A second major problem of metaethics is to ascertain whether there are criteria for judging competing systems of value. Are certain normative standards more appropriate than others? If so, how do we go about validating or vindicating our value judgments? A significant number of criteria have been introduced by philosophers to help us in the decision-making process.

In one sense, this inquiry is epistemological, for we are concerned with ethical knowledge and the question of truth. Is there any such thing as an ethical truth—analogous to an empirical or scientific truth—and if so, how do we go about establishing the veracity of an ethical claim? Ethical truths appear to be far more difficult to establish than ordinary factual truths. We can prove to someone that a table is made of wood or that it is hard, but not as easily that it is beautiful or valuable. I think that there are objective criteria to which we can refer and that it is not simply a question of caprice or taste. The facts of the case are relevant to our ethical judgments, but not sufficient in themselves, since normative attitudes are present. Apples and pears may be graded on the basis of objective qualities, and this does not depend solely on the taste of the beholder, although that is an essential ingredient. There are objective properties of the fruit, on the basis of which we make a value judgment. Similarly, we may judge the moral worth of an action in part by relating it to the facts of the situation. Complete skepticism or nihilism are indefensible, for we make normative claims throughout life. Someone who refuses to examine the objective factors intended by a normative claim we may say is normatively blind or deficient.

Philosophers have introduced criteria for making value judgments: Aristotle defined happiness as the ultimate good, Bentham and Mill used the greatest good for the greatest number criterion, and Kant employed the catagorical imperative. I do not think that the effort to find a single standard or criterion as the touchtone of ethical choice has succeeded. All these efforts are simplistic, for they attempt to reduce ethical choice to an ultimate principle or value, whereas ethical choice is pluralistic. It is far more complicated than most ethical philosophers have allowed, for it involves a multiplicity of considerations that we need to draw upon within a situation. The great philosophers have made contributions to ethical inquiry, but the principles they have introduced usually provide only one criterion to be considered along with others. I am here suggesting a kind of ethical eclecticism, in which we draw from the best insights of a variety of theories.

For purposes of our analysis I wish to focus on the fact that there usually are a great number of moral principles to which we may be committed. Indeed, in an ethical situation, it is often the clash of our values and principles that is at issue, and we need to weigh and balance all of them in making our choices. Societies have evolved any number of moral principles to which people become committed: it is our task, often, to adjudicate between them.

But what do I mean by the term *principle*? I would define an ethical principle as a rule we appeal to in order to guide conduct. An ethical principle is *general* in that it designates an entire range of actions which comes under its rubric. I am unwilling to say that it is absolute or universal, for any one principle may clash with others, and there may sometimes be exceptions. The term *general* is sufficient, for principles can be generalized in the sense that they are introduced to govern various forms of conduct that have similar characteristics. W. D. Ross used the term *prima facie* to apply to the general duties to which we are obligated, at least presumptively, unless other considerations outweigh their application. I would extend his terminology to say that there are sets of *prima facie general principles* to which we are obligated in the sense that we ought to follow them. These principles are not *actual* or concrete obligations. Whether or not we have an actual obligation can only be determined after a reflective evaluation of competing principles and values within a context of inquiry.

These principles are normative in the sense that they establish norms to guide our conduct. They are recommendations for action, and have an "oughtness" attached to them. Moreover, they are both emotive and cognitive in force and function. To say that someone is committed to a set of moral principles means that these have some internalized influence upon his motivation; they have the force of a psychological disposition. To say that a man or woman has principles that he or she stands by suggests some deeply rooted convictions.

These principles are also cognitive—or at least can function as such—for they can be tested in part by their consequences and modified or altered as the result of a process of inquiry. Thus, reason can be constitutive in the attitudinal state and be deeply interwoven with and influenced by psychological attitudes. Deliberative thought enters into the process by which we validate and vindicate our ethical principles and make them part of our being.

I submit that there are two main sources for the ethical life. First, there is a set of ethical principles, which are general rules governing our behavior and to which we are *prima facie* committed. And second, there is a wide range of values to which we are also devoted. How our principles and values relate to one another is a problem I shall address; I would only suggest for now that we need to weigh both our principles and values in any situation in which we have embarked upon a course of ethical inquiry.

Notes

1. See Lawrence Kohlberg, *The Psychology of Moral Development* (New York: Harper & Row, 1983); and Jean Piaget, *Moral Judgment and the Child* (New York: Free Press, 1932).

2. See Peter Winch, *Ethics in Action* (London: Routledge and Kegan Paul, 1972), p. 8.

3. John Dewey, *The Theory of Valuation* (Chicago: University of Chicago Press, 1939).

4. David Hume, *An Enquiry Concerning Human Understanding.*

5. Book 3.

6. G. E. Moore, *Principia Ethica* (Cambridge: Cambridge University Press, 1903).

7. See A. J. Ayer, *Language, Truth, and Logic,* Victor Gollancz, ed. (London: Oxford University Press, 1946); and C. L. Stevenson, *Ethics and Language* (New Haven: Yale University Press, 1943).

8. Ralph Barton Perry, *General Theory of Value* (Cambridge: Harvard University Press, 1926).

9. See C. I. Lewis, *An Analysis of Knowledge and Valuation* (LaSalle, Ill.: Open Court, 1946); John Dewey, *The Theory of Valuation, op. cit.;* and Paul Kurtz, *Decision and the Condition of Man* (Seattle: University of Washington Press, 1965).

Part II

3
The Common Moral Decencies

Principles, Moral and Ethical

I will focus now on moral and ethical principles and the role that such principles play in the life of the individual, especially as he or she relates to others in society. Although the terms are often used interchangeably, there is some difference between them: *Ethical* principles may be said to differ from *moral* principles insofar as the former have been explicitly modified by critical cognition and intellectual inquiry. Both moral and ethical principles, however, are rooted in human behavior.

Are there any general ethical principles that apply to human beings, no matter what the society? Do we have an obligation to follow them? Can we, in other words, discover any *common moral decencies* that have emerged in human conduct?

As we have seen, our moral and ethical principles are general *prima facie* guides for conduct. Etymologically, the term *principle* comes from the Latin *principium,* which refers to the beginning or foundation, that is, the source or origin, or primary truth. To refer to a person's *principia* in the moral sense is to designate the most basic norms by which he lives, those he cherishes and considers most fundamental in his life. A *principled* person has moral principles, which he is willing to stand on, and support when need be, and perhaps, if he has the courage, even to fight for. He is faithful to his moral convictions as to how life should be lived. He is reliable and trustworthy—unless he is excessively self-righteous. One may not agree with the principles he lives by, but at least he can be counted on to behave in terms of them. An *unprincipled* person is without scruples; he has no qualms about violating the standards of equity and probity.

Individuals whose principles fit into one kind of morality—that is, a religiously based moral code—take their principles to be absolute and universal God-given rules that they are duty-bound to follow. For critical ethical inquirers, a principle will not be taken as an unalterable regulation; it does not lay down a directive for everyone to follow uniformly. One has a conditional, rather than a categorical, duty; it is more like a hypothesis than a dictate, amenable to critical interpretation and appraisal before it is applied in a concrete context. This does not mean, however, that a general principle can be easily violated; once it is discovered or developed it cannot be taken lightly or abandoned. If it is deeply rooted in conduct, it cannot be blindly ignored or rejected without some justification. A general principle ought to be followed unless good reasons are given to demonstrate why it need not be.

We recognize a number of moral decencies that should apply to our conduct, especially in relation to other people. I am referring to forms of conduct that are generally appropriate and fitting. Our moral principles indicate what these are. In principle, for example, we ought to be kind, but sometimes an individual may take advantage of one's good will or be undeserving of our largess. In principle, we ought to be appreciative of what others may do for us, though the recognition of their help or recompense for it may be insufficient or too late in coming. That there are general rules of human conduct is one thing that a developed moral being recognizes; how these relate to one another, especially when they conflict, and which should be fulfilled, is another. We may, for example, make a sincere promise which in a time of adversity or altered circumstances may be difficult to fulfill or, were we to do so, would make it impossible for us to realize other equally binding principles or values.

Among the reasons we give to demonstrate why we ought or ought not to do something is the relevance of the principle to the case. Utilitarians emphasize the fact that in deciding what we ought to do we judge an action by whether or not it maximizes good and contributes to pleasure or happiness. This is an important consideration we need to take into account. There is a danger, however, that some utilitarians, especially in regimes tending toward the autocratic, may be willing to compromise certain elementary and well-established moral principles in order to achieve what they consider to be a greater good, or certain social goals they perceive to be desirable.

But moral principles have an autonomy of their own, in the sense that they are not simply instrumental, to be appealed to or dispensed with at will. They have an intrinsic worth, and are not to be considered simply as means to fulfill certain ends; they are part of the ends themselves. Our moral principles may indeed function as values treasured for their own sake. We cannot, for example, choose to be honest or dishonest simply to serve our own purposes or even a greater purpose; honesty is valued in itself as part of a person's character and is a high principle on the scale of human values. Principles and values may thus overlap. Still, principles and values are not necessarily the same thing, for values are not general, nor do they lay down *prima facie* rules of conduct.

The central question about moral and ethical principles concerns their ontological foundation. If they are neither derived from God nor anchored in some transcendent ground, are they purely ephemeral? If they are simply relative to human interest, can they be violated with impunity? What happens if they clash or conflict; how do we decide which have higher priority and legitimacy? Will morality collapse if there are no ultimate first principles resident in the womb of reality?

I think not. The moral and ethical principles that we live by and to which we are committed are "real;" that is, we can make factual descriptive statements about their centrality in human behavior. In that sense, they are part of *nature,* as are all qualities. Second, such principles are *relative* to human beings, to their interests, needs, values, and concerns. To say that they are relative does not mean that they are purely subjective, or that they can be dismissed at will, or abandoned by caprice. It simply means that they are functions of human behavior, and that they emerge in human interactions. It makes no sense to talk of them in an isolated abstract way, separate from their consequences in human conduct. Indeed, the commitment to moral principles becomes so significant in human civilization that they begin to take on a special kind of objective reality and are an integral part of the bio- and socio-cultural spheres. They have natural and objective foundations.

Objective Relativism

The term *objective relativism* perhaps best designates ontological status: moral and ethical principles have some kind of *transactive* function, applying to men and women as they interact in a natural and socio-cultural environment. This applies equally to so-called transcendental systems of morality; even though believers may choose to attribute them to some abstract divine order, these too are products of human culture.

When I use the term *relative*, I do so in three senses. First, moral and ethical principles have social and cultural referents and some deep institutional framework. Second, they take on meaning and force only because they are based on inherent propensities developed or inculcated in specific persons. Accordingly, they are also relative to a given individual. Third, such principles are *relational*; that is, they take on meaning and have content only because they *relate* to human beings.

The term *relativism* has been used as a term of opprobrium by its critics, and the adjective *mere* has been applied to relativism because of the fear that to consider the foundations of our moral code relativistic might lead to its being gravely weakened or endangered. Relativism should not be confused with subjectivism, however, for relativism refers to the empirical fact that principles are rooted in human experience and are not separate from it, whereas subjectivists can find no basis for criticizing or appraising principles. But I should point out that I think there are objective criteria for doing so—hence the term *objectivism*. Thus objective relativism is distinct from subjective relativism, and although the latter may lead to utter skepticism or nihilism, the former does not.

The term *cultural relativity* has been introduced by anthropologists to describe the wide range of principles and norms in human culture. Out of this has come the view that we ought not to impose our standards on other cultures—certainly not when studying them—and that one set of standards is as morally viable as another. That metanormative theory does not follow, as we shall see, and although principles are in some sense relative to cultures, this does *not* mean that we are led to cultural relativism in the sense that cultures are immune to critical ethical scrutiny, or that they are all at the same point in their level of ethical development. Again, there is a kind of *objective* cultural relativity distinct from subjective cultural relativity.

What are some of the objective features of relativism?

First, moral imperatives have some *socio-biological* basis; they are rooted in the nature of the human animal and the processes of evolution by which the species adapts and survives. Human beings are social animals, and our young require an extended period of nurturing for survival. Given this, a number of moral rules that govern behavior have developed. For example, ingrained in the species is maternal care, the instinctive urge of the parent to feed and protect its young. Another is the relationship between the sexes, which includes some affectionate regard for the object of one's amorous advances (delight in warmth and touch, fondling, embracing), as well as a number of concomitant psychological affections. These instinctive tendencies are not unique to the human species. E. O. Wilson found similar rudimentary patterns in other social species: Ants will die to defend the queen ant, and their relation to the corporate entity is such that they cannot exist apart from the colony. Of course, this is instinctive and not self-consciously ethical, but similar patterns can be found in higher-level species, such as the bonds of affection of primates, wolves, lions, and other species, for their young and for each other.[1]

The roots of moral conduct and the recognition of the elementary moral decencies requisite for face-to-face interaction thus already lie deep within the biological framework of the human species. Although there is diversity in the kind of moral rules accepted by different social groups, *some* such rules emerge—for example, in the relationship of parents to their young, or of sexmates to each other. Given the fact that individuals have common biological needs and face similar problems of survival, common norms have developed in spite of wide cultural diversity. Humans need to gather or hunt or plant food to survive, to shelter and clothe themselves against the elements, to protect themselves from predators or other marauding tribes, to relate to each other sexually, to reproduce, to deal with the aged who are no longer capable of self-care, and to face adversity and death with equanimity and fortitude. Given the common tasks of living, some common moral rules have developed. Given the nature of the human being as a social animal, it is thus essential that social groups establish certain rules governing the way in which the members would live and work together and delineate the parameters of acceptable social behavior, so that some clear sense of roles and expectations are understood.

Moral codes thus have an adaptive function; one can postulate that those groups which had some effective regulation for conduct were better able to survive, reproduce, and compete with other species or human groups, and thus transmit this favorable trait and these learned behavioral responses to others. One can imagine a possible scenario in the dim past of our forebears, when the glimmerings of what I shall call the common moral decencies emerged: be kind and considerate to the members of your tribe; be honest and truthful; do not maim, injure, or harm them needlessly; be sincere and keep your promises, etc. The test of the truth of these principles was their consequences. Those tribes that developed such rules had less discord and could better survive than those that did not. It is far more beneficial for everyone to cooperate; it works pragmatically in the long run. This is not a universal characteristic which has always dominated, for our propensity for moral behavior has to compete with other tendencies and temptations in the human breast. Still a minimum of moral relationships needs to operate if the social group is to survive.

We can see analogous forms of moral behavior in other species that bear striking resemblances to human conduct. For example, a mother duck will furiously seek to protect her ducklings from harm. Moreover, species establish pecking orders. Groups of chimpanzees, for example, are ruled by a dominant male who protects his females against other threatening males. Eventually he may be ejected by another male, ousted from his group, and left to die. Socio-biological and genetically rooted behavior has its analogue in the first development of moral patterns in primate groups and extended families. Thus there is a kind of biological relativity for morality conditioned by the constraints of adaptation and survival.

Second, of course, is the emergence of complex *socio-cultural* rules that go far beyond the basic biological imperatives. In the human species, it is sometimes difficult to distinguish the full range of social functions from simple socio-biological functions, but at some point, complex socio-cultural systems evolve. With the development of language, especially the use of symbols and metaphors, human mentation expanded, and learned experience could be preserved and transmitted to future generations. This especially applied to the development of sets of moral rules. In time, morality became nuanced with complexity. Higher levels of moral rules developed, superimposed still further, as it were, on our basic biological equipment and needs, or the immediate survival function of the rules. It is at the level of culture that morality acquires a new dimension, for it is elaborated upon, extended with finesse and distinction. It becomes ingrained in human conduct. Although within the tribe certain moral rules needed to be enforced if the entire tribe were to survive, these did not always apply to other tribes as they interacted and often battled.

It was then that a new stage of morality developed: We should treat the stranger in our land as our brother; we should not mistreat the alien in our midst. One can see this noble affirmation of a new moral principle in the Old Testament, discovered and enunciated by the Hebraic prophets. The first glimmerings of the universality of morality began to appear.

This points to the fact that moral principles are relative to the level of civilization that has developed. The emergence of a higher stage in moral awareness was no doubt forced on our forebears by the fact that as tribes of people intermingled, there were various forms of intercourse, including commerce and trading. When warfare and conflict threatened, there was the perceived need for establishing some conditions of peace and harmony, or no secure life would be possible.

Narrow tribal moralities thus had to be transcended. That this moral truth has still not been fully apprehended today is one of the great tragedies of the human condition; for nations, religions, and ethnic groups still are at war with one another and are willing to use dastardly means to gain an advantage. Yet ethical cognition points to the need for a universality in conduct, and it speaks to all men and women no matter what their social or cultural backgrounds.

Third, moral principles that have emerged have deep *historical* sources: they are the products of civilization, and eventually sweep over nations and become the common heritage of large sections of the globe. A good illustration of this is the revulsion against slavery. The moral principle emerged: Do not enslave another human being, even though he is of a different race, or comes from a poverty-stricken class, or is a member of an ethnic group too weak to resist capture and enslavement. The fact that there is little or no condemnation of slavery in the Bible or Koran, and that it was accepted and was widely practiced well into the nineteenth century by Christian and Arab nations vividly demonstrates the point: Many moral principles have developed only late in human history. This is also true for the recognition that females have equal worth and are thus entitled to equality of treatment, although this is by no means universally accepted or even practiced where it is given lip service.

Moral principles emerge at certain stages of historical development. They are relative to the culture and civilization in which they first appear and are given a hearing. They cannot be violated with impunity by a tribe, nation, or race, without condemnation by a major portion of the community of humankind. Today they have a profound claim on human conscience. To deny them a transcendent or divine basis does not mean that they are any less deeply rooted in human history.

The recognition of a moral or ethical principle may require a long and arduous struggle. Indeed, some principles are deemed so crucial in certain epochs of human history and the opposition to them is so intense that they can only prevail after long and bloody battles. This means that the moral decencies we come to recognize as necessary, at least on a minimal level, are enunciated and extended to all humans, and that a doctrine of human rights is developed for humankind in general. The moral codes of various cultures are not equivalent, and we can with some justification maintain that some have reached a higher level of ethical awareness than others.

One of the most profoundly disturbing facts about the human species is the partiality that individuals have for their own kind. There is perhaps a natural and even necessary favoritism that individuals display to members of their own breeding community. Parents have a unique obligation to protect and nourish their own children, and this is a stronger obligation than to the children of others; filial obligations are felt in return. This close relationship is no doubt advantageous and necessary for the survival and growth of the species. The same favoritism is generally shown also to the extended family: sisters, brothers, grandparents, grandchildren, cousins, nephews, nieces, aunts, and uncles. Again, this no doubt has some kind of bio-sociological function, particularly where members of consanguineous groups have a bond based on common interests and needs, and are confined to a common locality.

What is unsettling is the extension of this bond of loyalty to the wider community—the tribe, nation, or race of which one is a part— at the expense of other groups. This marks some moral advance, for at least it takes us beyond our immediate, face-to-face encounters and parochial attachments and brings us to a wider community. Nonetheless, a cause of much misery in human affairs is the fact that intense hatred can develop toward those not within one's own group, and this can erupt into violence.

Konrad Lorenz has found that members of a rat colony are able to tell by their common nesting smell which other rats in the colony are blood relatives, and to afford them more pacific behavior, while they will display intense aggression, kill, and tear apart unrelated rats who might stray into the nest from another colony.[2] One would hope that there is no strict analogy between human and rat behavior in this regard, but empirical evidence suggests a similar human affection for the inbreeding tribal group and hostility to perceived aliens. That this is not simply rooted in consanguinity, however, is clear from the fact that large nation-states sharing a common cultural heritage may in fact contain a multiplicity of breeding groups, and that they can maintain group loyalty within and exude venom outside with equal strength. Witness the bloody carnage in Europe between France and Germany in three wars and in the bloody war between the two Islamic nations, Iran and Iraq.

There are fortunately less dangerous forms for group rivalry to take, such as the competition between sports teams. Football teams from two different cities or countries may be locked in battle for victory or glory, and their fans, in viewing them, are aroused to intense levels of often irrational fervor, but warfare does not ensue.

The clash of group loyalties and the emergence of moral claims over and beyond parochial identities has been a slow process. And there is still a long way to go before a truly moral community of all humankind can or will be established. Is human behavior aggressive and destructive by nature, and is partiality and loyalty to one's own kind so deep that it can never be overcome? The history of civilization clearly evidences the indelible influence of ethnicity in human affairs, but it also demonstrates that it can and has been overcome, at least to some extent. The strict rules prohibiting intermarriage between different religious, ethnic, or racial stocks have broken down in some societies, which enables the development of new nationalities and loyalties. In this regard, economic, political, and social interaction—and especially mobility and travel—make it possible to meet people of different nationalities. In addition, critical ethical intelligence plays a vital role, for there has been the emergence of the recognition of universal (or general *prima facie*) human rights.

This is related to a key ethical principle: *Each person is entitled to equality of consideration as a person, and as such has equal dignity and value.* This claim is independent of his or her group membership, racial, religious, ethnic, class, national, or sexual orientation. Thus there are a set of human rights we can delineate that realize the fulfillment of basic principles. The term *right* means that persons are entitled to recognition and respect within the community of humankind, and their liberties and opportunities should not be denied or transgressed. In Chapter Seven I will specify what the most basic human rights are;

these include not only ethical rights but economic, political, and social rights as well.

The Justification of Ethical Principles

The question that can now be raised is this: If we grant that moral principles, including the common moral decencies and a doctrine of human rights, have evolved and are related to our biological human condition and to our cultural history, how do we determine which should be accepted and what is the standard by which they can be warranted? This is a difficult epistemological question, which philosophers have debated. Let me suggest what is *not* the case:

1. *Ethical principles cannot be deduced from the concept of God.* First, the existence of God is questionable. Second, not all men and women of different cultures share the same religious beliefs. Third, granting the fatherhood of God is no guarantee that uniform moral codes will emerge. Theists have "deduced" any number of moral codes at variance with those held by other believers. For instance, witness the sharp differences of opinion held by Jews, Christians, and Muslims regarding marriage and divorce.

2. *Ethical principles are not self-evident or intuitively certain.* The difficulty we find with the argument of intuition is that not everyone finds ethical principles self-evident. Often what is taken as intuitively obvious is simply a mask for established cultural attitudes, customs, habits, and beliefs, or for uncritical common sense. The appeal to self-evidence is not without merit, however, for ethical principles come to play such a vital role in human culture and are considered to be so important that those who flout them or fail to see their obligatory character are rightfully blamed as immoral.

3. *Ethical principles are not simply subjective emotional attitudes or states unamenable to any critical justification.* There are important objective criteria that we use to evaluate ethical principles.

How then would one go about appraising or justifying a principle? Even to ask for a justification is to initiate a course of ethical inquiry and is to presuppose some degree of objectivity. In this process of deliberation, cognition assumes an important role, supplementing mere faith or authority; it means that reason, in some sense, becomes constitutive in any judgment that emerges from the inquiry. Insofar as rules and principles are tested by rational considerations and by the relevant evidence, they are transformed from unexamined moral assumptions and principles into critical ethical principles. The moral principles that govern our behavior are rooted in habit and custom, feeling and fashion. Ethical principles emerge in the same rich soil of human experience, but are now consciously watered and pruned by critical intelligence.

In this process, one does not begin at the beginning, but *in rem,* in the midst of life and in the context of established and antecedent sets of the rules and norms. Intelligence translates arbitrary rules into informed judgments that are fashioned in the light of reason. This point is vital. The radical revolutionary, particularly in corrupt societies, wishes to destroy all preexisting social structures that he considers morally degrading; he wishes to wipe the slate clean and begin anew. One can appreciate the abhorrence of corrupt, oppressive, and hypocritical *ancien régimes;* and at times, drastic actions may need to be taken to restore social justice. Still, this does not mean that all norms, principles, and values can be overthrown; only some should be, and others should be retained as expressions of the collective ethical wisdom of the race.

Hence, my first point is that humankind, including the specific societies within it, already possesses a number of principles that are recognized and accepted as binding. This refers to precedence, to common law, and to the acceptable modes of conduct approved of by a social group and perhaps even enacted into law. The moral experiences, values, and principles already accepted by humankind in a historical context provide a starting point for morality.

If reason begins here, it does not mean, however, that it must remain here, because what is given is based on the problems of the past and on the solutions of earlier generations. The moral behavior of the past functioned in accordance with the philosophical and scientific outlook that then prevailed; and insofar as the scientific or practical knowledge may have been mistaken or limited, and has since been revised or added to, so the moral conceptions of the past may require modification. Similarly, many moral principles were introduced or slowly evolved to help people cope with their problems, but they may no longer be effective today, and indeed may be dysfunctional. Moreover, new problems may emerge, which the old-time religion or morality is unable to deal with. The old verities may not apply to present realities.

There is a glacierlike lag that persists in the moral domain: habits become so deeply entrenched that they are difficult to change. *Some* principles of moral order, no matter how archaic, are no doubt better than none, and are, in any case, essential for social cohesion. Yet many habits, no matter how venerable, ossify into mere prejudices and may need to be revised or abandoned if the society is not to stultify in repression.

How shall we change and for what reasons? First, I submit, by an appeal to *factual evidence*. To illustrate: Many people believe in capital punishment as the general moral principle that applies to the treatment of murderers. They may support their beliefs by referring to the old biblical adage, "An eye for an eye and a tooth for a tooth," which they utter as an article of deep-seated faith. The belief that murderers should be executed by the state, however, may also be related in part to the conviction that only capital punishment will deter murder, and that if a society were to abandon this method of punishment, the community would be at risk.

The factual question can only be resolved, if it can be resolved at all, by scientifically conducted sociological and psychological studies. Do societies that enforce the death penalty have lower rates of murder than those that do not? This is an empirical question. One can speculate about the answer, but only detailed scientific inquiry can resolve the question. But another key point is this: Would a person who believed in the death penalty because he thought it deterred crime be willing to abandon his belief if it were definitely established that it did not? And, conversely, can those who are opposed to capital punishment as a barbaric and ineffective method of treating murderers be persuaded to change their minds, if it could be shown that capital punishment did significantly deter crime?

I shall not present the evidence pro and con. I am merely pointing to the significance of factual data in modifying moral attitudes. I do *not* wish to argue that one can deduce ethical principles from the facts—that would be a form of the naturalistic fallacy—but only that our knowledge of the facts is relevant to our judgments. One cannot simply derive what "ought" to be the case by knowing what "is" the case. Nonetheless, knowledge of the full facts in a situation does help us to make wiser decisions.

Another illustration of the point concerns the question of whether homosexuals should be entitled to the same rights as heterosexuals, and whether, for example, sodomy should continue to be prohibited by the law, as it now is in many states and in some other nations. A crucial factual question is relevant: Is homosexuality genetically determined? Are those who express a preference for members of the same sex so disposed by biological causes that in effect a person's sexual orientation has been established at birth? There is some evidence that homosexuality exists in other species, which might suggest a genetic basis. E. O. Wilson has even postulated a possible socio-biological adaptive function for the appearance of certain homosexual members of the species. Whatever the truth or falsity of this claim, if people were born with their sexual orientation or developed it so early that they have little or no control over it, is it right for the community to condemn and/or prohibit such conduct?

The Roman Catholic church considers homosexual conduct sinful and urges continence and celibacy for homosexual individuals. Similarly, the effort to stamp out homosexuality by legislation is based on the premise that such individuals have voluntarily selected their lifestyle and can choose not to be gay. No doubt some element of choice does enter into the picture: Everyone must choose how to express their sexuality, regardless of their sexual orientation; one must decide whether to be promiscuous or to pursue a monogamous relationship. Also, under certain conditions, such as in the army, in prison, or in a monastery, homosexual conduct may be exacerbated among individuals who otherwise might not express a same-sex preference. But still, some scientific knowledge of the causes of homosexuality are relevant. For if we were to find that such individuals are unable to change their sexual proclivities, it would be oppressive of their rights as human beings to expressly deny what is for them part of their "natural" selves.

This does not mean that society may not regulate homosexual conduct that is overtly promiscuous, especially where the health of the community may be at stake, nor that it should not seek to protect the young from nonconsensual behavior. The issue of health especially raises factual questions. For example, the high incidence of certain diseases, such as AIDS, among homosexuals introduces questions of social control: Should bathhouses be closed, male prostitution regulated or prosecuted, or mandatory testing and treatment be required as a way to control the disease? If many or most homosexuals are unable to change their sexual orientation, should they have the same rights as heterosexuals to satisfy their needs? Such complex issues must be approached through fact-finding and analysis, and decisions should not rest simply on whether heterosexuals find homosexual behavior repugnant.

A second important test of an ethical principle is *comparative:* it lays down a general prescription for treating people or for behaving in relation to them. But principles may have to be modified if better principles are to be discovered. Some people no doubt think that there are, ideally at least, a set of ethical principles—such as those relating to justice or fairness—which at some point we can discover, and that these would reflect the norms of all human beings. This was Plato's quest in the *Republic,* as he sought an ideal, utopian definition of "the Good." I think that we need to be very cautious in this regard, for there is great danger that a fixed authoritarian model may be imposed. As I have said, morality and the principles of ethics should be open to modification as societies encounter new problems different from those of the past. Hence the need for revisionary and experimental approaches to many ethical questions. However, it is clear at the same time that many of the moral and ethical principles that have evolved, insofar as they deal with common human problems and needs, will remain the common heritage and moral wisdom of the human race and cannot be tampered with easily or abandoned in a cavalier manner.

Third, the most significant test of an ethical principle has not been stated yet, and that is the need to examine the *consequences* of proposed rules of conduct. We can judge principles not simply by what they state or enunciate, nor by our pious fidelity to them, but by how they work out in practice. The biblical adage is relevant: It is by their fruits that we best may know and judge them.

This appeal to consequences is a pragmatic test. A principle may seem fine on paper, but once put into practice, its end result may be disastrous. An illustration of this is the idea of participatory democracy, to which many people in the modern world are committed. The ethical principle postulates that all individuals in an organization should have an equal voice in determining the policies of that organization and the manner in which they are governed. Does that mean that everyone should have an equal vote? This seems eminently fair at the political level, particularly in guarding against oppressive governments; for the right of dissent and the legal right of opposition are strong bulwarks against tyrannical regimes.

But whether the participatory principle can be extended without qualification and in the same way to all institutions of society is highly questionable. For example, the movement for unlimited participatory democracy in universities and colleges can bring about confusion and lower standards of excellence. Students should participate in discussions of policies and curricula. They should not be treated as mere passive consumers without the ability to intelligently evaluate the content of the education being offered. Bright students, in particular, will be demanding of course offerings and quality of instruction.

Still, the application of participatory democracy, without recognizing the demonstrated competence of faculties in evaluating the educational content of programs, can lead to foolhardy behavior, as was the case in the 1960s in many universities.

By referring to the test of consequences, I do not mean simply the utilitarian greatest-happiness principle. If taken literally, this can lead to unfortunate results. Can a majority, for example, deny rights to recalcitrant minorities, if this would lead to the greatest good for the greatest number? Surely not, for there are certain principles and rights that should not be eliminated, no matter how beneficial the results would be to the majority. Some might say that the reason we are unwilling to deprive minorities of their rights is because of the long-range negative consequences, and that the ultimate test is still the greatest-happiness principle. This argument has some merit, but one might respond that one ought not to deprive others of their rights on intrinsic and not simply utilitarian grounds.

In any case, I would argue that the test of consequences is *plural* and not singular, for we cherish *many* values and principles that we wish to preserve; and hence to seek to derive a single principle may endanger the entire body of our values and principles. As a matter of fact, a wide spectrum of values and principles in a particular context of inquiry may be at stake; we may desire to preserve or enhance them, and it is important to examine carefully what a particular principle will do to them.

Here the consequentialist test is also empirical, because presumably the results can actually be observed in the world. We may, it is true, speculate about what might happen if a certain principle were adopted, but only concrete testing of the principle is decisive. Sometimes we may not be able to embark on such a course of experimental action, for it may entail too much risk; and so, our only test would be a hypothetical one. For example, a powerful political leader might ask, in weighing options, what would happen if a nuclear exchange began between the major powers? Would the human species be annihilated? Such a test would hardly be feasible.

There is a fourth criterion for appraising the worth of a principle, and that is the appeal to *consistency*. Kant's famous test of the validity of an ethical principle was its universality; before we commit an act, he said, we must ascertain whether the maxim under which we propose to act could become the universal rule for all mankind. He considered this a purely formal logical test. If the rule would contradict the entire framework of morality, we would not be entitled to make an exception for ourselves. We cannot lie, cheat, or commit homicide, for example, for if these were to become universal laws, moral conduct would be impossible.

Critics have pointed out two main difficulties with Kant's criterion. First, it is difficult to maintain that any maxims are absolutes, for exceptions may be justified on ethical grounds. This is especially the case where there is a conflict of duties. Hence, rules should only be interpreted, as I have already argued, as general *prima facie* duties and not absolute imperatives. Whether we actually have an obligation to do something would depend upon the context. Kant's categorical imperative is thus too formal and empty to serve as the sole guide for conduct. Second, the test of a rule is not formal consistency with the moral order, as Kant thought, but depends upon the examination of the consequences of action. It is because consequences are viewed as destructive to morality in an empirical sense that a rational agent decides to forbear. Kant's categorical imperative does serve us in ethical decision-making as one factor to consider, among others, but not as a decisive or single criterion.

Nonetheless, there is a logical test that is important, and that is the test of the *internal* consistency of our principles. No single ethical principle should be judged in abstract isolation without considering its logical effect upon other principles to which we are committed. Thus, we need to ask whether a new or old principle contradicts other principles we hold. If so, we may find ourselves to be hypocritical or holding a double standard. If, for example, we posit that all human beings are entitled to equal consideration but exclude women from this principle, we are limiting our definition of human beings to males, and it is obvious that we are disregarding half the human species. Thus we either have to abandon our general principle or reinterpret it to extend it to women. The appeal to consistency is a fundamental method for evaluating, revising, and extending principles. It is used by judges and courts of law, particularly in democratic societies, and has historically been involved in the battle for the recognition of new liberties and rights. Consistency thus is an essential criterion in addition to the appeal to facts and consequences in appraising principles.

One caution needs to be introduced at this point: it is the need to guard against the tyranny of principles. A moral principle, once it is enunciated and reaffirmed, may be considered so vital to human justice that it is thought no exception can be made to its application. In some cases, however, the rule of consistency can become oppressive, for when applied in actual life a principle may be destructive to the constellation of other values and principles that we cherish, a kind of self-righteous fervor may take over and moral fanaticism may rule.

One can think of firmly held moral principles that became slogans for radical revolution or reactionary repression. "All power to the people" may sound fine in theory as a universal rule, but when put into practice by an unruly mob or a revolutionary tribunal, it may lead to despotism.

"All abortions are wrong" is declared universally binding by the right-to-life groups seeking to preserve what they view to be the sanctity of life. They wish to defend the "life of an innocent fetus," but are willing, in a cavalier fashion, to undermine women's rights to reproductive freedom. In some situations, bringing a pregnancy to term might harm the woman (as in the case of rape or incest), or produce a seriously deformed fetus; right-to-lifers do not propose to pay the medical bills in such situations or raise the infants themselves. Still, these pro-life groups insist on absolute fidelity to their principle. Their opponents point out, using the consistency criterion, that many of those who are against the killing of fetuses defend other forms of killing such as capital punishment or the killing of innocent civilians in times of war.

Another illustration of the appeal to consistency is the attempt to apply the libertarian principle with nondiscriminatory universality and without viewing its consequences. That "individuals ought to control their own lives" seems a persuasive rule to govern our conduct, one that we ought to respect. Yet if it is taken as an absolute and without exception, it may in some cases harm both the individual and the community. I remember questioning a well-known libertarian who insisted that all addictive drugs, including heroin and cocaine, should be legalized; to be consistent with the primacy of individual liberty, he argued, the state should not seek to regulate private conduct in any way.

"What if the legalization of such addictive drugs would most directly

harm disadvantaged minority youth living in poverty in the ghettos?"
I asked.

His reply was, "I guess they'll have to learn their lesson. Perhaps
an entire generation of young people will have to be lost." He thought
this policy was consistent with his libertarian philosophy, but it seems
to me that in not allowing any exception, he was a victim of his principle,
unwilling to appraise it in the light of other principles and values he
undoubtedly cherished and failing to judge it by its actual consequences.

In summary, even if we abandon transcendental morality, and even
if the new ethics are relative to human interests and needs, we are not
thereby led to subjectivism in ethics. There is a kind of objective relativism
that we can and do appeal to, and there are objective standards for
judging the ethical principles that govern our lives.

A Catalogue of the Common Moral Decencies

Can critical ethical intelligence discover any *prima facie* general principles
that transcend the limits of cultural relativity and apply to all human
beings, no matter what their social condition? Are there any ethical
principles that we can affirm to be objectively true, independent of whether
there is a God who has declared them to be binding? I submit that
there are and that they are so fundamental to human intercourse that
they may be characterized as the "common moral decencies." Indeed,
virtually all human cultures have now come to recognize their significance,
for they lay down moral imperatives necessary for group cohesion and
survival. Individuals who abide by them are commended and praised,
and those who flout or transgress them are condemned and blamed
as immoral, wicked, or evil.

To state that certain forms of conduct are decent, admirable, or
proper, and that other forms are indecent and improper, even despicable,
is not simply subjective caprice or an expression of cultural bias, but
is, I think, a function of a level of moral development that has cross-
cultural dimensions. There is still wide diversity in human conduct; there
are numerous disputes about what is considered decent or indecent
behavior, and there is much variation in moral judgment. Nonetheless,
there is a basic core of principles that we have come to recognize as
binding in human conduct. We may apply the term *common* to these
"decencies" as a qualification, for we speak only of the most fundamental
principles that are widely held, leaving many other layers of moral

principles open to further critical examination. I use the term *moral* rather than *ethical* because I think the recognition that there are fairly basic moral principles that ought to govern conduct between civilized individuals has become deeply ingrained in long-standing social traditions. These principles are supported by habit and custom, are enacted into law, and are even considered sacred by various religions.

Far from being derived from some transcendental source, the moral decencies are taken as divinely revealed precisely *because* they are considered so basic to the human community. The fact that they have been converted into the language of divinity is a further sign of how highly esteemed they are. They can, however, have an authentic cognitive and independent ground; these principles are justifiable by rational considerations and are based upon practical ethical wisdom. Indeed, they express the deepest wisdom of the human race and can be discovered by anyone who digests the fruit of the tree of knowledge of good and evil. Interestingly, theists and humanists share in their commitment to the moral decencies, for people of all persuasions inherit a common wisdom, even though they may dispute the ultimate foundations of morality.

The following catalogue of moral principles should not be taken on a scale of ascending or descending priority. The order in which they are listed is simply one of convenience, for in any particular situation, one or more may assume higher priority than another. They should be interpreted as general guides for conduct rather than absolute or universal commandments, but this does not mean that their obligatory force is weakened; for a rational moral being can recognize their significance no less than can a God-intoxicated believer. It is important that we present them explicitly, since ethical philosophy should not be a metatheoretical and abstract exercise but should have a normative relevance to conduct. It is especially important for humanism to provide a catalogue of the moral decencies, in order to counter the unfounded charge that it has no moral principles.

Moral principles concern our relationship to other human beings living in communities; they would have little meaning for a hermit living in isolation in a cave or on a desert island. Some can also be applied to other sentient species, so that it makes some sense to talk about animal rights. Although moral principles are forms of social behavior, they need to be structured within the character of the individual if they are to have any efficacy or force.

There is some overlapping of these principles, and some are subsumed under others. Nevertheless, it is important that they be separately defined and classified. The following list should not be taken as exhaustive or complete. There are no doubt other principles that might be added. But at least the following provide a basic framework for ethical conduct and choice.

I. Integrity

1. *Truthfulness:* the quality of being truthful; veracity; accuracy in representing reality. This quality is basic to all human social relationships, for people cannot live and work together if there is a deliberate effort to withhold, falsify, or erase the truth. Negative: to lie; to be deceitful.

Interestingly, this principle does not appear in a forthright statement in the Ten Commandments, although one variant does appear: "Thou shalt not bear false witness against thy neighbor." Nor is it central to the Sermon on the Mount.

Nonetheless, telling the truth is a common moral decency expected in all civilized communities and probably in the majority of so-called primitive societies. When people deceive each other, it is difficult to count on them. Lying makes true communication impossible. When we do not know when to believe a person, we cannot rely on any aspect of his or her behavior.

People may disagree about what the truth is. They may differ as to what the facts of a particular case are, or how to interpret them, or what their causes are, but they are obligated to state the truth insofar as they know it—or believe they know it—without any deliberate intention to deceive others. The person who does not follow this principle is a liar.

The question of telling a harmless white lie is not an issue here; nor are the moral dilemmas that may arise when lying to someone may be considered—that is, not in one's self-interest but for the other person's good, especially when *not* lying conflicts with other general ethical principles equally binding. There are exceptions to any general rule, but such transgressions need to be justified before the rule can be overridden. Still, this does not deny the widespread human recognition that, all things considered equal, we have a *prima facie* obligation to be truthful.

In social contexts, one may swear an affidavit, take an oath, certify that one is telling the truth, or even take a lie-detector test, if it is believed that such will guarantee truthfulness. Truthfulness is basic to science, philosophy, and any discipline concerned with discovering the truth. It is fundamental to an open and free society but lacking in totalitarian and authoritarian societies, in which the elite attempts to cover up inadequacies, suppress dissent, and censor any attempt to speak or publish the truth. Such lying is a violation of a basic moral principle, not only from the standpoint of the individual but also from the standpoint of the community.

2. *Promise-keeping:* honoring a pledge; living up to one's agreement. In everyday life, if one makes a promise in good faith to another person, then it would be immoral to break that promise. Negative: failing to honor one's commitments; to be derelict and unfaithful; to not be true to one's word; to exhibit bad faith.

A promise is a declaration made to another person, who then expects that it will be fulfilled in the future by either performance ("I promise I will repay you") or forbearance ("I promise not to tell anyone"). It is a commitment other people may rely upon. It may include a solemn oath, vow, or assurance. The one who makes the promise has a responsibility to the person to whom he makes the promise. Implicit in this is the recognition that in some cases circumstances may become so altered that one does not have the means to fulfill a promise made in good faith.

This may involve the fulfilling of *contracts,* where two or more parties enter into an agreement or pact, in which both parties agree to perform or avoid certain acts, and in which one party, should he fail to fulfill his contractual obligations, stands in breach of contract. We not only have a moral but a legal duty to abide by agreements entered into freely and without duress. These include convenants entered into freely between contractual parties such as oaths of office, and vows of marriage. If one party to a contract violates it substantially, then the other party may not be bound to honor the terms of the contract. Some people make some promises they cannot possibly keep. They may do so to please others, in which case their motives are beneficent; or perhaps they do so to deceive others, in order to get them to buy a product or contract for a service, in which case their motives are malevolent.

3. *Sincerity:* the quality of being candid, frank, free of hypocrisy, and sincere in one's relations with others, especially on a one-to-one, personal basis. Negative: to be insincere, hypocritical, false, deceitful.

Sincerity is essential to building trust. It is a sign of moral integrity. A sincere person is truthful in his dealings with others; he is not disingenuous or artful in concealing ulterior motives. Between lovers and friends, sincerity is essential if confidence is not to be broken. If a person cannot trust what another says, then it is difficult to cooperate on common tasks. An insincere person takes another in and misuses him for his own purposes. In extreme cases he may be cunning. On the other hand, there may be some limits to the degree of sincerity possible in human relations. One may be artless and too self-effacing in his dealings with others. He may confide too quickly in another or confess his affection or love too readily, so as to disarm or embarrass the other person, who may not share his feelings. Sincerity is a necessary bond in human relations, and we have an obligation to follow it, though we need not bare our inner soul to anyone and everyone at the first opportunity.

4. *Honesty:* the quality of integrity or fairness in dealing with others. "Honesty is the best policy" is an aphorism widely accepted in common parlance, but often flouted in behavior. If no one could be trusted, all social interactions would break down. Negative: to be dishonest, deceitful, fraudulent, false, crooked.

I am using the term *honesty* here to pertain primarily to not using deceitful means to take material advantage. In human relations, it is important that we be able to trust another person's word. If someone says one thing and then turns around and does something else, such a person is without integrity. If he conceals a hidden motive, and is seeking to beguile or deceive another, then he cannot be trusted. Dishonesty is distinct from insincerity, though these vices overlap, because it is resorted to in order to gain some advantage. A dishonest person is willing to commit fraud. He may cheat or sell out for a price. His behavior is not honorable and he soon loses his credibility and our respect. The temptation to dishonesty is for the profit or prestige that one can reap. Dishonest people are hypocritical and duplicitous; they are insincere and willing to lie and break promises. Conversely, an honest person will tell the truth and fulfill his contractual obligations insofar as he is able to do so. Probity in dealing with others is essential if we are not to lose our reputations. Once one has a repututation for false dealing, his career may be ruined.

In the economic sphere, selling adulterated products, lying to consumers, or cheating them are pernicious forms of dishonesty. On the political and economic level, the opposite of honesty is graft and corruption.

II. Trustworthiness

1. *Fidelity:* the quality of being loyal; showing allegiance, fealty. This principle applies to one's attachments to friends, relatives, and the community. Negative: infidelity, treachery, perfidy, or betrayal.

In human relationships we build up bonds of common interests, we share values, and we are committed to similar goals to which we all strive together. A person is expected to continue his loyalty to another in a one-on-one relationship, or to a group if he has pledged allegiance and has received mutual benefits. He is not to betray the trust—particularly for personal gain or advantage—unless he has an overriding justification. Our obligation to be faithful is based on our previous commitments, which we have the responsibility to uphold.

Fidelity is an essential principle in a viable marriage, where the partners have demonstrated trust and love for each other. It also applies to brothers and sisters, parents and children, and other members of the family. Fidelity is the bond that also holds friends together through adversity or prosperity. This means that there is some constancy of commitment and steadiness of attachment, rather than capricious or infantile behavior. Fidelity not only applies to persons but to an individual's commitment to a cause, to his principles, or to the group or nation. We are not talking about blind allegiance or fanatic loyalty, but fidelity that is responsible and devotional. It is a mature commitment, opposed to fecklessness, vacillation, and disloyalty. No matter what a person's relationship to others or to a group, he or she is expected not to betray them. The principle of fidelity needs to be extended to ever-wider communities of humankind, though it has its origin in small interpersonal relationships.

Where the trusted individual or group has committed a grave moral transgression (e.g., treachery, murder, etc.), then one may deem it permissible to waive fidelity in the name of a higher principle or cause, but a clear justification must be given for this.

2. *Dependability:* the quality of being reliable and responsible. The importance of reliability in human affairs is well-recognized. Negative: to be untrustworthy, undependable, irresponsible.

We depend on other persons to do the things they promise to do, for which they are employed or with which they are charged. People assume different roles in society, and in the division of labor we come to expect that they will discharge their obligations and duties honorably. Parents have responsiblities to properly nurture and care for their children. Teachers are charged with the education of the young. People in public life have the duties of their offices to discharge. We expect that workers, office personnel, doctors, lawyers, administrators, etc. be trustworthy and do their jobs well. If they are undependable, lazy, indifferent— if we cannot count on them—especially when they have agreed to assume a job, then they are negligent and can rightly be criticized. In human relations we bestow confidence on certain individuals; if they betray our trust in them, then it is difficult to live or work cooperatively with them. Irresponsible behavior is blameworthy. Accordingly, once one is specifically entrusted with certain duties, he is obligated to fulfill them or to responsibly notify the appropriate person if he cannot.

III. Benevolence

1. *Good will:* to have noble intentions, a virtuous disposition; to demonstrate trust. In our dealings with others, it is important that we have a positive attitude toward those who are deserving of it, and that we express good intentions toward them. Negative: to be malicious; to show ill-will, hostility; to be distrustful, suspicious.

This principle means that we should have good feelings about others, wishing them well and not seeking to do them harm. It suggests that we should always think the best of others unless they are scoundrels, and even then, they may have some redeeming virtues that we can discover. We should always try, if possible, to find something good to say about another person, and seek to appreciate his virtues rather than to criticize his faults. Moreover, we should be glad when he prospers and be pleased when he is happy. We should not exult in the misery of others. In general, it means that we show some care, concern, or thoughtful regard for the needs of others.

The antonym of this is *malice,* to wish people to make fools of themselves, to fail in their efforts, or indeed to suffer harm. The Tenth Commandment says that we should not *covet* another person's belongings. Among the most difficult of human vices to control is *envy* of what someone has, or *jealousy* of his achievements, talents, or possessions. This passion may be all-consuming and destructive to viable relationships of trust, or to effective learning, working, and functioning. If allowed to grow unimpeded, it can destroy persons and corrode nations.

The principle of good will is the willingness to allow others to live and let live. A person with good will does not wish to deny other persons good fortune or success because he himself may lack them. Instead he hopes for the best for everyone. A person of genuine good will often finds that his motives are misinterpreted by people who lack good will; though he is sincere in his aims, others may accuse him of the same perfidy to which they are prone.

The opposite of good will is *hatred*, which can lead to an all-consuming and seething rage between enemies, jilted lovers, former friends, or competitive rivals. Though one might compete against rivals in a sports contest or commerce or in time of war, one should strive to maintain *some* degree of fairness and courtesy toward one's opponents. If one loses, it should be with some grace; one should not wish to get even or bear undue resentment. This means that *vindictive* conduct is patently wrong. One should not seek to retaliate, or to make others pay for their wins or for one's own misfortunes.

One form of good will that is more general than its expression on the personal level is *benevolence*, the love for humanity and the desire to increase the sum total of human happiness. This is expressed in a philanthropic, charitable, and humanitarian devotion to worthy projects.

2. *Nonmalfeasance as applied to persons:* refraining from harming or injuring others. This principle is related to good will; it denies the right to inflict harm on other persons, without necessarily requiring that we confer benefits upon them. Negative: harmful or malefic actions or evil deeds against others.

Nonmalfeasance involves the following important list of prohibitions that are necessary in any civilized community. Anyone who flouts them transgresses the most basic principles of moral conduct. This applies not only to the members of our own inner circle, tribe, or nation, but to all men and women, whatever their ethnicity. It is the principle of brotherhood, which unfortunately is violated constantly in times of war, when the rules of decent behavior are usually abandoned.

Do not kill other human beings.

Do not inflict physical violence or bodily injury on them.

Do not deprive them of food, shelter, clothing, or other necessities of life.

Do not be cruel, spiteful, vengeful, or vindictive.

Do not inflict harsh or inhuman punishment on anyone, even those who have severely transgressed these principles.

Do not torture or inflict unnecessary psychological suffering upon them.

Do not kidnap persons, take them as hostages, or hold them against their will.

Do not terrorize innocent persons by threats to life or limb.

Do not rape (see "Sexual consent" below).

Do not libel, slander, defame, or seek to destroy the careers of others.

Do not harm others by gossip or innuendo; do not spread false rumors or calumny.

Do not abuse children, the helpless, the weak, or the disadvantaged who are unable to fight back or defend themselves.

Do not harm by revenge or carry on a vendetta for past wrongs.

3. *Nonmalfeasance as applied to private and public property:* showing respect for the property of others or of the community. Persons have a right to possess property they acquire honestly, without fear of theft or plunder. Negative: to rob, steal, plunder.

The act of theft of lawful possessions is considered a crime punishable by law in all societies that sanction the holding of private property. The most extreme form of robbery is the use of force or intimidation to compel a person to give up property through acts that may involve threats to life or limb. Plunder or pillage in time of war involves spoilation and extortion, often on a vast scale. In extreme cases, this involves sacking and ravaging an area. It may also occur at the hands of bandits who loot, pirates who seek booty, kidnappers who seek ransom, or even arsonists who maliciously destroy property.

Robbery may occur surreptitiously when the victim is absent, but it is obviously still wrong. Another form of robbery is the deliberate effort to defraud persons of what is rightfully theirs.

When we say that persons ought to respect the property of others, we are referring to property that is rightfully obtained and not unlawfully gained by misbegotten means.

The principle similarly can be extended to public property. The prohibition here is against the purposeful looting, defacing, misusing, or neglecting the common property of a group or association, or the public property of the state.

4. *Sexual consent:* to have mutually consensual, voluntary sex. This

is a form of the nonmalfeasance principle as applied to private sexual conduct between adults. Negative: to rape, require sexual submission, to abuse or harass sexually.

The act of rape is a violation of an individual's rights as a free person and is abhorred by the civilized community. This means that sexual relations depend upon consent given by both parties. It means that there will be no use of physical coercion to seize or force a person to have sexual intercourse. Included under this is the use of intimidation or duress to force a person to submit to any degree of penetration of any orifice of the body. Whether this applies to marriage partners is open to dispute. Generally, it has not been applied to marriage partners, and those who force their partners to have sex have not been considered rapists; today many women think that the definition of rape should be extended to protect them from brutal husbands—and certainly from estranged ones.

Included in this principle is the recognition that sexual consent explicitly excludes children below the age of consent. (See Chapter Eight, on privacy.) The use of force or deception in order to have sexual relations with children is specifically proscribed and considered even by hardened criminals to be the worst crime. It is severely punished by the civilized community.

A broader form of the principle of sexual consent is now under intense debate, and that is whether society should permit private, nonmarital, and especially homosexual, relations. Historically, many societies have regulated what they consider to be deviant forms of sexual conduct, prostitution, anal or oral intercourse (whether hetero- or homosexual), and sadomasochism, even though it is difficult to police most forms of sexual conduct, since most sex acts occur in private.

The extended principle would permit any type of sexual relationship between consenting adults and prohibit the state from intruding into the bedroom and prosecuting the varieties of sexual preference. Another problem that emerges is whether the state should regulate sexual relations between adult members of the same family (brothers, sisters, aunts, uncles) and all forms of sadomasochism, even where there is consensual agreement between the parties. (See Chapter Eight.) These expressions of sexual orientation, however, are generally not recognized under the common moral decencies, and the extension of the principle of sexual consent to them is a recent development.

5. *Beneficence:* kindness, sympathy, altruism, compassion. To perform a good deed, to be helpful or thoughtful, to be humanitarian, and to bestow gifts are acts of beneficence. This is the positive desire to help others, to improve their lives, to confer benefits, to reduce misery, to spread happiness. Negative: to be malevolent, harmful, selfish, uncharitable.

A beneficent attitude toward others is deserving of the highest praise. Some individuals may be so limited in means that they are unable to contribute very much to charity. But a beneficent person is willing to go out of his way to do a good deed. This involves empathy with the needs of others. It means that we ought to be considerate of the feelings of other human beings and seek to assist them if we can. This may not cost very much: to give up one's seat on a crowded train or bus, to help a blind person across the road, to lend a helping hand to someone injured or in need of solace are all beneficent acts. It means also that one should do what one can to reduce a person's misery or suffering, and even, if possible, to contribute to his care, education, nourishment, pleasure, or happiness. Many people discover that it feels better to give than to receive and that the pleasures of altruistic behavior outweigh the pleasures of self-seeking gratification.

Moralists have pointed out that the principle of beneficence, or doing good to others, is less binding than the principle of nonmalfeasance, or not harming them. Within the family unit, however, relatives have an obligation to assist family members in distress, and if possible, to afford the means for them to prosper. The more spontaneous this is, the more satisfying it is; the more satisfying it is, the easier it becomes. Altruism among friends and relatives is expected, and one condemns egocentric behavior in this context. We call upon those we love to assist us in time of need, to make sacrifices of time and money. Jesus' admonition that we should "love one another" is the noblest expression of this principle. A morally decent person recognizes, for instance, that if we are all seated around a table, no one in our midst should want for food; he will willingly break bread with others.

Beneficence has two dimensions: (1) an injunction to assist mercifully in order to alleviate pain, suffering, or deprivation for those we are able to help, and (2) a positive prescription to increase the sum of the goods a person can attain in life. The real question, again, is how far the principle of beneficence shall be extended: to all men and women—including the starving in Africa and the diseased in the slums of Asia—

or only toward those within our range?

The state can enact legislation to protect individuals from harming one another; for example, force or fraud is considered a crime and can be punished. Thus although the state can regulate negative behavior, it can hardly legislate altruism in those individuals who lack it. In some societies, it provides tax-incentives for voluntary contributions to charity, thus encouraging beneficent action. The principle of nonmalfeasance is considered too important to be left to private action and is thus enforced by the state. The principle of beneficence, on the contrary, cannot easily be enforced.

IV. Fairness

1. *Gratitude:* the quality of being grateful, of having friendly and warm feelings toward a benefactor. In human relationships, it is important that we show some appreciation for favors done for us. Negative: ingratitude; to be ungrateful, unappreciative.

Many individuals are pleased to bestow a gift or a favor, or to lend a helping hand to someone who needs or wants it. They may not wish recompense nor expect anything in return, but would welcome some sign of appreciation. The recipient should manifest some gratitude, by thanking the person or acknowledging his help. Perhaps at some future time, he may return a favor in kind or render a service. Those who are oblivious to good deeds bestowed and act as though they believe they have favors coming to them are ingrates, insensible to what others have done for them. If a good society is to prosper with beneficent actions, the quality of beneficence is watered by signs of appreciative response. In some cases, the help proferred may be long overdue, niggardly, or inadequate, and may not deserve recognition. Where it is worthy, however, it merits gratitude. The recognition should be dignified, without obsequiousness or groveling; for the benefactor to demand this would itself be indecent.

2. *Accountability:* the quality of being answerable for conduct. There is a deep sense that a person who commits a foul deed that harms another, particularly an act such as murder, robbery, or rape, should not be allowed to remain unpunished. Negative: not being answerable for conduct.

Implicit in this principle is the idea that individuals should be held responsible for injuring others and should be called to account for it. For a grave moral crime to go unanswered may be considered unjust. Moreover, there is the conviction that if a criminal is allowed to go unpunished, the societal order will degenerate. The victim or his relatives or the community at large may feel so aggrieved that unless some accountability to the public is rendered, moral outrage may only be compounded.

In the strong form, this includes the demand for revenge, whereby one inflicts equal suffering, pain, or loss so that the punishment fits the crime. The penalty imposed either may be invoked as an act of retribution for its own sake, or, in more developed moral communities, may be used to deter future moral transgressions and crimes. In this way society attempts to protect itself, and if possible, to reform the criminal. In civilized communities, cruel and unusual, barbarous, or degrading punishment is deemed inappropriate.

One form the principle of accountability takes is the demand for damages. Where culpability has been established, and particularly where there has been an attempt to harm another through malice, it is felt that some form of reparation ought to be made. When someone has injured another person or harmed his property, the victim can sometimes sue for damages.

The whole effort of civilized conduct is to establish procedures for determining guilt and then seeing to it that there is a just application of the laws. In extenuating circumstances or for first-time offenders, society recognizes that there are some grounds for mercy. Related to this is the need to forgive and forget at some point and to avoid vindictiveness or revenge, especially when a person has made a mistake and admits it, shows some remorse, or has learned from his errors. In such cases the better part of valor is to be forgiving, not carry a grudge, and even at some point to welcome the reformed criminal back into the community.

3. *Justice:* fairness, equity, rectitude. That justice ought to prevail is widely held in civilized communities, even though there may be widespread disagreement about what it is. Negative: injustice, unfairness, partiality.

In its simplest sense, justice refers to meting out just deserts, that is, punishment for misdeeds and reward for merit. The principle of accountability enters here, as do notions of equity and rectitude.

Also involved in the principle of justice is the idea of equitable compensation for work performed or services rendered. This involves a normative standard for distributing the goods and services of society. People should be paid an honest wage for an honest day's work; income and/or wealth should be equitably divided among those who have earned and/or deserve what they have received. The principle of fairness is present here. In democratic societies, other manifestations of justice have emerged: the rule of law, equality, and liberty. All individuals are considered equal before the law and should not seek to obtain special privileges and immunities which others in the community lack.

The modern democratic principle thus suggests equality of consideration: each person is equal to all others in dignity and value. Similar is the principle of liberty and the opportunity to pursue happiness without undue interference. New ideas of economic equality have been introduced in modern society. Implicit in the principle of justice is the belief that there ought to be penalties for discrimination based upon racial, religious, ethnic, or sexual differences. Should those who are unable to work receive some support from society? Should the basic needs of the disadvantaged be satisfied? Should society help those who through no fault of their own are unable to care for themselves? The dispute between capitalism and socialism takes us far beyond the elementary moral decencies to a more complicated doctrine of human rights and equality of opportunity and of treatment. Justice also requires an appeal to the use of peaceful methods of adjudicating differences equitably and harmoniously. It means that we should reason together in order to solve our problems and not resort to force or violence.

4. *Tolerance:* the quality of sympathetic understanding and broadmindedness. The toleration of individuals or nations who differ from us in values, manners, customs, or beliefs becomes an essential method of achieving peace and harmony in a civilized world. Negative: prejudice, bigotry, hatred, discrimination, narrow-mindedness, mean-spiritedness.

One of the faults of human beings is the tendency to reject and deny equal access or rights to individuals or groups who do not share our beliefs and practices. This can happen within the community, where we may disapprove of the lifestyles or values of other individuals; or it can apply to other groups, cultures, races, or nations, whose customs and beliefs we find alien to ours. We may disapprove of their tastes or norms, and think that their beliefs are false, bizarre, or wicked. The tendency is to seek to censor or prohibit differing values and beliefs.

We may even fear them or believe that they are a great danger to our community. We may feel that if they are allowed to go unchecked, our own cherished values would be undermined. Thus the desire is to suppress them.

The tolerant person may differ with others in his community, yet forbear any effort to suppress them. He believes that he has a moral obligation to allow diverse styles of life to express themselves. To tolerate does not necessarily mean to approve; it merely means that we will not seek to prohibit differences by legislation, nor use force to root them out. Tolerance need not imply permissiveness. An open and pluralistic society will permit some measure of freedom so long as those to whom it is extended will not seek to prevent others from enjoying the same rights. It does not necessarily mean that "anything goes" and that no standards of criticism are possible.

Tolerance applies to a broad range of subject matters: moral and religious beliefs, practices and ethnic customs. It is opposed to any discrimination on racial, religious, economic, social, or sexual grounds. It also applies to philosophical, scientific, or political forms of belief.

To tolerate means that we accord other individuals or groups some respect—not that we agree with them, only that we recognize the rules of the game, and allow them some degree of liberty of belief, taste, and pursuits. In biblical terms, to tolerate the alien or the stranger in one's midst is to recognize that one may sometime be an alien in another land, hoping for the same measure of sympathy. Tolerance is a basic humanistic virtue. In modern times, humanists have defended the right of dissent of nonbelievers and heretics against the demands for conformity. It is a generalized moral principle and an expression of moral decency.

5. *Cooperation:* working together for peace, harmony, tranquility, or the social good. Maintaining a state of peace and amity between individuals within a community, between factions or states, is essential for the human social order. Negative: the inability or unwillingness to work with others to prevent or diminish war, hostility, strife, conflict, discord, and enmity.

That we should attempt to keep the peace and not resort to violent means in order to achieve our ends is a cardinal rule that all individuals and nations recognize in principle but unfortunately all too often violate in practice. We should use every effort to work out our differences peacefully. Negotiation is preferable as a mode of preventing strife or conflict, but to resort to power or force in human affairs is common.

The moral principle is that we should seek to avoid this and not impose our will upon other individuals or nations. Aggression against others with whom we cannot agree is destructive to all human values. If allowed to get out of hand, it leads to the killing or maiming of individuals or the despoiling of their property. Defensive measures of self-protection are justifiable against an aggressive enemy.

Warfare, though common, is hardly the best or most effective method for resolving differences. Aggression or the fear of it leads to retaliation or encourages preemptive strikes. It engenders intense hatred against one's enemies and a seething desire for revenge. People have resorted to war for any number of reasons: for territorial expansion, financial profit or plunder, to promote a cause, to convert heathens or barbarians, ostensibly to aid mankind, and to bring down tyrants or madmen. The toll of violence often can be terrible in human suffering and misery.

We ought to beat our swords into plowshares, says the Old Testament. "Turn the other cheek," says the New Testament. But both injunctions have been violated with impunity by Judeo-Christian nations. The Koran has been used as a justification for the Jihad, or the Holy War in the Middle East.

The principle of cooperation beseeches us to find an appropriate resolution for our differences, to strive as mightily as we can to negotiate, and to reach compromises that all parties to a dispute can accept. We need adjudication rather than confrontation. Unfortunately, men and women often sing praises to peace as they march off to war.

Under certain conditions a war can be a just one. This is particularly the case when it is a war of self-defense. It is difficult to justify a war of aggression, undertaken in order to achieve one's political ends or to seize power or amass riches. Under certain conditions, one may not be able to reach an understanding with an invading army or a menacing individual. One should try to negotiate or compromise, and war or violence should only be a last resort. It is only in a situation of clear and present danger and in order to protect oneself that appropriate force can be justified. The general rule of moral decency is to cooperate as best we can, to tolerate the differing views of others, and to negotiate. Whether in fact it is always possible to do this remains to be seen, but it should be both the rule and goal of conduct.

Although the preceding list of common moral decencies has merit and is widely accepted, at least in principle, by most civilized communities, how they work in practice will depend upon individual circumstances or different social situations. That they are not fully realized in human conduct should be evident to everyone. No one is perfect. These general principles only establish norms of decent conduct; they do not promise that everyone will observe them. Indeed, given the conflicts that may sometimes arise in life, individuals may violate their norms and principles. But this should not weaken our obligation to recognize their binding nature, and whenever possible to seek to live in the light of them.

Many more ethical principles have lately emerged in some societies, and some that we have discussed are still open to dispute in others. Both are products of a revisionary humanistic morality.

These include the doctrine of human rights, the right to privacy, an ecological concern for the environment, an imperative to seek to preserve other species on this planet, obligations to future generations, the need to transcend the limits of ethnicity, and a need to extend our ethical concerns to the wider world community.

Notes

1. E. O. Wilson, *Sociobiology: The New Synthesis* (Cambridge: Harvard University Press, 1975).
2. Konrad Lorenz, *On Aggression* (New York: Harcourt, Brace & World, 1966).

4
Excelsior:
The Ethics
of Excellence

What Is Value?

Thus far we have been discussing the common moral decencies that civilized communities have recognized and that critical ethical intelligence should take into account in order to reach wise decisions. Although we have dealt with the individual's moral behavior, we have left aside the question of the personal realization of the good life and the role that values play in ethical choices.

Some moralists have ignored questions concerning value, for they have thought that the center of morality must be our obligations to one another and the relationship of the individual to society. Kant fits into this category, for he believed that morality must be concerned with fulfilling the moral law, and not with considerations of personal happiness or of the good. But he was mistaken, for we do not live simply so that moral commandments be obeyed in and of themselves; rather we obey them because of their instrumental role in contributing to the good society, in actualizing individual human happiness. There is something disingenuous about deontological theories, whether religiously motivated or not, that take virtue and duty as the center of the moral life and minimize the need to realize the widest constellation of values that we cherish.

Many philosophers historically have focused on the good. They have sought to define its nature and delineate what it is and how it can be enhanced. A paradox has emerged, particularly sharp between humanistic and theistic approaches to morality: Is the central question of ethics maximizing goods, or doing what is right; realizing values, or obeying moral principles? Both the good and the right are, no doubt, essential to any complete theory of ethics, but central to our concern is the need to discover some measure of creative enjoyment and enrichment in life.

Value has a more specifiable meaning than the classical idea of the good, and it can be given a behavioral or operational definition. Good is a far more abstract concept, often related only to the moral good, whereas value encompasses a wider range of human activities (economic, social, aesthetic, etc.). Value, as I interpret it, does not exist independent of the processes of preferential behavior expressed by an organism. Wherever there is selective teleonomic activity,[1] valuing is going on. The worm has value for the bird, the carrot for the horse, the T-bone for the dog. Organisms engage in a number of focused activities, such as ferreting out objects and consuming them. Here, value has a biological basis; it is mixed with instinct and conditioned response. Certain goods have functional survival value for the organism, and it learns to strive after and appropriate them for its own purposes. Pleasures that accrue in the process of consumption also serve as a motive for future action, and there is an effort to engage in activities and seek out objects from which enjoyment is derived.

Valuing activities are also essential for the maintenance of human organisms. Built into the genetic endowment of the species are biological processes essential for its survival. During the processes of evolution, certain forms of behavior contribute to survival and have adaptive value. Eating, copulating, fleeing from danger, and fighting all trigger appropriate responses in behavior and have important biological functions. Every normal member of the species develops deep-seated somatic and homeostatic needs, and these have to be satisfied if the human organism is to survive and function. Pleasure is attached to the satisfaction of our basic needs, such as feeding and copulation. Human beings, as complex social animals, can only survive in groups; they have built-in bio-cooperative mechanisms to enable them to do so. Our biological stimuli are modified, however, in socio-cultural contexts, and new values emerge in civilization. Food and liquid are essential to sustain life, and humans embellish them in a variety of ways. The variety emerges from the geographical regions and socio-cultural traditions under which we live: from spaghetti or rice to escargot or filet mignon.

Similarly there are a whole range of bio-psychological needs and interests: sexual activities, art, music, poetry, sports, politics, and philosophy. We thus have a double nature: Our values are structured by our given genetic endowment, but they are also malleable and modifiable as conditioned and learned responses. Indeed, there are virtually unlimited varieties of tastes and appreciations cultivated within the cultural contexts in which humans are born and flower. In complex social systems, economic activities are geared to producing and distributing an incredible number of goods and services consumers will find enticing. Humans become so dependent upon such goods that they actually come to need them to live. Their worth is given a price and we engage in barter and trade in order to obtain them. We come to crave and exult in the fineries, delicacies, and luxuries afforded by civilized life.

Value may be defined as the object, or goal, of any interest, desire, or need on the part of the human organism. Value is biogenic and psychosociogenic in origin, content, and function. In any valuing process, there are goals (ends, purposes) that we seek to attain, and satisfaction and/or pleasure in their consummatory achievement. Valuing involves both objectives and activities. It is a transactional concept, for we interact with objectives in an environment, and the objects and experiences are fused and intermingled. Thus valuing is relational. It includes a perceived or imagined objective (expectation), a conative striving process, and some immediacies of enjoyment and satisfaction in achievement.

Some values are largely instrumental; that is, we pursue goals because of their results. We mine for coal or work the soil not for mining or digging's sake, but for what such acts lead to: warmth and food. The concept of intrinsic value refers to that which we seek in itself. There is rarely a sharp delineation between instrumental and intrinsic values, but rather a continuity. We may come to like our work and find it intrinsically worthwhile. Moreover, intrinsic experiences have consequences and are themselves instrumental, positively or negatively, to what follows. We may enjoy good food, music, wine, sex, or play for their own sakes, but some of these activities have physiological and psychological consequences, especially if taken in excess. There is a means-end continuum in behavior. Although we seek out means to achieve our goals or objectives, our ends are themselves functionally related to, influenced by, or modified by our means. What we wish to achieve is contingent upon what is possible or probable.

In human behavior, valuing processes are not simply instinctive or unconscious; these are surely present (as in the newborn's sucking response), but most involve conscious awareness. Our motives and intentions thus are expressed in emotive attitudes and are fused with cognitive states of consciousness. Processes of deliberation and reflection intervene to structure our values. Valuings that are purely conative or motor-affective are thus transformed into purposeful *valuation* processes, whereby we come to define, interpret, and evaluate our values. We seek to appraise them in the light of knowledge of the situation in which we act. We learn that to successfully fulfill our desires, we need to calculate the likelihood of achieving them. We thus weigh the consequences and costs of our actions. We make predictions of what will ensue were we to embark upon a course of action. And we formulate various strategies to attain our ends. The objects we choose to pursue often depend upon our estimates of the likelihood of achieving them. In Edward Arlington Robinson's poem "Miniver Cheevy," a man longs to be a knight of old or a Medici prince. And because he can't be, he abandons rationality, lapses into self-pity, and becomes a hopeless drunkard.

Rationality is essential to the processes of human valuation and volition. How does it proceed? By considering the facts of the situation, the objectives desired, the goals we wish to achieve and how they fit in with other motives, the circumstances under which we act, and an estimate of the effort, time, or cost needed to achieve our ends. A wise choice involves balancing the worth of one object against others, a prediction of the consequences of achieving it, and an imaginative exploration of its net effect on the other values that we and others hold. We often ask ourselves whether we need an object or merely want it, and, if the goal is difficult to obtain, whether it is really worth the effort. Here the evaluative process brings in short-range and long-range considerations.

A reasonable person will not wish to place in jeopardy or risk a long-range interest (for example, a marriage or career) for an immediate and transitory value (for example, an affair). He learns the economizing principle, namely, to forgo expenditures and enjoyments today for capital investment in tomorrow. On the other hand, he asks, should he sacrifice *all* immediate enjoyments for a future that might never come? The essential question, given the wide range of human interests and values, is to balance competing values and interests and to judge which ones are worthy of attainment. A rational person soon learns that if he wishes to preserve his health, restraints on eating, drinking, working, and even playing are essential, and that if he wishes to achieve mental equilibrium, some temperance in his passions is necessary. Or, as the ancient Greeks said, nothing to excess, in all things moderation.

There are many disputes about values and about the objectives that are worthy of pursuit. One can catalogue the great number of valuable things that we enjoy experiencing—virtually all of the goods for which people express preferences. Which of these ought to be considered most beautiful, satisfying, or fulfilling, and which are ugly, unsatisfying, and worthless? At this point, considerations of ethical values emerge, and we may attempt to develop a hierarchy or scale of values, a set of priorities, a hedonic calculus. Is there a *summum bonum* that we should seek above all else?

I may like watching football games, going to the opera, taking vacations in the Caribbean, collecting stamps, reading Wittgenstein, singing in a chorus, working for a cause, making love to my wife, exercising daily, supporting a worthy charity, doing my job well. But I cannot do them all at the same time and may have to sacrifice some for those with more enduring ends.

Why do I seek these goals? Is there some ultimate goal that I desire more profoundly than any other? At this point begins the philosopher's quest, and the most common response to the query is, yes, there is a highest good: it is happiness. But what is happiness and how is it achievable? Is it creative self-actualization, hedonic pleasure, service to our fellow human beings, or the attainment of a state of eternal bliss in the hereafter?

What is the humanist response to these questions? Given the wide diversity of interests, values, and tastes, and the different motives expressed in human culture, it may be thought arbitrary to seek to define one set of values as superior. Which is "better": shooting dice or reading poetry, basking in the sun daily or hard work, a life of dedication to the service of others or solitary meditation, heroic adventure or withdrawal from the world? Students in my philosophy classes always resist the question. In wishing to be fair-minded, they end up as subjectivists: "Who are *we* to say that one style of life is *better* than the next?" I ask, "Is there a difference between the life of great nobility and enterprise in which a statesman conducts the affairs of a nation, and that of a lush who spends his days on a barstool consuming vast quantities of alcohol?" Granted, we risk the danger of exalting one set of values over a wide range of experiences and enjoyments and perhaps even of censoring tastes by legislative or cultural dictate.

Yet we may ask: Is there a difference between a Florence Nightingale, who dedicated herself to caring for wounded and dying British soldiers in the Crimea, and a prostitute who also ministers to soldiers in other ways and for other reasons? Is there no way of comparing the life of an Albert Schweitzer, for example, with that of an S.S. trooper? To claim that there are no criteria for evaluating interests, tastes, and preferences would reduce us to nihilism, where all values are equal because there are no values, and no distinctions can be made, and where there are no differences in quality and nobility. Is that a reasonable posture to take?

This debate has raged for centuries. It is central to the history of ethics. Plato and Aristotle denied that all pleasures were good, and found that only some were; John Stuart Mill made a distinction between higher and lower pleasures. From the standpoint of humanistic ethics, both sides of the argument have merit. We need to tolerate alternative lifestyles and the richly diverse range of human enjoyment, and not seek to prohibit or legislate them out of existence. Nor must we identify that which is simply accepted as a higher form of life by an Establishment that may be blind to its own hypocrisies and rail against meaningful nonconformity. Still, there are some norms that we can use as guides, and some standards of evaluation. Would a Bluebeard who dissolves bodies in lime or a drug addict qualify equally in dignity with a Jesus Christ or an Abe Lincoln? It would be ludicrous to argue that anything is as good as anything else, and the fact that some sentient being is interested in an object or activity and enjoys it does not thereby mean that it has value equivalent to some other object or activity.

Some values are more precious than others; some interests are demeaning and unworthy of human attention. Some forms of life are vulgar and banal, and others have sterling qualities that evoke our admiration. We recognize that certain kinds of activities are trivial, and that others are more significant and ennobling. Indeed, we critically appraise values all the time, and in a wide range of fields. Within each field we use comparative judgments: we say that there are good and bad artists, poets, skiiers, chefs, political leaders, musicians, mechanics, philosophers, and scientists. And we appeal to aesthetic and moral standards of criticism. The standards we appeal to may not be fixed or absolute, and they may be relative to the context or field of inquiry, but nonetheless we assume that they exist. They are the standards of civilized taste, discriminating appreciation, cultivated connoisseurship, and professional competence.

Standards of Excellence

Indeed, criteria for grading values and performances are introduced in virtually all fields of human endeavor; these involve qualitative standards of excellence. What is excellence? How do we know it when we see it? How can we attain it? These questions are particularly important for the ethics of humanism. Its critics, especially the theists, charge that it has no standards or values, and that insofar as it advocates tolerance, it is permissive toward the vagaries of human tastes, including those of voluptuaries and egotists. But this is not the case.

There is, as Mill pointed out, a difference between the levels of taste of a developed adult in comparison with that of a child or a savage. Mill says, "It is better to be a human being dissatisfied than a pig satisfied; better to be Socrates dissatisfied than a fool satisfied."[2] If the pig or fool differs with this judgment, it is because he knows only one side of the question. The fully realized human being has tasted both kinds of pleasure—the developed (intellectual, aesthetic, and moral), and the underdeveloped (purely physical)—and according to Mill, invariably prefers the former. Thus, basic to the concept of value is the idea of realization, for this enables us to distinguish levels of maturation and growth. The standard here is what a person who has fully actualized his talents would judge to be worthwhile. This leaves room for the higher reaches of intellectual, aesthetic, and moral pleasures.

Although Mill's argument is not unreasonable, I think it can be overstated; one should take a balanced view. It is not always the case that intellectual, aesthetic, and moral pleasures are superior to the natural biological pleasures derived from food, drink, exercise, physical contact, or sex, and that if given the choice, most people would prefer the former to the latter. One might say that it depends on the time, place, and circumstances. Sometimes one would prefer to make love rather than visit an art museum, jog rather than read a book, enjoy a good dinner and drink fine wine rather than listen to a lecture by a colleague, or spend money at a football game rather than contribute to the Salvation Army.

Many so-called moralists are deceptive, especially when they label the so-called biological pleasures as "lower" forms of human experience. There is an underlying *hedonic phobia* gnawing at the bowels of such moralists, who, though they may have developed the capacity for enjoying literature, the arts, mathematics, or spiritual pursuits, are incapable of enjoying good food and drink or experiencing an orgasm. These individuals are so repressed that they cannot appreciate the excitements of physical and biological pleasures without a sense of guilt or sin, and they live out their lives in impoverished sublimation, spiritual substitution, or other forms of ascetic desperation.

I would argue that in order to achieve the full life, a person has to satisfy his or her basic biological homeostatic and survival needs, and this includes the need for sexual love and orgasm. When these needs are dammed up, the potential for tragedy simmers. In the past, diseased views of sex—such as St. Augustine's—have been celebrated and emulated. The Roman Catholic or Buddhist emphasis on celibacy and asceticism is essentially pathological. To fight against natural desires or consider them evil, to be at war with one's own body, or to turn in wrath and hatred against it will often produce serious illness. What untold misery and desperation this view has caused the poor souls whose bodies were considered so corrupt that they were forced to suppress their natural desires! Perhaps I have overstated the case. Some people have resorted to sublimation seemingly without ill effects. Some say that orgasm might not be necessary for everyone. Some people claim to lead fulfilled lives as celibates, whether by deliberate choice or the inability to find a suitable partner. Perhaps "pathological" is too strong for all of them. Yet is a celibate not like a person who would rather be blind or deaf because of the quiet afforded him; and may not we say that his capacity for enjoying physical pleasure is underdeveloped?

Nonetheless, if there are disturbed individuals who are incapable of appreciating their biogenic tendencies, there are also those who have never developed other potentialities—intellectual, aesthetic, moral, and social values, the so-called civilizing virtues. No doubt the terms *higher* and *lower* are here misleading, for we wish to develop fully as personalities, and it is difficult to assign priority or posteriority on a scale of values. It is not either/or, but *both* that we ought to cultivate in any kind of rounded life. I have elsewhere called this the *exuberant* life, or robust hedonism, for it does not involve simply passive enjoyment but creative actualization. The ideal here is the person who is able to realize and appreciate a wide range of biogenic and sociogenic values. One must be cautious, however, about defending a hierarchy of values, as A. H. Maslow did,[3] unless one makes it abundantly clear that biological pleasures are as essential to one's well-being as those of higher levels of creativity.

The normative concept of *excellence* is applicable here; it refers to the various dimensions of experience. We say, for example, that a person enjoys excellent health, meaning that his physiological system is functioning well. He gets proper nutrition, takes sufficient exercise, and is free of any major ailments or diseases. By contrast, another person may be in poor health. These categories have some objective basis in testable fact. Although conditions of health are relative to each person, some empirical criteria are relevant to the evaluation. We can also appraise a person's social relationships, to see if they are dysfunctional or harmonious. There are, for example, some families rent with emotional conflict. A husband and wife may be incompatible and live in constant friction, and their children may suffer as a consequence. Although such normative judgments are relational in the sense that they refer to specific individuals with diverse idiosyncratic tendencies, we nonetheless can characterize some relationships as healthy and others as unwholesome.

The philosophers have traditionally referred to the vital role that reason plays in ensuring happiness. But a key element they have sometimes overlooked is the need for developing emotive compassion. In mature relationships, some affectionate bond is present, and there is some empathy for the needs and interests of other persons. All of this suggests a double normative standard. First, there is the need to satisfy our basic needs and desires, both biogenic and sociogenic. The inability to do so leads to unhealth. Second, there is the need to achieve some degree of harmony or compatibility in the social environment, particularly in the intimate, face-to-face relations of the family.

It is apparent that the idea of excellence can also be applied to the so-called higher creative functions, to our intellectual skills, for example. Some individuals are slow learners, poor readers, or are unable to do mathematics or science, whereas others seem gifted, well-motivated, and capable of high performance. We grade students on a scale of academic achievement. We praise aesthetic creativity. We recognize the musical genius of a Mozart or a Beethoven, and the artistic talents of a Leonardo or a Van Gogh. Standards of critical judgment enable us to appreciate a work of art and to evaluate it in terms of its aesthetics. Thus we use standards of excellence throughout life.

Ethical Excellence

The central question is whether there are standards of *ethical* excellence. Is it possible to contrast and compare the wide variety of tastes and appreciations, and to adjudicate between them? Can we judge between various styles of life and apply to them the terms *better* or *worse*? If so, on what bases?

The first point to make is that all evaluating procedures are *comparative*. Few absolute standards can be discovered. All standards, thus, are relative to a class of persons and their performances. We can, for example, rank track-and-field athletes, but only in relation to the performance of other athletes. We might do this by first examining the Olympic records. Only those who have broken new records or been awarded gold medals, such as Roger Bannister, Fanny Blanken-Koen, Paavo Nurmi, or Rafe Johnson, would qualify for excellence in the field. *Excellence* is thus a thoroughly relative term, applicable to human beings engaged in some activity and used to compare their capacities and achievements. Here we are talking about athletic excellence, not ethical excellence, but analogous processes apply.

Another test of excellence is *consistency* in performance. It is not a single success—important as that may be to record—but achievement over a period of time that most impresses us. A child prodigy, however great a talent, may burn out early and be heard from no more. Not everyone is a Yehudi Menuhin, who displays virtuosity throughout his life. Thus we say that Wordsworth and Whitman are great poets, that Mies van der Rohe and Frank Lloyd Wright are great architects, that Einstein and Newton are great scientists. Such individuals are considered geniuses in specific fields of endeavor because their work broke new ground. Their performances or discoveries came to be recognized as preeminent, towering, or unique, and eventually each was publicly acclaimed. Does excellence require public approval? They are considered excellent not because they achieved recognition, but because of the intrinsic qualities of their work, which manifests creativity, innovation, discovery. They are noteworthy because they have exceeded our expectations, and have made an outstanding contribution.

I should add that there are countless creative persons who have not been recognized during their lives but whose excellence and creativity are eventually acknowledged. Van Gogh, for example, was not recognized as a genius during his lifetime, and Nietzsche was reviled as an evil man.

No doubt we can also quantify some forms of excellence, as when a person receives a perfect score on an examination. Often the evaluative concept is qualitative and difficult to characterize numerically; yet the excellence gleams through, much as a polished crystal, and we are dazzled by its sparkling beauty. Standards of ethical excellence are relative to a person's own level of talent and accomplishment. A person may not be a genius, nor make new breakthroughs, yet working with the materials he has, a kind of excellence may emerge. In focusing on excellence, I should make it clear that we should not concentrate on only a small elite. We should not judge the quality of a person's life by his or her fame or eminence, nor by the criterion of whether he or she is a genius or has made significant discoveries or contributions to the world.

Excellence is a relativistic standard applicable to the individual on his own terms, given his personality, the biological and environmental factors in his life, and the social circumstances in which he finds himself. The life of nobility that I am talking about has a dignity and grandeur, not as befits only monarchs and presidents but also persons of the lowest station. Excellence emerges whenever there is a harmonious blending and symmetry. Even through pain, suffering, adversity or tragedy—and perhaps in spite of it—the life has been worthwhile. Such a person does not live in a degraded state of failure and self-deceit. His life exudes exquisite qualities. His life is *precious,* to himself and to those about him. One doesn't have to paint a Mona Lisa to excel in life, but only one's own home. Nor does one need to build a monument; it can be one's own career nurtured with loving care. A person can express a kind of artistry and virtuosity in living, even if it is in modest circumstances.

Perfection cannot be attained by any person; all humans have flaws. It is in spite of a person's limitations and character defects that a kind of qualitative worth may still express itself. A human life, if well-lived, is a wonder to behold, a sublime and illustrious entity, like a spendid chestnut tree or a stately lion. We need to appreciate what it means to be a human being, and not mistakenly believe that one has to be a genius or a saint—for we are all only human.

We come back to the question: From the standpoint of *ethical* value, in what sense is it meaningful to apply the standard of excellence?

Can we apply the terms *exquisite qualities* and *high merit*? Yes, we can. Here we appraise: (1) the *kinds* of values that a person cherishes and that activate him or her, (2) the *style* of life that he or she has adopted, and (3) how he or she *relates* to other persons within the sphere of interaction. In dealing with ethical excellence, I am not referring simply to a person's chief occupation or career—as important and satisfying as that may be in achieving the good life—but to the total constellation of values and principles manifested throughout the entire life. A person can be a great physicist and lead a miserable life, a great mathematician and not know how to get his car started, a sensitive poet and a terrible husband. I do not wish to focus on the part-man or part-woman but on the total life of the developed personality. What are the ingredients in a life which enable us to say that the person is exemplary, and/or that he or she is capable of some nobility? What are the admirable qualities, the signs of perfection and excellence that manifest themselves?

From the standpoint of the humanist, the fruition of life is to live well and to achieve some modicum of happiness. For the individual, happiness involves some sense of achievement and of having reached the fullness of one's being. A person's life is like a work of art. We are involved in the creative process of giving form and structure, unity and harmony to our plans and projects. We have blended colors, tones, shapes, and forms, and affixed them to the canvas. Our life is in part our own creation. What results is due to the choices and actions we have taken over many years and decades. Is the end product our own doing? Are we able to bring the parts together, to complete our dreams and projects, and to give a kind of unity and coherence to our world? Not everyone can create a masterpiece, build a noteworthy career, or lead an exemplary life. Many persons have failed. Their lives are wasted, they are overcome by fear and timidity, they are drowned by years of sorrow. They can never find a niche for themselves in the scheme of things. And so, they are condemned not only by the fates (to speak metaphorically) but also by their own inability to achieve great things. By this I do not mean social expectations, but their own. How many failed careers, dissolute marriages, and lives of quiet desperation are there?

Could a person's life have been otherwise? Yes, perhaps to some extent, but if so, how and in what sense? The full ethical life, measured in personal terms, involves a sense of achievement and accomplishment, a conscious recognition that we have, however modestly, contributed to the world, expressed our talents, and done something useful and productive in terms of our own ideals. To be able to do so can lead to a joyful and creative life, the bountiful, outgoing, adventurous life. Happiness, in some sense, can be achieved by most men and women, but it depends upon what we do. It depends on our being able to fulfill our basic needs, but also in our being able to express our creative talents in whatever fields we choose.

There are, of course, great tragedies, unforeseen accidents, and calamities. Someone is struck down by the ubiquitous tide of events, and through no fault of his own is unable to complete his life satisfactorily. Thus luck plays a key role in life: being in the right place at the right time, or being absent from the wrong place at the wrong time. But still, what happens to us depends on what we do, how we respond to challenges, whether we deal with them wisely, how we plan our lives, the choices we make, the people we relate to, our interests and activities, our occupations and careers, how we adapt and persist in spite of adversity, and how we respond to new opportunities.

Some of the classical religious models, I submit, are in a profound sense antihuman, and the source of deep-seated misery and unhappiness. I am referring to those systems of morality that preach withdrawal from this world, such as some forms of Buddhism, which advocate the extinction of desire in order to achieve a state of quiescent nirvana, or some aspects of Christianity, which emphasize salvation in the next life. The Promethean ideal is to challenge the gods and the fates, to adopt the outgoing posture, to dazzle our own world with achievement. Living outside the Garden of Eden, having eaten the forbidden fruit, we need the courage to persist despite adversity. That is what human culture is about; it is the product of our hopes and inspirations, of our imagination and resourcefulness, and of our determination to fulfill our highest visions. The sum and substance of the creative life is expressed in the heroic virtues: the unwillingness to accept defeat, and the determination to create a new world in which we realize our aspirations.

The key to the life of excellence is not found by simply satisfying our needs, or even in fulfilling our nature, but in exceeding it by leaping forward and performing courageous deeds. Ethical nobility best exemplifies itself by taking the first step into the unknown when all others fear to do so, by lighting a candle instead of suffering the darkness, and by seeking to reach new horizons for ourselves. A creative person is capable of *existential* choice, is willing to master his or her fate as far as possible, to dream of new frontiers, and to expend the effort to bring all of this into being. The creative person is not fixated on the past, nor is he overwhelmed by the present moment, but instead focuses his energies on attaining his future. He does not bask in Being nor is he mired in Nothingness, but he is eager to enter into the exultant process of Becoming, for that is the dynamic key to life.

In writing these lines, I am not unaware of the possibility for some skepticism, for I have described a style of life that has been emphasized in certain cultures but not in all. It is expressed in contemporary American and European life, where creative scientists, artists, entrepreneurial builders, and high achievers are praised. But not all cultures have focused on this; some have sought other ideals, such as religious quietude or spiritual release. Is what I am presenting universal in the sense that it expresses a common human capacity, no matter what the culture? Not all individuals in all careers are capable of high achievement. Yet I say it applies to everyone. Would it apply to the office typist, farm laborer, or factory worker who has a job to do that leaves little room for creativity? Some individuals seem to exult in the adventurous life of challenge, while others would prefer comfort and security. Is the ideal I have presented only available to a creative elite?

These objections are worrisome, for, if true, they would mean that the exuberant life is an expression of my own personal predilections (or even physical makeup), and though I may have found such a life exciting and ennobling, others may find it stressful and tiring. Is there any objective justification for it, or is it simply a matter of taste? Some of these criticisms appear to have merit. Perhaps I am only talking to those individuals who have a Promethean temper and who can find grandeur in a life of risk-taking and exertion. Yet, in support of my argument, I submit that if one scans the entire human drama, one finds that creativity plays the key role as the mainspring of civilization, and that each person can contribute to creative development, no matter how modestly. It is the creative surge that marks the indomitable human spirit, the fact that men and women are not content to rest, but can strive to master events and turn them to advantage. The human animal is a builder and doer, and is by its very nature creative. I readily concede the need for order, harmony, for savoring the immediacies of experience, and for times of release and relaxation from the strenuous life. Nonetheless, creative activity and the achievement motive are deep impulses within the human species, the sources of greatness and inspiration, which enable us to transcend the limits of our nature and to build culture. Many theists war against such impulses; they wish to save us from the ambiguities and challenges of living by postulating an eternal life of blessedness. But insofar as they try to deny the creative adventure they are antihuman and the enemies of human realization.

Excelsior

Can I be more precise? What constitutes ethical excellence? It is not simply a life of pleasure or enjoyment but one of creative achievement. Is it possible to delineate the qualities and characteristics that such a life of excellence entails? Perhaps the term *excelsior* best describes this state of creative fulfillment. No one can attain perfection, and yet there are degrees of magnificence that each and every person may discover and express. I shall adopt *excelsior* to mean a concrete, empirical state, one that can be achieved here and now. One doesn't have to wait for nirvana or salvation in the next world.

First, we may distinguish those states of excellence that apply to the individual as he seeks personal realization and exuberant achievement. Second, there are excellences that apply to the individual as he relates to other human beings within the community. For no one can fully achieve a state of excelsior without sharing values.

I. Excellence Primarily in Regard to Oneself

1. *Autonomy.* Among the highest human excellencies is a person's ability to take control of his or her own life. This means the willingness to accept responsibility for his own future and the recognition that it is the person himself who will ultimately decide how he wants to live and what he wants to become. This is not to deny that by living in communities we make cooperative decisions, but since we have only one life to live, we should not waste it by refusing to make our own choices or by forfeiting that opportunity and allowing others to choose for us. The autonomous person thus has some sense of his own independence. He is self-directed and self-governing. His autonomy is related to the affirmation of his freedom.

Can he control his own destiny? Can he change or redirect events?

Is he so structured by impersonal forces that he can do nothing other than submit to them? The great failure in life is an individual's acquiescence to his fate, his willingness to escape from freedom, and his refusal to make choices about his own vital interests. Theists demean human power when they maintain that we are nothing in ourselves but are dependent upon God at every turn. They insist that we can do nothing outside of God's dictates. We cannot overcome the tragic character of the human condition; the only solution for man is divine salvation.

The humanist differs with this pessimistic appraisal and psychological retreat by providing a positive alternative. We *can* cope with the problems of living. But we need to deal realistically with the world as we find it, and not seek to flee to a mythological deity for help. Only by extending our best efforts can we hope to overcome adversity, conflict, tragedy. We need to be willing to do what is necessary to understand the processes of nature and to seek to redirect them for our own purposes. If we are to succeed, we need to have some confidence that we can make a difference, that our activities will be effective, and that at least we will try.

Thus autonomy is personal freedom extended to control the events that impinge on our lives. I am not talking about our ability to influence other people or society at large, but to control our own private life and the acceptance of this as an ongoing project. One must think: I am at the center of choice and decision, and I must decide what I wish to do with my life. I will make my views known, and when possible I will attempt to act upon them. This involves courage, not simply the courage to be, but the courage to become. It involves audacity and verve.

The opposite of this attitude is conformity, withdrawal, and in its extreme, fear and trembling. Here one is defeated before one begins. A person feels that there is nothing that he can do except submit to his fate and the Furies. Yet a person with an autonomous, self-affirming, assertive outlook refuses to give in without a fight. The autonomous person has pluck, energy, and some strength of will, which enables him to forbear and to prevail.

Autonomy is not antisocial; indeed, the open, democratic society encourages the growth of autonomous persons. The best society is one in which people are willing to accept some responsibility for themselves and to behave intelligently in making their choices. Autonomy does not mean that I may not work in concert with my wife or husband, sister or brother, mother or father, friend, colleague, or fellow-citizen. Insofar as I am autonomous, I can respect other persons as equally entitled to autonomy over their lives.

2. *Intelligence.* Classical philosophers have emphasized the essential role that reason plays in the good life. In doing so, they have perhaps underestimated the significance of the conative and passionate dimensions of human experience. Aristotle delineated five intellectual virtues that he thought contributed to rational excellence: philosophical wisdom, scientific demonstration, intuition, art, and practical wisdom. Our intellectual abilities are far more complex and extensive than that. I have elsewhere catalogued twenty-one such intellectual qualities, including everything from abstract intelligence and logical ability on the one hand, to technical skill, artistic virtuosity, and mechanical dexterity on the other.[4]

Aristotle perceptively recognized the significance of practical wisdom in making ethical choices. One can possess high intellectual skills and manifest significant intellectual attainment in one area, and lack it in others. It is difficult to find one person possessing all the intellectual talents. From the standpoint of the ethical life, however, the most important quality is that of practical critical intelligence. Common sense, or native understanding, enables us to cope with the dilemmas encountered in life and to make sensible choices. I call this *good judgment,* the ability to evaluate alternatives and make intelligent decisions.

Whether this ability is a gift of the gods (that is, genetic) or a product of experience, capable of being cultivated by education and training, has been debated by the philosophers. Why are some people able to hit the bull's-eye, as it were, and to know the best thing to do in a situation, whereas others are *taugenichts* (good-for-nothings), poor fools constantly embroiled in disasters and unable to make wise choices? Practical wisdom is probably a result of both talent and training; fortunately we can learn to improve our capacity to engage in critical thinking and apply it to ordinary life. What I have in mind here is *prudential* intelligence; that is, the ability to make plans, fulfill projects, and reach decisions after a deliberative process. This includes an estimation on our part of the costs and consequences of alternative actions. Cognition becomes constitutive of the process of choosing. The ethics of excellence depends upon our ability to make *informed* judgments based upon knowledge of good and evil.

We had better be honest about this excellence. No one is perfect, and even the most rational person may at times succumb to passion. It is surely appropriate to fall in love, cheer the home team, or enjoy oneself at a banquet. Intelligence provides an ideal model, a comparative method for evaluating values and principles, and balancing competing claims within a situation. Critical ethical intelligence is not purely formal or abstract. Its content is concrete: One should not counter reason against desire. It is not a question of cognition mastering or dominating desires, as the ancient Stoics would have it, for all motivation involves our wants and is deeply bio-psychological in content. Our motives, fused with desires and reasons, stimulate us to action, not to thought alone. All that awareness can do is bring about an equilibrium between the various phases of our psychological impulses. Intelligence itself is a biological state. It is not an interloper; it is an intimate part of our entire physiological makeup, though only one ingredient in the preferential process of valuing. Nonetheless, we may say that we ought to prize intelligence as an excellence, for insofar as it can play a causative role in helping to modify intentions and interests, it can contribute to a better life. It is essential, for it is the fullest and the most complete expression of what we are as human beings.

Intellectual activities are a deep source of enjoyment and enrichment. This is surely the case with pure research, the quest for scientific explanations of how nature operates, historical investigations, philosophical understanding, and so on. Many individuals have dedicated their lives to intellectual pursuits and have discovered the intense satisfaction they can afford. Aristotle recognized that one needs some measure of leisure in order to pursue the life of the mind. Every man and woman is capable of some degree of intellectual activity, whether it is going to school, reading books, listening to lectures, or trying to discover something for themselves. There is a fascination in attempting to solve problems and puzzles; some of the most challenging games test our mettle as we become engrossed in their solutions. Man is a curious animal and he wishes to know. Some people are so eager to be well-informed that they wish to learn everything they can about a certain subject. They may travel or read widely; they may wish to meet new people or go to exhibitions or lectures. This expression of our intellectual interests points to the fact that we place a high value on knowledge, both for its value in our lives and as a source of enjoyment.

3. *Self-discipline.* This is an important virtue to develop. It is related to intelligence and good judgment, but it goes beyond them. It applies to the life of desire and passion. Unless one can control his emotions and direct his efforts to constructive purposes, his energies are apt to

be squandered and dissipated in unproductive and self-defeating activities. One is in danger of being obsessed with a given pursuit, like the food addict, who eats to exhaustion, or the nymphomanic, whose desire for sex is uncontrollable. The habit of self-discipline needs to be cultivated by education and training. Once achieved, moderation is used in satisfying one's desires. Self-discipline also enables one to channel his efforts creatively in order to achieve his purposes in life. Discipline draws upon intelligence and practical wisdom. It fuses thought and desire. More than a cognitive state, it applies to the character of the whole person. It involves strength of will and the determination to persevere.

The undisciplined person is prey to every haphazard whim and fancy; his lusts and cravings dominate him. He may be overwhelmed by his desires for sex, food, drink, drugs, or trivial entertainment, to which he may give in with abandon. Self-restraint is an essential guide for mature individuals, who are able to resist the lure of momentary temptations for long-range goals. It may entail some measure of stoic resignation, but also involved is the ability to face adversity and the determination to overcome challenges. This does not mean that one does not enjoy life or ever give in to desires. Rather, he seeks to balance the various desires and decide which ones will be fulfilled. To lead an effective life, one needs to guide and control external events, but also to learn how to master and control one's inner drives so that they do not dominate.

4. *Self-respect.* The ethics of excellence involves the development of a decent respect for oneself. We are constantly being told that we ought to respect other human beings, our elders, the law, and those dependent upon us. This may be well and good, but in the process some individuals forget that they are entitled to the same kind of care and consideration they confer on others.

The focus on self-respect can become exaggerated if an individual develops an over-inflated sense of his own worth. These are the egotists and egoists. I am not talking about them, for their self-concern has been inflated beyond reasonable measure, and society has a right to complain about this and guard against them. These individuals often behave in an infantile fashion, which may lead to megalomania and self-glorification.

Contrasted with this state is absence of self-esteem and an impoverished sense of identity. Having been beaten down by others, perhaps over-criticized by censorious parents or teachers, a person may rebel and flout even the most reasonable demands of society, or, on the contrary, he may withdraw, lacking any sense of independence. Such a person simply conforms to what is expected of him. I find that a deep and abiding concern of college students is whether their talents compare favorably with those of their peers. Poor or average grades or parental disapproval can arouse great anxiety. They have an underlying fear that they may not succeed in life.

Some individuals, lacking self-confidence, give up early. Unfortunately, such individuals often find it difficult to live fully, because they lack minimal respect for themselves, their talents and abilities, and what they can achieve or attain. Those who lack self-assurance may constantly need to prove themselves, and so they wear themselves out in fruitless efforts to seek approval in the eyes of others, and abandon what they would like to do in life. The opposite of self-respect is self-hatred. For some individuals it can so corrode their sense of worth that they constantly criticize themselves for failures or defeats—or even for their inability to succeed gloriously. They may be perfectionists, never content with the tasks they have chosen or their level of accomplishment. They have no inner peace. They may even give up in quiet desperation, seeking to find some quiet haven that will afford them warmth and security. Despite the lip service paid in our culture to openness, tolerance of differences, and emphasis on individuality, there is an appalling pressure to conform, which is not conducive to self-respect.

No one can succeed in everything he undertakes in life. One tries his best, hoping to learn from defeats. But the person who lacks self-respect can never accept failure: he turns against himself. Although he can make allowances for those about him who fail, he will not do so for himself. He may love others, but he doesn't love himself. Christianity certainly helps to foster this self-guilt by advocating values that are completely unobtainable on earth, such as perfect virtue, and then castigating its adherents for not obtaining them.

The humanist responds to the perfectionist: You are the only person you have to live with all your life, from the beginning to the end. Hence, you might as well come to terms with yourself, enjoy yourself, and think well of yourself. Although hopefully you can recognize your virtues and limitations, you may need to make some allowances. This doesn't mean you are not accountable for your errors of omission and commission, or that you shouldn't constantly strive to improve.

Some self-respect is necessary for building one's identity and to expanding one's powers of autonomy and independence. Pride in oneself is not a sin. Self-effacing humility is not an appropriate response for a free, autonomous person capable of some action in the world and desirous of deserved respect.

5. *Creativity.* The creative person exemplifies the most eloquent expression of human freedom: the capacity for originality. Creativity is intimately related to autonomy and self-respect, for the independent person has some sense of his own power. He does not submit to the obstacles he encounters in nature. He is able to invent or to bring into being something new. He not only can apprehend new possibilities but bring them to fruition.

Creativity has many different facets. One often thinks of the creative scientist on the frontiers of knowledge who makes some monumental discovery or proposes some new and daring theory. It is also the driving force of the great artist or sculptor, who is able to take the raw materials of nature and impose new forms that fulfill his creative vision. The poet, novelist, and composer, using the materials of language or harmony, weave captivating works of art that inspire us. Similarly, the inventor or engineer creates a new instrument, machine, or device. Statesmen who draft constitutions, builders of new industries, explorers of uncharted seas, continents, or galaxies all express similar creative impulses. The designation *creativity,* I reiterate, should not be confined to exceptional geniuses, for it applies to ordinary people who display talent for innovative behavior.

In one sense, all organic life has creative dimensions. The first union and fertilization of egg and sperm and the processes of creative growth that flow from it illustrate the creative processes intrinsic to organic matter. Wherever there is learning and adaptation by life-forms to environmental problems, there is some degree of creativity.

Creativity is one of the defining characteristics of the human species. No one is entirely without it, for it is the necessary means by which we overcome adversity and adapt or respond to stimuli in the environment. There are, however, degrees of creativity; perhaps it best manifests itself in teleonomic activities consciously directed. Creativity involves both insight and imagination. It appears wherever thought strives to solve problems by introducing alternative means, and manifests itself wherever we seek to combine old materials in new ways. It is the key stimulus to culture-building. Insofar as each person is unique, some creativity is expressed in his idiosyncratic behavior, and in how he learns to cope with and adapt to the world on the everyday, pedestrian level.

There are degrees of excellence attached to creativity. Some persons are more adept than others at discovering new possibilities. They are overflowing with new ideas; they have fertile imaginations. Unfortunately, someone can be a creative genius in one field of endeavor, or show enormous talent and achievement at one time, yet lack the creative outlook outside his field or for the remainder of his life. Thus we should focus not on narrow creativity in a specific area but on the creative life in general, which is approached adventurously and openly.

The uncreative person tends to be a conformist, prone to follow rituals or be obsessive in observing rules. A creature of habit, he is unwilling or unable to try something new. He resists change or novelty. The creative person, on the contrary, is a fountain of ingenious ideas. He is fruitful, constantly bubbling over with new thoughts, schemes, and plans. A problem with one form of creativity is that people have brainstorms but end up as visionary dreamers who never implement their ideas. An effective creative person is one who can follow through. He is not simply an ideas man but a doer, able to realize his dreams. To be effective, his ideas must be grounded in reality. The great creators of history have not simply had random flashes of insight, but have been able to express them, give them form, and ground them in reality. They do not simply conceive or apprehend in their inner souls alone, but can give birth to their offspring. Creativity thus involves a generative process of organization and realization. Many creative persons are not on the frontiers of knowledge, nor do they contribute to civilization's advance. They may not be gifted with special talents, yet in their chosen areas they are creative: finding and following new recipes, redecorating a room, planting a garden, repairing the roof, breeding horses, or teaching a course. I am not talking about pseudo- or pop-creativity, which follows the whims of fashion, but genuine creative expression. The creative person has some confidence in his powers and willingly meets the challenges of life with self-assurance and zest.

Creativity ought to be encouraged in the young, and nourished and cultivated throughout life. Unfortunately it has its enemies. Creative persons often arouse envy and jealousy, and since they are at times unpredictable, they may be difficult to live with. If allowed to vent all their enthusiasms, they can be exhausting to those around them.

From society's standpoint, the most important use of creativity is its application to work. Some forms of work are drudgery. The creative person is able to make his work exciting. His work is not separate and distinct from himself, but flows forth as an expression of his own interests. Drudgery most likely ensues when means are disconnected from ends, and one is given orders to fulfill that hold no interest. A slave or peon has no mind of his own, or at least is not permitted to introduce his own purposes and fulfill them. His labor is thus humdrum, rote, or mechanical. Creative activities thrive best in a free environment, where people's efforts are directed toward their own goals. Given the division of labor, it is often difficult to permit creative persons free rein to luxuriate in their inspirations. One needs to work to make a living, and this work may be boring, yet it needs to be done. That is why developing opportunities for creativity in the marketplace is important. But if this is not entirely feasible, then the expression of creativity in leisure time becomes all the more important for the ordinary person. A creative person, in any case, is resourceful, in that he can deal with life's problems, using both imagination and effort to achieve what he wishes.

6. *Motivation.* Some individuals are highly motivated. They are always ready to undertake projects without wasting time or engaging in delaying tactics. They are resourceful in both ideas and deeds. Other individuals are lazy and ineffective. They never seem to have sufficient energy or interest in doing something, but get by with a minimum of effort. They have low levels of motivation and hence low levels of activity. They do not wish to stand out. They would much rather rest quietly in a garden than weed and plant it or venture outside of it. They seem to withdraw from the hustle and bustle of living.

The motivated person, on the other hand, is self-directed. He has courage, stamina, and the will to do something. He is not loath to dirty his hands and do the things necessary to get the job done. There is an old saying: "If you want something done, ask a busy person." A lazy person never succeeds because he lacks the determination and drive to do so.

There is an excellence that characterizes the well-motivated person. He is able to gather together the things he will need in order to attain the goals he appropriates as his own. He has autonomy, self-discipline, self-respect, and a capacity for creative, inventive, and adaptive response. But he also has the ability to fulfill his goals, whatever they are. Individuals often shy away from tasks they do not like or that are given to them by others. They are only happy when they are doing what they want to do. Unfortunately, some people are limited by narrow horizons and restricted interests. They demonstrate, not only at work but even at play, that they have impoverished imaginations. Low levels of motivation characterize them. They never seem to find themselves. Their drives are wanting. They never develop a career—for them a job is a job, not a *profession.*

A well-motivated person *professes* a specialty or expertise, and is committed to it. He is achievement-oriented. But more, he finds some pride and satisfaction in his accomplishments. The underachiever is bankrupt as a person. He is easily bored, which means that he is boring. His reactions are infantile, for his only interest seems to be "having a good time." Unless he can point to some contribution he has made to his own life, some deed or accomplishment that is creative and rewarding, then he is underdeveloped and will clearly have a lessened sense of self-respect. Well-motivated persons are dependable, for you can count on them to get something done. The unmotivated person is given to sloth and indecision. In extreme cases, he literally ends up a bum.

7. *Affirmation.* Living the full life depends, to a great extent, on a positive outlook. This means having some degree of optimism, believing that life can be good and bountiful, that it can be ameliorated and improved. Opposed to this is negativism, pessimism, and a tragic sense that life is difficult, that things cannot be changed and will only get worse. There always seem to be impossible Bastilles to storm. This attitude is defeatist and depressive.

The affirmative person takes life as a challenge. He looks upon it as an opportunity. He wishes to do many things and to experience widely. Exuberant happiness cannot be achieved without some sense of one's own power and the ability to solve one's problems. An affirmative person's attitude is apt to be a cheerful one, for he looks to the future with high expectations. His attitude also expresses humor, laughter, and an appreciation for fun. If we have self-respect and some creativity and are well-motivated, then our outreach is ongoing and there is a willingness to explore, experiment, innovate. The optimist tends to look at the positive side: he focuses on the good in people, not their faults. Living is exciting; horizons are unlimited; there are not enough hours in the day to do all the things he wants to do.

The pessimist is forever focused upon the tragic aspects of life. He worries about, without seeing solutions to, the problems of the world—hunger, suffering, pain, and sorrow. He is timid and fearful of what people will say about him. Thus he is permeated by negativity, paralyzed by fear, and more apt to retreat than to advance.

The affirmative, outgoing, optimistic, bouyant person finds life to be joyful. There are so many wonderful things to accomplish, so many future achievements that beckon us. Life is full of great promises and opportunities: whatever ills we now encounter can be improved upon and ameliorated. The optimist is never bogged down by feelings of impotence, but has a sense that human effort can be effective, and that we can make this a better world in which to live. A new turn of events is taken as a propitious opportunity, a bright prospect for success. He willingly meets new challenges with anticipation and enthusiasm. He is full of the will to live, to overcome, and to attain new heights of creative enjoyment.

8. *Health.* High on the scale of excellence, perhaps even first, is the realization of personal good health. Perhaps it is a truism to emphasize health (though philosophers have often overlooked it), but any realistic view of happiness must take health as its starting point. If one is to live and live well, one must be in reasonably good health. If a person is grossly handicapped, sick, or in constant pain, he may not be able to function well, nor be able to accomplish all that he wishes to, yet many individuals have been able to live significant lives in spite of debilitating pain or physical handicaps. In situations of poor health, a person should attempt to do the best he is capable of doing. It is interesting to note that many professed humanists lived long and comparatively healthy lives. What's more, they remained active until their deaths. John Dewey pursued a vigorous career until the age of ninety-three and Bertrand Russell, who died at ninety-seven, was arrested for demonstrating against the atom bomb when he was in his nineties!

There are important principles we should follow if we wish to live healthy lives. It is particularly essential that health education be an important part of our upbringing, and that children should learn from the earliest age about their bodies. The widest dissemination of scientific knowledge should be readily available. This means that there be adequate information about (1) proper nutrition; (2) the importance of daily exercise in maintaining physical and mental fitness; (3) ways of avoiding unnecessary stress and attaining periods of relaxation and rest; and (4) exercising moderation in the life of pleasure. All of this is within the range of preventive medicine. For the humanist, the neglect or abuse of the body is immoral, particularly by those who seek the idle pleasures of hedonism, or who waste their talents in indolence and sloth. This means that drug addiction or gluttony in food or drink—growing obese or eating or drinking to reduce one's anxieties—are also to be condemned.

The test of whether an action is good or bad lies in its consequences. The emphasis in medical science has been on diagnosing and treating illnesses once they occur, and though this is vital, we also need to understand how to avoid risks to health and prevent illness. We now know that the excessive intake of alcohol, cholesterol, or cigarette smoke is dangerous, and only a foolish person ignores the warnings. In any case, every individual is responsible for his own health. The body is the most important possession that we have, and it is our responsibility to see not only that it is not abused and that preventive measures are observed but also that proper care is taken once an illness develops.

The achievement of good health is not simply physical or biological; it involves an important psychological dimension. Psychiatric disorders are the bane of human existence, the source of anxiety and depression, misery and unhappiness. The treatment of the whole person is essential: no doubt many mental illnesses have their origins in biochemical malfunctioning. Psychiatry needs to seek the causes of manic depression, schizophrenia, and other debilitating illnesses. Which of the various methods of drugs or psychotherapy are most effective in treating mental or emotional disturbances remains to be determined. Severe cases of psychosis may have a biochemical basis, so the sick individual may not be helped much by counseling, although his family may benefit from it. Such illnesses are tragic in their destructiveness, rendering the victim unable to cope by simple acts of will power.

The fulfillment of a person's psychosexual needs seems to be an important factor in health. Does the satisfaction of libido fantasies and the avoidance of repression enhance a person's ability to enjoy life? The answer appears to be yes, though of course within reason. It is difficult to discover a single model of sexual realization, for tastes and enjoyments are wide-ranging. Different individuals are "turned on" by different fantasies. What appears odd or vulgar to one person might be exciting to the next. Richard von Krafft-Ebing, who in the late nineteenth century catalogued "deviant" sexual practices, devoted an entire chapter to foot fetishes. Without delving into intricate questions here, I merely wish to state that the capacity to satisfy the sexual libido, culminating in orgasmic release, seems to be an important contributing factor to health.

9. *Joie de vivre.* The French terms *joie de vivre* and *bon vivant* refer to joyful living. All work and no play is not the be-all and end-all of life. The affirmative outlook, important as it is, focuses primarily on the future. Yet the present moment is intrinsically worthwhile, and we need to appreciate fully the immediacies. The *capacity* for enjoying life is an important excellence; it manifests itself in the hedonic and the erotic. The ability to enjoy pleasure without excessive guilt or the sense that it is evil is a positive virtue. I am thinking primarily of those pleasures in personal life, innocent and robust, that do not injure or harm others.

Many moralists have exiled hedonism, eroticism, and the *bon vivant* from their moral universes. Theists have railed against the body and condemned sexual pleasures. In so doing, they betray their own *hedonic or erotic phobia,* which expresses a disease of the soul. Various terms describe the failure to appreciate hedonism: asceticism, self-denial, repression. The inability to savor the delicacies of life is a corroding psychological malady, and can be a source of neurosis and misery.

There is a wide range of pleasures that we should enjoy as part of healthy living. First are those that involve the satisfaction of our basic urges and needs: food, drink, sex. Built on these are the developed pleasures of moral, altruistic, intellectual, aesthetic, and even spiritual joys. A person with *joie de vivre* can find pleasure in a wide range of activities. He can enjoy a feast, drink heartily, make love, read books, travel, listen to music, work for a cause, enjoy sports, poetry, the arts— indeed, experience everything that is worthwhile.[5]

However, excessive concentration upon hedonistic delights, abstracted from the activities of life and to the detriment of other excellencies, is not conducive to the well-lived life. The glutton, fleshpot, drug addict, or libertine mistakenly focuses on the immediacies of enjoyment as the sole end of life. Fixation on the hedonic-erotic is infantile and destructive to the total personality, especially insofar as it dominates other creative activities. The hedonist is the prisoner of his own pleasure-seeking desires; there is an inner tyranny at work.

One must steer a course between two extremes: on the one hand, theistic morality, which rails against the body and makes war on natural enjoyments, and on the other hand, amoral hedonism, which abandons all self-discipline and allows us to become prey to our cravings. One cannot fulfill all of one's fantasies. Self-restraint and moderation are signs of personal maturity. Still, the satisfaction of one's sexual needs must be rated high on the scale of values, and this means some orgasmic pleasure and sexual release. Masturbation is a common method of sexual enjoyment. Kissing, petting, sexual foreplay, and sexual intercourse involve the fullest expression of the libido, for these relate to other persons.

No doubt the strength of sexual passion is connected to the need of the species to reproduce itself. But in human affairs, reproduction is no longer the primary reason for sex; the desires to achieve pleasurable orgasm and to enhance love and intimacy are the chief motives. These matters become enormously complicated, given the wide range of pleasurable activities people seek; thus what is "normal" or "natural" is not easily determined. Romantic love is no doubt among the highest of human pleasures. Infantile forms of love wish to possess or even use the other person as a source of sexual gratification. The intensity of psychosexual longing can drive men and women to madness and desperation—especially in the case of unrequited love (such as in *Carmen*)—but also to the most rewarding forms of fulfillment. In one sense, an individual is never fully realized unless and until he or she is capable of achieving some kind of romantic attachment to another.

Is man polygamous and is promiscuity to be accepted? Mankind has long since discovered that jealous rivalries for sexual partners could lead to constant warfare. The institution of marriage, a monogamous relationship, with divorce as a safety valve, is a sensible solution. Although sexual pleasure can be derived from the physical act itself, one soon discovers that some kind of emotional attachment provides the most enduring form of satisfaction, especially when it is based on sincerity and trust. Sexual enjoyment appears to be more complete when it is experienced in a loving relationship with another.

Love is twofold: first, it helps to actualize our deepest yearnings, needs, and desires, especially to be loved by another human being; and second, if we are able to love another person, we wish him or her to prosper on his or her own terms. There is a general concern for the good of the other person, not for the reflected glory that he or she brings. Mutual love is both sexual and altruistic.

10. *Aesthetic appreciation.* Included in our capacity to enjoy life

fully is an appreciation for the finer things of life as perceived by the senses and enhanced by the intellect. The term *aesthetic* best describes these pleasures, which include the fine arts, poetry, drama, literature, and music. One's ability to appreciate great beauty enriches life. Unfortunately, some individuals never seem able to develop an understanding of the arts. They may be tone-deaf or color-blind or disinterested, totally unable to enjoy classical music, art, literature, or the theater. The appreciation of aesthetic values is a product of education, and parents should expose their children to these values at relatively early ages.

Appreciation presupposes a kind of growth and development of the personality: one admires the natural beauty of a brilliant sunset or a beautiful woman, and this does not require training. But the highest reaches of the arts require some exertion. To learn how to read requires early effort, and what a great source of satisfaction and joy it is to the person who masters it.

One's aesthetic sensibilities need not be limited to the arts, for tastes can be cultivated in other areas—in fine delicacies that the gourmet appreciates, in exotic varieties of flowers, or in embellishments in fashion. The aesthetic touch can be added with finesse and expertise to almost any field of human interest. The connoisseur of fine wine is able to discern subtleties that bring pleasure to his sense of taste. A simple farmer may not be able to tell the difference between a chablis and a bordeaux, but may have a subtle and distinctive appreciation for breeding blue-ribbon horses or show dogs.

II. Excellence as Related to Others

We have been discussing excellence primarily in regard to the individual. But we are social beings, and among the highest human values are those that relate to others: the excellences of ethical development. Although we are discussing the ethical excellences last, this in no way indicates any order of priority; moral or ethical development must stand high on the scale of values, and anyone who lacks it is missing something essential.

Some individuals are apparently blind to the moral decencies, much the same as some individuals are deficient in health or intelligence. Hence they may be said to be morally handicapped. Whether this is due to social and environmental conditions or some biological insufficiency, and whether moral decencies can be cultivated or taught are questions we have touched on and will return to as we deal with ethical education in Chapter Six. It may be that no human is fully deficient in this capacity, else he would be as a wild animal. Sociability is part of our being and defines our very nature. Perhaps morality is only a question of degree. We all need to belong to some community. Behavior outside it would be self-centered, autistic, or hermitlike. Our language and the symbols and metaphors by which we function are all transactional, the products of culture and community. The civilizing component of morality is as much a part of our definition as is our biological equipment. For example, we need to be loved and cared for by other human beings (parents, relatives, lovers) if we are to develop and flourish. Concomitantly, we need to love others, to be concerned about their needs, to share their values and dreams, to learn to live and work with them cooperatively. We not only need parents and sexual mates, friends and colleagues with whom we can identify, but in a broader sense, as fully developed moral beings, we need to be a friend to each and every person, within our community and outside of it. There is a kind of moral excellence that comes to fruition as we develop our ethical capacities.

Since the moral decencies are central to our social natures, they need to be internalized as values within the person if they are to be effective. Values and principles overlap, for in living by general rules, we incorporate them as part of our preferential structure, and learn to cherish them for their own sakes. They become moral excellencies for us to live by.

Values thus are not simply private soliloquies or idiosyncratic preferences. Nor are they selfish expressions of desire. They involve our sharing of common objectives and goals. Although one must respect the domain of privacy, among the finest values are those shared with or involving others; they are the moral decencies, which become part of our character and being.

The following list of the ethical excellencies is not complete, but enumerates those which lie at the core of our ethical behavior. They follow very closely the moral decencies discussed in Chapter Three.

1. *Integrity*. This term encompasses a whole set of the moral decencies. A person who expresses this excellence in his life is morally sound and uncorrupted. We can count on his being consistent.

—Such a person is *truthful* and is not given to lying or deceit.

—He keeps his *promises* as best he can, does not break agreements, fulfills his contracts, and pays his debts.

—He is *sincere* in his relations with others, not duplicitous or two-faced.

—He is *honest* in his dealings and will not deliberately cheat, steal, or seek to take unfair advantage.

2. *Trustworthiness.*

—A person with this quality shows *fidelity* to his friends, relatives, and colleagues who are deserving of it; he will not betray their principles or values out of self-interest and without rational justification.

—He is *dependable*, reliable, and responsible, and someone on whom we can count.

3. *Benevolence.*

—Such a person has a genial disposition and *goodwill*. He does not have ulterior motives, evil designs, or vested interests. He generally wishes only the best for other persons and is happy when they are happy, and pleased when they prosper.

—He bears *no malice* toward others, carries no ill will. He does not harbor hatred, jealousy, envy, animosity, resentment. He has no bitterness, anger, or rancor. He does not carry grudges. He has no desire to purposely inflict any harm on another person or upon another's lawful property, possessions, or family.

—He will not seek to force his attention on another person or seek to dominate her or him sexually; he bases sexual relationships on *consent*.

—He is *beneficent*, sympathetic, considerate, thoughtful, and compassionate. He makes a positive effort to reduce needless suffering or pain in others and to distribute, as far as possible within his means, some benefits. He strives to be altruistic. He is kind, charitable, and wishes to be helpful. He is friendly and shows affection. He is especially sensitive to the needs of the weak, the helpless, the forlorn, the disadvantaged, and the handicapped. He is not over-impressed by those who have wealth, power, fame, or position.

4. *Fairness.*

—A person with this quality will express *gratitude* to individuals who have helped him or deserve thanks. He will express appreciation for a job well-done, a deed well-performed, or a benefit rendered. He is not vindictive or given to petty jealousy or envy.

—By the same token, he believes in some measure of *accountability*. He believes that those who commit immoral deeds or inflict injury to others should be held responsible. Thus he has a sense of right and wrong, and seeks as far as possible to be equitable in his dealings with others. He follows rules that will establish a *quid pro quo,* harmony and order. He bears no resentment, does not seek revenge, and is willing to forgive and forget.

—He tries to fulfill, as far as he can discern them, principles of *justice* in his dealings with others. He wishes to treat each person with equal dignity and value. He attempts to be even-handed, to apply the principles of fairness to others, and to give rewards for merit.

—The fair-minded person will be *tolerant* of other lifestyles and will respect the right of others to be different. Though he may disagree with or find odd or offensive others' values, tastes, beliefs, or practices, so long as they do not harm others or impose on them, he will forbear. He will accord to other individuals the same rights he asks for himself, and though he may criticize and/or persuade, he will not seek to stamp out, denegrate, or suppress other styles of life, points of view, or value systems.

—The fair individual will not resort to the use of violence, force, or power in his dealings with other human beings. He will be *peaceful* and *cooperative.* As far as is possible, he will seek to negotiate differences and to work out compromises in which all can live together. He lives by the spirit of fair play and reasonableness.

Notes

1. For a fuller discussion of teleonomy see Paul Kurtz, *Decision and the Condition of Man* (Seattle: University of Washington Press, 1965).

2. John Stuart Mill, *Utilitarianism,* Chapter 2.

3. A. H. Maslow, *Toward a Psychology of Being* (New York: D. Van Nostrand, 1962).

4. Paul Kurtz, *The Transcendental Temptation,* pp. 63-64.

5. ———, *Exuberance: The Philosophy of Happiness* (Los Angeles: Wilshire Books, 1977), chapters 5 and 6.

5
Responsibilities

The term *responsibility* may be used in at least three senses. First, it refers to personal reliability. We say that a responsible person is dependable and trustworthy and that we can count on him to do a job well and fulfill commitments. Second, we can use the term to refer to accountability. When we hold a person responsible, we say that he can be praised or blamed for his actions and that society may punish him if they are considered egregious. These two senses of *responsibility* have been discussed earlier.

In the following discussion, I wish to deal with still a third sense of *responsibility*, not unrelated to the first two. I ask: What are a person's responsibilities, obligations, and duties to himself, to those in his immediate circle, to the community of which he is a part, or even to humankind as a whole?

Responsibilities to Oneself

In what sense can we say that one has a responsibility to oneself? Surely there are excellences of character that pertain to one's personal life. May we not say that one has an obligation to do what one can to cultivate and develop them? Does one not have an obligation to do those things that pertain, for example, to health—to protect one's physical and mental well-being? May we not say that a person should expand his horizons of knowledge, that he should develop his critical thought and his faculties of intelligence and self-discipline? Should he not strive to achieve some type of creative work and develop a career? Should he reasonably seek to satisfy his sexual libido? Should he seek to be well motivated and not waste his talents? Ought he to develop his aesthetic tastes and appreciations? These all involve personal values and choices. A mature person will recognize his responsibilities to preserve and enhance his own being, and will strive to be healthy and wise.

What if a person wishes to squander his talents in idleness? What if he does not want to work? What if he prefers the pleasures of immediacy, prefers to savor the present moment and not worry about tomorrow? In a free society we grant him the freedom to do as he wishes. One cannot legislate for another: a person should have the right to pursue his own values so long as he does not harm others. The right of privacy is an enduring libertarian principle. Still, one might remonstrate with such an individual. I especially have in mind the dialogue I often have with adolescents and young college students. The basis of personal responsibility, I say to them, is first and foremost prudential: One needs to consider long-range goals and not simply immediate desires. One learns from experience the necessity of that. At thirty-five, forty, or fifty, one may regret that he squandered his opportunities at eighteen, twenty, or twenty-five, though it is never too late to learn from one's mistakes, and certainly not too late to learn new things and to set new goals.

Can we say to another person: "You have an ethical obligation to realize your potentialities"? Parents constantly admonish their children, and teachers seek to instruct their pupils as to their duties: be friendly, brush your teeth, watch your nutrition, take care of your health, try to get an education, read as much as you can, be careful whom you marry, try to get a good job, plan for a future career. But youngsters do not always listen, or heed these admonitions; they perhaps would prefer to sail the seven seas, or become an artist in a Parisian garret, or volunteer for space research, defying conventional mores and bourgeois values. And of course there is some appeal in seeking an adventurous life of exploration and excitement, fulfilling one's own dreams and destiny. We should not object if they have high aspirations and may be able to realize their ambitions. They have a right to choose what they want to be and how they wish to live. And if they succeed in their unconventional choices, we may later admire them and say proudly, "My son the billiard champ," or "My daughter the poet." We must not impose conventional community standards on exuberant and restless minds, but must allow them to find their own way. That is what adventure and discovery are all about, and it is the rich soil out of which progress grows. Be that as it may, what if a son or daughter wishes to do nothing but waste time in idle pursuits and fancies? What if he is dirty, lazy, slothful, ignorant? We have the right to find fault with him if we have to live under the same roof. But what if he degenerates on his own terms? What if he is unable to hold a job or sustain meaningful inter-personal relationships? What if one's offspring is a virtual ne'er-do-well or a worthless bum in society's eyes?

From the social standpoint, of course, he has failed us. We feel he has some responsibilities to those about him, who may be concerned and even love him. But what of a young person's own standpoint? Yes, we say, he does have some responsibilities to himself, in relation to his own needs and desires, goals and aspirations—whatever they may be. Alas, many people fail in life and their existences become tragic. Perhaps events so weigh them down—they may come from broken homes or suffer debilitating diseases or become alcoholics or addicts—that it may be difficult or impossible for them to change. But in some sense and in the last analysis, such people still have some choices and some responsibilities to themselves. Perhaps the most basic personal duty a person has is *to be all that he is capable of being, to utilize his talents, and to realize his capacities.*

Capacities, of course, are multifarious, and generally cannot all be realized. Should one become a mathematician or a violinist, a great lover or a chef, an athlete or a businessman, a peace activist or a scientist? All require effort and concentration, and there are only so many hours in the day. Not everyone can be a Leonardo. Moreover, what we become depends largely on chance or luck. We may decide to pursue a certain endeavor, or to move to another area. Our decisions are cumulative, and they block out other opportunities. Could we have been different if we had seized an opportunity, taken a different path, or made a different decision? We can't go backward in life. But still, we may say that whatever we do, we have a duty to achieve some degree of *excellence* in our activities and our lifestyle, and to develop some pride in the way we live and some satisfaction in what we have already attained. The mystic may demure and seek to escape, preferring to sleep in poppy fields and allow his creative talents to lie fallow, latent, and untapped. There is also the hedonic libertine who would rather sniff cocaine than pursue knowledge. Who are we to say to any individual that he has failed, that he has dissipated his capital, exhausted his innate potential through dissolute living, or allowed it to rot in indolent squalor and inactivity, or in a futile quest for nirvana or salvation?

We have to be cautious and not censorious; we should be sensitive to the nuances of living, the diversity of tastes and pursuits, and the wide variety of passions and interests. Promethean men and women should not seek to impose standards of creative excellence on people who are indifferent or incapable of highly visible achievement. Perhaps we have an obligation to point out that a person should not waste his talents, whatever they are, and should instead seek to actualize them. But if our advice falls on deaf ears, there is little else we can or should do for that person. However, if one has children, one can teach them to strive for excellence and achieve all they are capable of. One method of appeal is evocative and persuasive. We might attempt to arouse within recalcitrant learners a desire to know. Perhaps we can plant the seeds of possibility in impoverished spirits, so that they will bear fruit. We can motivate and stimulate the desire for personal growth and achievement. But we can only guide; if the impulses are absent we can't generate them. One strategy is to say, "If you were to try it, you might like it!" I think, for example, that a young person who does not like French cheese, or Bartók, or T. S. Eliot, is missing something. Once he tastes, hears, or reads more widely, he may come to cherish such pleasures. One can learn to appreciate all the goods of the self-actualized life—from creative work, sports, travel, and adventure, to music, poetry, philosophy, and science.

Responsibilities to Others

If we cannot assert simply and in all cases that a person has some responsibilities to himself or for himself, we can surely insist that he does have responsibilities to others, and that he cannot ignore them in a cavalier manner. Here ethical issues are in the forefront, for they concern a person's relationship to other human beings. Obligations constantly emerge on various levels of social interaction. Every individual has a number of duties to discharge based on his interpersonal relationships and prior commitments.

1. *Parental responsibilities.* Most fundamentally, parents are responsible for bringing up their children. They have a moral obligation to protect them by providing adequate food, shelter, and health care, and making available opportunities for learning. They cannot with impunity abuse or neglect their children. Most parents, out of loving

concern, do wish to do what is best for their children. Unfortunately, some parents are derelict in their duties, and they warrant moral condemnation.

Parental love has its roots in part in natural instincts—shared with other species—but also in acculturation. There is a bonding process of child to mother that begins when the mother feels the fetus kicking and moving about. As the child is born, this is strengthened by smell, touch, eye contact, and the child's awareness of his or her mother's response to a need for food and warmth. All the child's senses are stimulated by maternal and paternal contact, and this dependency-intimacy relationship continues throughout the child's upbringing. A parent has a right to bring up his child as he deems best. But he also has the responsibility to give the child proper care. Society has an obligation to protect children who are willfully neglected or harmed by their parents. The rights granted parents are correlative with the implicit understanding that concomitant duties are to be discharged. If they are not, parental rights to bring up their own children can be set aside by society.

Perhaps this is not the place to enumerate in detail what obligations parents have to their children. Suffice it to say that they must satisfy all of the survival and growth needs of the child. Parents should also attempt to contribute to their offsprings' intellectual, aesthetic, social, and moral education, to instill the moral decencies by example and practice, and make an effort to cultivate excellence. On the other hand, children too have rights, and parents have no license to violate them. In particular, children have a right to cultural enrichment and knowledge, and one must question the determination of authoritarian parents to protect them from exposure to different belief and value systems, ostensibly for fear of "corruption." Many parents want their children to share their beliefs and values, which is perhaps to be expected. However, this should not be at the price of individuality. A young person should not sacrifice or suppress his talents in certain areas because his parents disapprove of them. Loving parents will want their young sons or daughters to fulfill their own personalities and realize their own unique natures. The best way for a person to become autonomous is to find his own way. Morally responsible parents should want intelligent, mature sons and daughters, not robots who do their every bidding. Parents should not seek to create children in their own image—even if they believe that God so created them.

2. *Filial obligations.* Children also have commitments and duties to discharge in regard to their parents. The Ten Commandments spell this out: "Honor thy father and thy mother" is one of the most basic duties. An uncaring son or daughter is immoral, and this precept extends to most if not all societies. A thankless child can be sharper than a serpent's tooth, says Shakespeare. If a mother or father is obligated to do all that he or she can to further the welfare of the child, then the child—during childhood, adolescence, and throughout life—has concomitant duties. Many of these involve the moral decencies: to be loyal and faithful to one's parents; to be truthful, sincere, honest, trustworthy; to keep one's promises to one's parents; to be grateful for what they have done; to show appreciation of them. Surely the duties of nonmalfeasance are present: we should not threaten or harm our parents in any way. The duty of beneficence is especially strong: we should be altruistic and loving and have a regard for their interest and welfare. If they have a duty to protect and nourish us, then we have a reciprocal duty to do the same, especially as we get older and are able to do so. This especially applies to the years when our parents are sick and old. Why depend solely on the state to oversee their health care and welfare? Why should not their children do this first and foremost? This has been the case throughout the history of the race, and should be true today as well.

Whether an individual has a personal responsibility to himself to preserve his health and realize his talents, he surely has some kind of obligation to his parents. He cannot betray their trust. There may arise a conflict about values, particularly when the children differ with their parents about what career to pursue or whom to marry. A responsible parent may give advice and counsel, but he should allow his offspring to make their own choices (save in an extraordinary crisis situation), without insisting that they do what the parent wants. At some point a young adult may have to rebel and disobey his parents, particularly if they are unreasonable, and he needs to assert his own autonomy. In some crises the conflict may be so tragic that there can be no easy resolution. This is particularly the case when parents are overly demanding, protective, or selfish.

One should do what one can do to please one's parents and assist them if they need help, but at some point one has to cut the umbilical cord. In some situations, children may have to support their parents or sacrifice time and money to help them if they are sick. But where do we draw the line? I know of one young woman who gave up love and marriage and a life of her own in order to care for an ailing father, and a young man who felt his sense of duty to support his parents so keenly that he never established a family of his own. Fortunately, Social Security, Medicare, and nursing homes provide assistance in critical cases; and parents should not be infantile in what they demand from their children by way of sacrifice and dedication.

Nevertheless, given all of these qualifications, a child does have responsibilities to his or her parents, and should fulfill filial duties with love and devotion.

3. *Marital obligations.* One has the right to marry the person of one's choice, to enter into a contractual agreement, and to live together, sharing common goods and possessions, goals and values, and it is incumbent upon each partner to discharge his or her duties toward the other.

Marriage relationships need not be recognized by the church or the state to be ethically valid. Two adults who choose to live together as man and wife, as intimate companions or lovers, for a period of time on the basis of mutual agreement, constitute a marriage relationship. What is vital here is that it be a consensual relationship, not based on force or duress, and that the union not be arranged by parents or others without the agreement of the parties. If there is a consensual marital relationship, then the parties have certain obligations and duties to each other. Of primary concern is the need to abide by the moral decencies. If there is any place that such decencies are relevant, it is within the family unit: between sexual partners and companions and between parents and children. What this means is that the relationship must be based on integrity. There must be sincerity, truthfulness, honesty, and dependability. If the parties do not trust each other, it is not possible for them to live together in any kind of harmonious way.

Monogamy is among the most dependable of social institutions, for it provides a means of satisfying sexual needs in a stable and secure environment, and it protects individuals from the passions of fear, jealousy, and envy that enter in where there is sexual rivalry, competition, and uncertainty. "The heart hath its reasons, which reason knows not of," said Pascal. We may extend this to our personal lives. If the bonds of love and affection are totally absent, it is difficult for a relationship to endure. Some relationships may be purely sexual, entered into with a wild passion in order to satisfy erotic desires. Erotic satisfaction is vital in life and should not be demeaned. But purely romantic sexual alliances often diminish with age and time, and the frenzy of first sexual encounters often give way to tired and boring relationships. The flower of romantic youth fades with passing time, but it can be supplemented by deeper and more enduring bonds of affection. Although sexual compatibility is generally a necessary ingredient for a fulfilling marital relationship, it is not sufficient in itself, for there are other needs and interests that a marital relationship satisfies.

There is a whole catalogue of moral responsibilities that emerges in a marriage, as each partner is apt to point out—at times in carping tones—to the other. There is the basic moral excellence of fidelity. The marriage fails when there is persistant infidelity, and when a partner lies, cheats, or deceives the other. No relationship is perfect, and two partners may not have equal sexual needs. Where there is sexual compatibility, then the obligation is clear: in principle, one cannot or should not stray. Nevertheless there may be exceptions to this. People are only human; there may be an occasional affair or experience with someone else, and the marriage can still continue. That doesn't make adultery right, for if two persons are in love and are sexually compatible, then they have a general *prima facie* obligation not to break their explicit or implicit vows.

It is another matter when two parties in a marriage are not entirely sexually compatible, for one may be insufficiently satisfied by the other. He or she may still love the mate and enjoy sex, but wishes something more. I am not here defending adultery, but reflecting on the marital condition and how there may be a quest for alternative outlets. Some women may be frigid and some men impotent; no doubt they should visit a sex therapist or marriage counselor to see if they can correct these problems. Presumably the husband or wife can flirt and seek to persuade or entice the other to have sex, though rape or coercion can only lead to an embittered marital relationship, like that of Soames and Irene Forsyte in John Galsworthy's *The Forsyte Saga*.

We have already mentioned the case of Lady Chatterley. Her husband was unable to make love, having been wounded and rendered impotent in World War I. The gamekeeper was available. She was a woman with normal sexual desires and passions. Should she have suffered abstinence throughout her life? Though loving and caring to her husband, she deemed it morally permissible to have an affair with someone else.

This is a choice for an individual to determine, and no one can say *a priori* that it is absolutely wrong or unjustifiable. If erotic needs are essential for the good life, to insist that they be blocked for life is strong medicine that many individuals cannot suffer—even though celibates and Catholic priests insist on the merits of abstinence. The woman may be pregnant and unable to have sex, the man may be away on business or ill, an old lover may turn up unannounced; there are extenuating circumstances, as romance novels and films dramatize. In many societies, alternative solutions may be resorted to—such as prostitutes, call girls, and mistresses. There would no doubt be fewer prostitutes if every marriage provided equal satisfaction. One may still wish to be married, for, in addition to sex, there are other common interests and values in the relationship: shared lives and memories too beautiful to betray or abandon, careers and homes, sufferings and joys experienced together, and especially children and relatives that one knows and loves. Moreover, a wholesome marriage and family contribute enormously to the basic core of human values, and they need to be defended and preserved.

We thus ought to love and honor our husbands and wives, but whether we ought to obey them is another matter; obedience should not be made to apply to women. In much of the long history of the race, women were oppressed by men, forced to do their bidding. A wife has some responsibilities to fulfill in the home and so does the husband; and in post-modern urban and technological societies, both may have roles to play in the economy. The husband should not have hegemony over his wife. She is a free and autonomous person, equal in dignity and value, and her rights should be considered equal to the man's. A couple will work out marital tasks such as cleaning the house, shopping, making repairs, earning a living, cooking, and raising the children, and one or both mates may choose to assume one or another of these responsibilities. This also applies to unmarried couples living together, to people living together under common law, or to any other arrangements of cohabitation. In marriage or a family, there is an egalitarianism in respect to goods and services, for both share and share alike in accordance with their needs. Decisions between two loving persons should be jointly arrived at by a mutual process of give and take. In some marriages, one party may be domineering, always wanting his or her own way, and the other may be passive, always ready to accommodate. Perhaps this is a well-matched pair; but still the passive party has rights, and surely his or her needs or wants should not be submerged by the other's.

If there is any rule that should apply it is the principle of negotiation of differences and compromise. Thus we have a responsibility to appreciate the needs of the other, and to try to work out a *modus vivendi*. One learns from long experience that if a marriage is to be viable, one ought to bend, to not carry a grudge, to not lose one's temper; and if one does, to apologize, forgive and forget, kiss and make up, and not be so pig-headed or emotional that one can't discuss a problem. Each party has a responsibility not to be selfish, but to practice thoughtfulness and consideration.

No marriage is perfect, and each has its ups and downs. But if it is worth preserving, one has to have a sense of responsibility toward one's partner. It is not all give or all take. If the marriage fails, the recourse is separation or divorce, a state that is not in itself evil or sinful but is a reasonable way out of a bad situation. In my view, one should do whatever is necessary to maintain a viable marriage: divorce is a painful and disruptive experience. But if the marital differences are irreconcilable, then living apart and dissolving the union may be the only sensible alternative, and at some point in the future, either party may choose to remarry.

There are of course other arrangements between the sexes that people have resorted to: polygamy, bigamy, homosexual relationships, group marriages, trial marriages, open marriages. I have not been discussing these, only monogamous heterosexual relationships, but presumably in other arrangements, similar principles of sincerity, trust, honesty, negotiation, and cooperation should apply, providing a moral bond for the union. Marital arrangments—of whatever kind—entail responsibilities and duties based upon past agreements and present and future intentions to make them workable.

4. *The extended family.* Included in the class of responsibilities one has are those to other members of one's family, especially if one is fortunate enough to be a member of a large extended family. I am thinking of sisters and brothers, grandparents, aunts and uncles, cousins and in-laws. The relationship of sisters and brothers to one another is among the strongest and warmest of human relationships, upon which a good deal of human civilization rests. Though siblings may have spats, they are nonetheless expected to maintain their bonds of fidelity and devotion throughout life; these are second only to the bonds of parental

and marital relationships. But other kinship relationships also play a vital role in life. In primitive societies, the tribe includes all members of the kinship breeding group. In stable societies, individuals are brought up knowing all members of the family.

A personal autobiographical account is perhaps useful at this point. The love of my parents and my brothers and sisters came first, but this was extended widely to many other relatives in the broader family. In northern New Jersey, my father's family included seven brothers and one sister and several dozen cousins. My mother's clan, located primarily in New York City, were five sisters and two brothers. I knew my father's mother, a large and domineering woman who ran her clan with authority. My father was the youngest son—her baby—and so she had a warm place in her heart for us. My maternal grandparents were full of love and solicitude for their many children and grandchildren. I remember my grandmother as an adorable bundle of joy and my grandfather as a loquacious and smiling man with a beer-barreled chest and stomach, who lived to be ninety-two and always had a small cigar in the corner of his mouth. (The cigar was called "Between the Acts." I once put it in my mouth and became quite ill from the taste.)

Both families attempted to maintain close kinship ties. They decided to initiate—largely at my father's behest—a "Family Circle" after the sons and daughters had grown up. So they met once a month on a Sunday at someone's house, year in and year out, in order "to keep the family together." And we as children were able to get to know our relatives very well, not only at family get-togethers but at weddings, funerals, and other events. The attachments and affection of those years were precious and remain with me today. Unfortunately, given the mobility of modern society, most of my relatives retired to the south, and the children dispersed throughout the States, rarely seeing one another except perhaps at funerals. Virtually all of my aunts and uncles have died. They have ended up in two separate family plots—one with a high headstone and the name Kurtz over fifty gravesites, and the other in a different cemetery with the maternal name Lasser. They remain as monuments to the large extended families that are increasingly difficult to maintain in post-industrial urban societies.

Yet I cherish my moral commitment to each and every one of my aunts and uncles, who would always kiss and hug me upon arrival and departure. Though I would blush from ear to ear with embarrassment,

I nonetheless welcomed it. Each was a personality, with idiosyncratic values and beliefs. Most would send me a card or present on my birthday, and I in turn felt a sense of moral devotion toward them. I would commiserate with and console them when they described their aches and pains, and laugh with them when they told me jokes or when I played with their children, my cousins. My aunts and uncles followed my career and were always interested in and proud of my achievements.

How beautiful it all was, how rich and rewarding! And what a fertile setting for the moral decencies to take root, to be nourished, and to flourish. My many cousins and I have in turn had warm feelings of devotion—and of responsibility as well. To say a kind word, to console if there was an illness or death, to send a present if there was a new birth or marriage, to do a favor if possible, to recommend a job, to lend money when someone was in desperate plight—one did not have to be asked twice but gave quietly. If they suffered, we suffered. If they were joyful or thrived, we were joyful and exultant.

These ethical bonds are deeply rooted in the history of the tribe; to betray them is unthinkable. The moral decencies are displayed in their finest moments within the inner circle: brother to brother, sister to sister, living together, loving, sharing similar values, seeking new horizons. And the bonds of nephew to uncle or aunt to niece are also strong: as if a deep bond within the family breeding stock indelibly stamped us with a deep-seated piety to our ancestral heritage. Is it because we look alike and share the same traits? Does this set us apart from others? My relatives are decent to me, I have a concomitant fidelity to them, and it is my obligation to return consideration and love in kind. The moral principles, though undefined, are deeply etched in our consciousness.

There have been petty jealousies and envies, and at times feuds and spats, differences and rivalries. Yet in spite of this, there is a fabric of expectation and obligation within the family circle that is keenly felt. One had to go out of one's way to help a relative, especially in time of need. "Am I not my brother's keeper?" Indeed, we can argue that our primary moral responsibilities are here: to the family circle and its mores, and especially to one's parents, brothers, and sisters. But the principle can be extended: One can't expect others in society to do as much for us as we will do for ourselves. We eat and live together, celebrate marriages and graduations, commiserate at illnesses and funerals. How strong the bonds of compassion based on common sufferings and joys! Our obligations to a cousin or aunt, though strong, are not as demanding as to a parent or child, sister or brother. Are obligations weakened as the blood ties are thinned? What can we do for the Bushman in Africa, or the person in any faraway place? Very little in comparison with what we can do for those in our own small group, based on intimate face-to-face interaction.

5. *Friends.* Moral devotion does not depend upon our biogenetic attachments alone. Husbands and wives are of different genetic stocks, though the bonds of attraction and love are biosexual in origin. The same thing cannot be said of friends; yet we may have deep and abiding interest in and moral devotion to our friends, almost as much as to our relatives. Here is the real test of an ethical commitment: Can we extend it outside our own inner family to the stranger who becomes a friend to us?

Individuals may make many acquaintances in life on different levels. One may know someone casually, simply because he sees him occasionally in passing. One observes the decencies in encountering him; perhaps simply by saying "Hello," "Good morning," or "Thank you." Manners are important and one must be polite. These individuals may not be friends, but still we are civil toward them. Or one may know someone for a short period of time, for instance, as a fellow voyager on a train or plane, though he may soon be forgotten. Or again, one might make friends in the workplace—the office, factory, or school; a relationship develops, but it may be one of simple convenience. When working together we follow elementary civilities. If two people are at a water fountain, one defers to the other. Or if one is on an elevator, one does not push forward, but graciously gives way. All of this is necessary in the day-to-day transactions of ordinary life.

To be a *friend,* on the other hand, suggests a special moral relationship between two or more persons based upon *virtue.* I am not talking about alliances of convenience or utility, but of friendship based on genuine respect, esteem, and affection. A friend is a companion with whom one chooses to be, indeed, whom one seeks out. Friendship involves some intimate association. A true friend is a source of pleasure and satisfaction. In a sympathetic relationship, we experience laughter, wit, and fun in being together. A true friend is one who has a sense of loyalty to the other, is sincere, honest, and truthful with him and can be counted upon to stand with him through thick and thin. He is dependable and trustworthy, free of hypocrisy or pretense. He is genuinely concerned with the welfare of his friend, feels sorrow at his misfortune or pains, and is glad at his delights and gains. A friend does not have any ulterior motive, nor would he misuse the other for ill-gotten gain. He expresses a beneficent attitude and a sense of goodwill toward him or her.

Indeed, friendship is the first major step that individuals take beyond biological kinship ties to welcome the outsider into his moral concern. It is the beginning of a passionate regard for the good of others, and it is the cement that binds us to other humans beyond our own inner kinship group. A true friend will gladly do a favor, lend a helping hand, go out of his way, and even make a sacrifice without being asked or expressing regret; he has a sense of obligation and an altruistic regard. Thus, there are responsibilities and duties that we have to our friends, and this we discover by living and working together and sharing common goals and interests. We know that we must not betray or speak ill of a friend: to do so would be to break the bonds of trust. Friendship is intrinsically worthwhile for its own sake, but it also is confirmed by its role in heightening shared experiences and the positive benefits it confers on the parties concerned.

One aspect of friendship that is often overlooked is its generally nonsexual character. Friendship may exist between a man and a woman, though this may have romantic-sexual overtones. The bonds of friendship may be very strong, as between comrades-in-arms or schoolchums. If these ties are to endure, they must involve some affectionate regard between two or more persons. If affection is intense, friends may even be said to love each other in the best sense of that word, that is, to have a deep-seated emotional attachment and loyalty to each other and a regard for each other's well-being or prosperity.

The term *bi-affectionality* is relevant. This may sometimes be confused with bisexuality, that is, the capacity to be aroused sexually by both sexes. From the standpoint of this kind of relationship, it is not the sex of the person that is relevant, but the *person* of the sex. Another term to describe this affinity is *bipersonal,* that is, the ability to relate to another person, male or female, to genuinely desire that person to be fulfilled, and to truly love that person. That is the highest reach of moral friendship, perhaps the highest expression of spiritual *agape.* We may go still further, because we can relate to more than one person. *Pan-affectionality* allows a person to transcend the limits of biological determinism or sex roles, and to achieve *panpersonal* or *panamorous* devotional altruism. Not all friends reach this level, but when reached, it can be a profoundly ennobling experience. One can have many friends to whom one relates on many levels fully and completely. This state is among the highest states of human love, and when realized, it is treasured for its own sake.

The real test of our ethical principles, however, is to what extent we can carry our other-regarding concerns beyond our intimate network of relatives and friends to the stranger or alien in our midst and beyond.

6. *Small-group interactions.* We come to know and to deal with many different people in everyday life, as we move about and interact with them, and a set of responsibilities is implicit in our transactions. Though we may barely know many of our neighbors, common decency tells us that we will not, for example, purposely throw garbage on their front lawns or play loud music late at night, if for no other reason than that we do not wish to be offended by their retaliation. More specifically, the roles that we assume in our community, our daily activities and occupations, carry with them a concomitant set of duties based on our past and future expectations of those with whom we interact.

A teacher has a set of defined responsibilities to his students: to do his best job, to be punctual, to be considerate, to be conscientious in conveying knowledge, to have the interest of the child at heart, to seek to stimulate within the pupils the desire to learn and to develop important skills. With the job go obligations and duties that the teacher can either perform well or not.

This is also true for other people whom we encounter, for each occupation has its appropriate responsibilities. We would be shocked if the shopkeeper short-changed us, particularly if we are a regular customer, if the bus driver passed us by, or if the nurse in the hospital did not attempt to lessen our discomfort and pain.

Numerous obligations and duties emerge within the community. The roles that we play in the division of labor carry with them duties of performance, our stations in life concomitant tasks. These are not simply or even primarily ethical; they may be economic, as we assume tasks in the company, factory, office, team, or organization. We have a job to perform for which we are paid. If we do not perform well, we can be fired or replaced, or fail to receive a raise or promotion. But parallel to this is our sense of responsibility. We are obliged to discharge, with proper effort, the functions and services to which we are assigned. We may become dissatisfied, and so seek employment elsewhere. Here the common moral decencies of integrity and responsibility enter into the economic sphere. If we lack them our fellow workers will quickly discover that fact and refuse to work with us cooperatively. The employer has obligations to his employees to pay decent wages and to insure good working conditions.

Similarly, in other areas of economic life, we have our professional duties to perform. Whether one is a doctor or lawyer, a general contractor or stockbroker, there are expectations that follow. There are ethical standards that pertain to each profession: a code of medical ethics, a legal ethic, a quality and safety ethic, a business ethic. Coworkers, clients, and customers are able to sue us for negligence or malpractice, for which we may be liable. Our responsibilities follow from the network of activities that we undertake. The butcher must not sell us contaminated meat, but we should pay him if he has extended credit. The doctor has special responsibilities to his patients, and when he bills us, we have contractual responsibilities to pay him in return.

We also build up many other responsibilities and duties within the community. For example, if there is a fire, we feel an urgency to call the fire department, or if the fire department is not readily available, perhaps to help put the fire out if we can. If there is an emergency and someone is in distress, we call the police or an ambulance and see what we can do to comfort the person until help arrives. Living within a community, we develop a sense of mutuality that goes beyond our specific contractual duties. We may be concerned about what the mayor or the members of the school board do in discharging their responsibilities, implementing their policies, and running their administrations. We may join voluntary organizations and support co-operative efforts that we deem important: the Girl Scouts, Planned Parenthood, the local symphony, or the SPCA.

But do not our moral obligations go further and extend to others whom we may not know at all? There is the tragic case of Kitty Genovese, a young woman who was brutally murdered in an open courtyard in a Queens, New York, garden-apartment complex. Late one night she screamed for help as she was being assaulted. Dozens of neighbors heard her cries, but no one came to the rescue or even bothered to call the police. "I didn't want to get involved" was their pitiful excuse when later confronted by a shocked community. Mass society becomes impersonal, amorphous, and distant, but are we not our brothers' keepers, and do we not have an obligation to help those who cry out in need and distress? Ethical responsibilities express a deeper sense of community. They are deeply rooted in our fidelity to the well-being of the community—both on the local level and at large—in which we are nourished and sustained.

Beyond Ethnicity

Our sense of ethical responsibility may also apply to those who are of the same ethnicity, race, religion, or nationality as we, and with whom we may feel a special bond of kinship. This is especially true in pluralistic societies where individuals may identify with their ethnic or racial fellows. The ultimate ethical test is whether and to what extent we can carry our sense of moral community to those who live outside our immediate group or community or are of different ethnic or racial stocks. Since the moral decencies are first given birth in the small family or group, we may ask: Can we transcend the limits of our tribe, ethnic nationality, or race? Can we be faithful to the wider community of humankind? If we have responsibilities on the more intimate levels of life, do these apply in general to humanity as a whole? As we have seen, there are terrible examples within human history that demonstrate how hard it has been for this sense of identity to develop. Virtually endemic to the human condition has been intense and bitter intertribal, intergroup, and international rivalries and conflicts. Is the human species such that although there is moral devotion and compassion within the family, clan, or small community, it is virtually impossible to extend it to a wider realm?

It is surely the case that there are good empirical and pragmatic reasons why individuals operating on a face-to-face basis have some need for adhering to the rules of the game: these are necessary for survival. Is there at the same time a built-in instinct for aggression, which vents itself in hatred and animosity toward outbreeding or alien groups? The constant and bloody battles of conquest and defense would seem to support this dismal interpretation. Humankind has been unable to resolve the terrible scourge of war. I do not have any easy remedies. We cannot be certain that the tendency toward warfare will ever be entirely overcome.

The venerable religions have been aware of the problem. They have advocated the ideal of the brotherhood of men under the fatherhood of God. Missionaries have taken the "good news" of the Bible and the Koran worldwide in order to gain converts to the cause. This has had a positive effect in that it has sometimes helped to break down barriers and establish a truly worldwide outlook; similarly, economic, military, political, and scientific influences have become global in scope. All of these tendencies extend the concept of the human family so that it includes the family of nations, not simply *my* family or nation.

Unfortunately, at the same time that there has been the development of a global consciousness, there have been national power blocks and political, economic, and military rivalries. Religious traditions in particular tend to be highly divisive. Instead of building bridges, they often throw up ramparts, particularly where a religion is militant and its devotees true believers. A fundamentalist Christian or Muslim believes that only his fellow believers will enter the pearly gates of heaven, and Jews have felt that they are the "chosen people" of God. Hence there is an effort to convert, exclude, or condemn those who do not follow dogmatic faiths. The humanist virtue of tolerance is often lost in the process. Such religious fanaticism divides, rather than unites, humankind.

The crucial questions are these: Are we not each a citizen of the world community? Do we not each have an ethical obligation and responsibility to humanity as a whole, and does this not transcend our parochial loyalties?

The World Community

In one sense it is more difficult to make a case for an extended ethical consciousness than for our ethical responsibilities on a lower level of group interaction. Still, today there are powerful forces moving us toward a new ethical global consciousness.

First, intergroup rivalries, even if they are rooted in consanguineous, small-group loyalties, have diminished where large states have developed and where systems of law and order have prevailed. This has not been easy, and there still are ethnic conflicts within large nations. Still, many modern nation-states have developed that are able to encompass large territorial areas and a great variety of racial and religious ethnicities, and this has enabled conditions of peace to prevail. The Soviet Union, for example, has almost two hundred ethnic groups within its territorial confines. So has the United States. In the early days of the U.S., as immigrant groups flocked to the large cities, there were outbreaks of street warfare between gangs of Irishmen, Germans, Jews, Poles, etc. A century later, these conflicts have dissipated as the nation has become more homogeneous and new civic virtues developed, replacing the ethnicities of the old country. Hopefully the same process will occur for blacks, Asians, and Hispanic-Americans as they become assimilated within the larger community. Thus nationalism is able to take small groups to a higher-level order of patriotic obligation and responsibility.

Second, in the early days of human history, communication was slow and travel difficult. Thus, most people tended to live and die in one locality, as did countless generations of their forebears. Not only did customs and habits remain fairly stable and slow to change, but inbreeding groups tended to produce similar ethnic and/or racial types. But today there is widespread travel and mobility, and virtually instant communication. Moreover, racial, religious, and ethnic intermarriage is increasing as societies tend to integrate. Accordingly, the division of the globe into clearly defined ethnic enclaves or isolated racial stocks is gradually eroding, and new mixed races are emerging. Rather than "polluting the racial stock," as racists maintain, miscegenation is strengthening and enhancing it, and the ancient loyalties are being eroded. In America, Australia, Canada, and elsewhere, there are marriages between Scotsmen, Irishmen, Englishmen, Germans, Jews, Poles, Italians, blacks, Hispanics, Asians, and Indians. As blacks and whites intermarry, they produce mulattoes, and as Asians and Europeans intermarry, Eurasians—entirely new racial stocks. Similar processes can be seen in most of the European countries, which are no longer and may never have been lily-white and to which the workers from former colonies have immigrated and are breaking down racial barriers.

Third, and most surprising, is the fact that cultures are rapidly interpenetrating, and borrowing and sharing are going on at a rapid pace. Scientific research, technology, and industrialization, as well as Western democratic ideas and values, have reached many Asian countries. Similar work ethics and material values can be found in Japan, Saudi Arabia, Paris, Kenya, London, and Los Angeles. Moreover, there is intense interest in Asian cultural values in the West. Emerging then for the first time is a *world* culture, in which there are no longer separate and distinct pockets of isolation. Although there are still different languages, there is the ever-apparent need for a common world language, so that we can better communicate. Perhaps English is, for all intents and purposes, replacing French as the language of the diplomatic services and the educated classes who need to communicate across national boundaries.

Fourth, of equal significance is the fact that there are now powerful economic forces interacting on a global scale. No longer are there separate nation-states or regions able to develop their own economic resources, independent of world trade or world markets. Large-scale transnational corporations and conglomerates and powerful national governments with global interests have made the economic marketplace an all-encompassing one. Indeed, no area can hope to solve its economic problems in isolation. Unemployment, productivity, capital investment, currency exchange, and technology are all worldwide in scope.

Still—and this is most troubling—the world today is based on independent, sovereign nation-states, each with a law unto itself. The need for some kind of transnational political authority and a system of world law is more apparent than ever before. The twentieth century has seen the decline of traditional imperialist colonial empires. The scientific industrial revolution enabled the European nations to chart the Seven Seas, to dominate various portions of the globe, and to create vast empires. The wars for national liberation were progressive, for war freed national and ethnic groups from domination and allowed for some self-determination. But at the same time, the emergent nation-states have produced a lot of discord since World War II. A sense that there is some community of interest among nation-states has led to regional alliances such as the development of the European Common Market and the Warsaw Pact nations. But the issue that is emerging is: Do we not all have an obligation and responsibility to the entire world community?

It is clear that we do have responsibilities and obligations to the nation in which we live. As citizens of France, Japan, the Netherlands, or Argentina, we may speak a common language, and we share a common heritage and values. Patriotism and chauvinism have been powerful forces in the modern world, and many dreadful wars have erupted as a result. Many Americans claim deep devotion to the ideals embedded in the Declaration of Independence and the Constitution, and they feel it a privilege to be a citizen, by birth or naturalization. Polyethnic and nationalistic allegiances are thus facts of modern life. But is it not incumbent on us to become world citizens, and, if so, what would that entail? Do we not have a responsibility to that ideal? It is here that a revisionary and cognitive humanist ethics comes to fruition; for, I submit, we do indeed have such an obligation, above and beyond our lesser loyalties, and this entails the responsibility to preserve the natural ecology of the globe for future generations. It also carries with it an obligation to see to it—as far as we can—that human rights are protected everywhere on the globe. The ethics of humanism, if it means anything, must be planetary in scope. There is a difference between the small-group interactions—where the common moral decencies and our sense of personal responsibilities first emerge—and a larger global context. Whether humans are able to make this profound transition remains to be seen. It is the central issue of our time: how to build a global ethical consciousness.

Why Ought I To Be Moral?

We still have an important question to resolve on the level of small-group interactions, and so I wish to return to the basis of one's primary obligations and ask the question, "Why ought I to be moral?" What is the ground of my obligations and duties to my fellow human beings? This question is often hurled at the humanist by believers on the one hand, and by skeptics on the other. Theists maintain that they have solved the problem of obligation; we ought to obey moral rules because God commands it. This is considered a justification for moral obligation, and it provides the normative force. Without it, they insist, there would be no basis for behaving morally, and anything would be as right or wrong as anything else. Thus, naturalists and humanists seemingly are put into a quandary, for theists argue that if we remove God, we remove all grounds for morality.

We have seen the difficulty with this thesis. There is insufficient evidence that God exists. In the last analysis, such a conviction must rest on faith. To ground ethics in God only pushes skepticism one step backward and does not advance the argument. More to the point, many people who profess belief in God neglect their moral duties and actually break moral principles. Thus, belief in God has proved time and again to be insufficient ground for guaranteeing moral behavior.

Also, fear of punishment or hope of reward is hardly an *ethical* reason to follow God's commandments. It masks a basic self-interest: one is moral out of prudential considerations. Indeed, in one sense, the theists' argument is *immoral,* for it abandons the moral conscience for an authoritarian ground, and thus sidesteps the content of the moral imperative itself. Theistic morality is inadequate, for moral obligation is so important in its own terms, in and of itself, that it need not defer to a prior premise. To seek to bolster moral obligation by referring it to a still more fundamental nonmoral ground is to betray our deepest moral sensibilities.

The challenge we face is this: Can we justify responsibility *on its own terms,* for purely *ethical* reasons, without recourse to something independent or *a priori*? The ethical skeptic denies that we can. He looks for an "ultimate" justification for moral conduct, and can find none. But he is also critical of theistic attempts to justify obligation, for there is no necessary deductive relationship between God and our obligations; and the theist has not proven the *obligatory* character of the obligation. Thus the skeptic remains unconvinced, and rejects the view that God's commandments are morally obligatory.

But the skeptic turns the same guns on the ethical naturalist and humanist, because he does not see how one can derive the "ought" from the "is" without a leap in the argument. The skeptic wants a first premise and a foolproof justification for the "ought"; claiming to find none, he throws his hands up in a kind of subjectivistic despair. He asks the question, "Why?" *ad infinitum,* and since he can find no proof, he is dissatisfied with any and every answer given to the response. Why is this good? Why is it obligatory? he implores.

Let me attempt to deal with this problem by asking first: What does the question mean? And let me confess right off that I can make little sense of the question, "Why *ought* I to be moral?" as it has been traditionally formulated. For if it is meant as a universal question, it is hard to know what response would constitute an adequate solution, and even whether this question is intelligible. Moreover, it masks an underlying "quest for certainty," as John Dewey calls it, when none can be found.[1]

I submit that the question more appropriately should be phrased in specific terms: "Why ought I to perform *this* obligation or *this* duty?" At least then there is some concrete reference and hence some identifiable response. "Why should I pay back the money that I borrowed from my friend?" "Why should I be truthful to my clients?" "Why shouldn't I rob the little old lady on the street corner?" Each of these questions is contextual. Yet each of them has considerations and reasons which are relevant in concrete empirical terms.

Let us deal with the first question. Let us suppose that your friend loaned you money when you asked for it, and now she has asked you to return it because she needs it. This is a claim that is being made in a situation, and you have a corresponding duty to satisfy it. Generally, relevant contextual reasons are sufficient, and any sensible person will not dispute them. Of course one may ask, "Why should people repay their debts?" If someone were to raise that philosophical question, we might smile and wonder whether he were putting us on or whether he lacked ethical insight or was deficient in some way. He may be fixated on an infantile level of moral development and truly lack cognitive insight, or more seriously, he may lack a proper compassionate regard for the interests or needs of others. He thus would be morally illiterate. Nonetheless, we may wish to argue and try to convince him. How would we proceed? What is at stake is the fact that the *prima facie* general rules and moral decencies that we've learned from experience apply here. The rule "Keep your promises" is reinforced by another rule, "Pay your debts," and both pertain to the aforementioned situation. We could, of course, argue the merits of these general principles. For if these principles were constantly violated, no one would want to lend anyone anything in the future, and all borrowing might soon come to an end. If people did not keep their promises and pledges, then no one could be trusted in the future. The consequences would mean a breakdown of human confidence and a kind of disaster in human relationships would ensue.

To thus reason, we are referring to a second-order presumptive rule of a higher degree of generality. In arguing with a moral skeptic who questions whether he has such an obligation, we would first ask whether he did indeed borrow the money. If he said yes, we would then ask whether he agreed to pay it back. If he again said yes, we would say, "That is a sufficient ground for you to return the money." Within this situation, his obligation is reinforced by the fact that he has an *added* duty especially incumbent upon his relationship as a friend. But there may of course be extenuating circumstances in the situation, and he may point them out. He may not have the money, and, being in dire circumstances, hope that his friend will allow him to default. Being a friend, perhaps she will go easy on him. Or perhaps she has borrowed money from him in the past and failed to repay. Clearly, arguing on this level is sufficient. One need not invoke God or metaphysics to unravel the moral dilemma. If forced to, however, one can move on to a second-order proposition. The ethical principle is: "People ought to repay their debts." But that, we have seen, is not an absolute, only a contingent general duty, for other principles may come into conflict with it, and debt-repaying or promise-keeping may give way. For example, perhaps I cannot pay my debt because I gave the money to another friend who is very sick and needs it badly. One ought to repay unless there is a higher duty or good to realize. And so there may be a conflict of duties. All of this is at least arguable.

Nevertheless, both the theist and the skeptic may join forces and literally shout, "But why obey any ethical principle at all? Why not reject them all? Why believe in morality? Prove to me that one ought to behave morally." These questions are as old as philosophy. In Plato's *Republic,* Glaucon and Adeimantus ask Socrates the same question: Can you prove that justice, morality, or virtue is intrinsically good, not for the instrumental or utilitarian reasons that they will lead to the good life and hence be useful, but in and of themselves? What is my answer to this question? Again, the question usually does not arise in the ordinary course of living, for obligations are concrete, and they grow out of our social roles, the claims and demands made upon us, our prior commitments, and our future expectations. Yet the questioner is looking for the ultimate root for the moral life. Such questions may arise in desperate people who are opposed to the Establishment, and who are willing to flout all norms of common decency. Or again, they may be raised by a philosophy student who is looking for an epistemological guarantee for the entire framework of rights, duties, and obligations.

One must make a distinction between *reason* and *motive.* One may give arguments for the moral point of view, but these may or may not have psychological force within the life of the individual, who may still ask, "Why be moral?" My response, if that ensues again, is that this is not a meaningful question unless given content by reference to a *specific* claim. Moral decencies, goods, rights, duties, responsibilities, and obligations are grounded in a person's prior commitments and loyalties, and in his place within a concrete network of social relationships: as parent, child, lover, friend, client, practitioner, teacher, professional, etc. It all depends on one's personal relationship to others and various occupations and roles within a social scheme. It is within that institutional framework that the *prima facie* general principles and the common moral decencies resonate. These emerge in our consciences: to be truthful, to not steal or inflict pain on others, to be kind and helpful. Why? Because we learn by living together that there must be some rules governing expectations and duties. The basic moral rules are the lubricant that makes harmonious social transactions possible. Each of these rules is tested by its consequences in action. To deny them would lead to chaos and disorder.

"Why ought I to be concerned with harmonious social transactions?" may be the response. The answer here is twofold. First, because it is in each person's *self-interest,* for virtually everything that a person wants in life involves other human beings. Accordingly, there have to be some accommodations and some amity. These are instrumental and pragmatic considerations that a reasonable person will accept on purely prudential grounds. A rational person assumes the role of the impartial spectator and recognizes the generality of moral considerations, on *prima facie* grounds at least. A general principle is not an actual duty, and what one should do depends on a deliberative weighing of all the factors within the practical situation.

Second, ethics does not and cannot rest solely on egoistic consideration. If it did, it might reduce us all to Machiavellians, cunningly using morality for our own crass self-interests, and willing to set it aside if conditions warrant. There is a deeper aspect to the ethical life, however: moral awareness is rooted within our nature as human beings. There is a built-in dependency relationship based on socio-biological roots and cultural conditioning, and this reflects itself in our emotions. We generally or potentially have compassionate regard for others. Thus, *social interest,* and not merely self-interest, can motivate us. Lovers spontaneously feel an empathetic concern for each other. Two friends develop altruism through companionship and mutual interests. A mother has a deep affectionate regard for her child. One is considerate of the butcher, the baker, and the candlestick maker.

If a person does not see that he has duties and responsibilities, then he is morally blind and cognitively deficient. Some individuals may never get the hang of mathematics, and may have difficulty understanding geometrical proofs. We can only take them so far in syllogistic reasoning, and if they do not have the insight, I suppose there is nothing we can do except repeat ourselves. "If a = b and b = c, therefore, a = c" is a simple enough syllogism, and we assume that at some point, the student will get it, though more complicated mathematical reasoning is not open to everyone.

Similar considerations apply to empirical questions, where we attempt to evaluate evidence for a factual claim. In regard to elementary descriptive propositions, there must be some agreement: "It is raining outside" can be tested by simple observation. The merits of more complicated empirical hypotheses or theories are open to debate about whether there is sufficient evidence for them, but not about the empirical given of sense data. Similar considerations apply to the proof of elementary moral responsibilities. If a child or adult does not understand that he ought not to lie or inflict senseless harm on another person, then he or she may be morally deficient (generally from psychological or physiological damage) and lack the rudimentary moral insights requisite for social compatibility. We may have reached an impasse, for we are dealing with a person who, for whatever reason, has a low M.Q. (moral quotient).

The perplexing problem in human affairs is that moral insight is not equally distributed. It may only be partially present in some people, and they may only apply it to members of their intimate group. Ethical motives compete with other impulses and temptations within the personality.

Let it suffice now to make the following theoretical points:

1. Moral behavior is part and parcel of our nature as social animals.

2. Moral motivation is largely a potentiality, which develops only under optimal conditions. There are stages of moral growth.

3. A person's moral development may be thwarted, suppressed, or submerged by other influences.

4. There may be deviations from the norm of moral empathy, and these may be due to subtle biological, psychological, or sociological causes.

5. Whether a moral sense or social interest will develop depends on the genesis of character cognition and compassion.

Lawrence Kohlberg, Jean Piaget, A. H. Maslow, and other educational psychologists have maintained that there are stages of development, but whether actual stages conform to their lists is debatable. I wish to present the following analysis of the phases of growth and development—though the order of development may not always be the same in each individual. (For a fuller discussion of this, see Chapter Six.) The real issue is whether and why the latter phases of development are absent in some individuals.

Infantile amorality. In such individuals there is no inward sense of right and wrong. The individual lives in terms of instant gratification—almost as an infant, unable or unwilling to accommodate to others. There is no moral awareness. This stage applies only to psychotics or gravely handicapped people who cannot be fully socialized. Insofar as some socialization usually occurs, few people fully represent this stage.

Obedience to rules. Here moral conduct develops, based primarily on conformity to rules and habits, imposed and enforced by social commands—much as one housebreaks and trains a puppy. Any deviation from the code is severely punished. The moral code is conditioned, and the person is inculcated to obey it, much as he obeys the law. He is rewarded for fulfilling his duties, and sanctions are applied for deviation. The relationship between agent and teacher is one of passivity to authority. Much religious morality never gets beyond this authoritarian stage. Everyone must go through this learning phase as a child, especially if they are to acquire the basic moral decencies.

Moral feelings for others. There develops within the normal individual some internalized concern for the needs of others. There is a regard for the moral decencies and a desire to fulfill them. This may function on the interpersonal level, as between lovers or friends. It may be thwarted or blocked or be deficient in some individuals, especially where their psychophysical development is retarded and their basic needs are frustrated. Moral feelings are a normative expression of the social nature of human beings. It may be low or absent in distorted personalities. If it is, the motivation for ethical conduct is more difficult to stimulate. The development of feelings of empathy during early upbringing is perhaps the best stimulus for the growth of genuine moral sympathy later in life.

The ethics of self-interest. Decisions of what to do may be based solely on considerations of self-gain. The ethical agent makes rational calculations about his future conduct, and will sometimes make exceptions to general ethical principles, especially if he believes that he can escape detection. Very few people are totally immune from such temptations. Some people do this to excess, and they are cunning in planning for self-profit. The decision to restrain one's impulses and enter into cooperative social contracts may be done, however, out of a consideration for one's long-term benefit. Here the selfish person is willing to abide by ethical rules, for his main concern is ensuring his own long-range happiness. The excellencies are often sought as a way of maximizing one's personal values. Such individuals may be deficient in moral sympathy for others and may be primarily self-centered. This need not be the case, however; formulating choices on the basis of self-interest does not necessarily imply a lack of moral concern for others.

Union of moral feeling and rational self-interest. On this level there is a genuine feeling of empathy and loving concern for others: The love of one's family, team, tribe, or nation can all fit within one's self-interest. One desires his social group to prosper even if it is sometimes at the expense of other groups. Here altruism is planted in one's cognitive and affectional attitudes.

Humanistic ethics. A fully developed ethical system involves a concern for the broader community on a more universalistic basis. It is able to transcend the level of small-group relationships, and has the following ingredients:

—There is devotion to general ethical principles, and one does not break them without just cause.

—There is an inward feeling of moral sympathy and beneficence, and a desire to not needlessly hurt other human beings.

—Reason is used in guiding one's own conduct in terms of the excellencies. This may involve some consideration of self-interest, but it includes the interests of one's group as well.

—There is in addition an ethical awareness of the need to extend ethical considerations beyond one's inner circle to a wider community of human beings. This ethical concern is for the preservation and well-being of the world community and for humanity as a whole.

Note

1. John Dewey, *The Quest for Certainty* (New York: Minton Balch, 1929).

6
Education for Character and Cognition

Ethical Education for Children

We have argued that human beings in general have the potential for moral behavior and that this is deeply rooted in our nature as socio-biological animals. To survive as a species and to function in human communities, we need to learn how to work cooperatively and live by basic ethical principles. This is the source of the common moral decencies that serve as the bedrock for any human community. These moral imperatives transcend the diversity of cultures; they become so ingrained that they are often sanctified as divine by religiously based communities. They are, however, the common heritage of human civilization, and are shared by theists and secularists alike.

Moral principles compete, however, with other impulses in the human animal: self-interest, aggression, competition, the desire to dominate others, etc. Moral sensibilities may be masked, thwarted, or suppressed by other drives. In some individuals, moral conduct may be overwhelmed by fear, selfishness, or the desire to inflict suffering on others. Human beings are capable of cognitive responses, which can moderate passions and help us to tolerate and negotiate differences and cooperate with others in achieving common tasks. We can understand how nature operates and attempt to modify conduct in the light of critical intelligence. Reason thus adds to our species's native impulses; it provides us with a restraining component. Moreover, reason can also modify custom; it can introduce progressive ethical principles by which individuals learn to lead lives of excellence and in terms of which they widen their ethical concerns beyond their immediate circle of acquaintances and become aware of their responsibilities to a greater community of humankind.

The basic topic I wish to raise in this chapter is how we may realize the moral decencies, exercise self-restraint, and develop a rational respect for ethical principles. How can we ensure that moral conduct is not suppressed or thwarted by self-interest, hatred, the quest for self-aggrandizement, or power? There is within each person a struggle between negative and positive impulses; in some individuals, wholly selfish or even demonic tendencies dominate. How can a society develop intelligent, thoughtful, considerate, other-regarding human beings?

This difficult question is fundamental to every social system. Historically, humankind has attempted to instill virtues in its children, and to instruct them about proper moral conduct. Practical lessons learned from experience are eagerly shared with children. We want to raise productive sons and daughters; we want them to be capable of personal growth so that they can realize their creative talents, but we also want them to be morally responsible and sensitive to the needs of others.

How we achieve these ends is a question that has engaged parents, teachers, and civic and religious leaders alike. This is an issue that is intensely debated in the public schools today. Should the schools attempt to teach morality? If so, what should be the goals of moral education? I submit that the goals of ethical education are twofold: First, to develop *character* in the young, so that they are able to observe and express the common moral decencies, both in their own lives and in their relations with others; and second, to nurture the capacity for ethical *cognition* and the ability to engage in critical ethical inquiry.

The first goal is elementary, a process that parents begin early, perhaps at birth, for tenderness begets tenderness, and perhaps only a baby who is loved can grow up into a moral being. How a baby is fed, bathed, played with, talked to, and allowed proper rest is the beginning of molding character. Parents toilet train their babies to teach control of rudimentary biological functions. They also instruct them in table manners. Children are put to bed early, they are taught to restrain their impulses, not to make loud noises when their parents are sleeping, to wash their hands before eating, to brush their teeth. In time, they may be assigned chores around the house. They are taught to straighten up their rooms and make their beds, perhaps to cut the grass, do the dishes, or feed the pets. At school children are taught to read and write and are instructed in the proper use of their mother tongue.

The point is that habit-formation is essential in all human conduct, and we cannot easily live together unless we learn to restrain our impulses and direct our desires along constructive, socially accepted pathways. All of this proceeds unconsciously in all civilized societies, and moral training thus begins in the earliest months in the nurturing process of raising our children.

Some parents fail in this endeavor. They may be so disorganized or distressed in their personal lives that they are unable to bring up their children in a loving and wholesome way. Perhaps they themselves were abused and so they abuse their own children, thus perpetuating a syndrome of neglect and, in some cases, of violence. Some may be authoritarian despots, seeking to impose their own rigid standards of right and wrong; they are insensitive both to the needs of their children and the complex nuances of moral choice. Nonetheless, there are moral models that decent parenting exemplifies, and I wish to outline what I think is appropriately involved in this process. I am talking about *ethical* education that is appropriate to the twenty-first century and beyond, and I submit that the processes I describe can, in large part, be accepted by theists and secularists alike.

A great deal has been written about the content of primary- and secondary-school education, whether the schools should engage in moral education or religious training, and if so, what the schools should teach. Some parents are apprehensive lest the schools undermine the beliefs and values of their religious or ethnic group, and so they oppose any moral education in the schools. They are fearful that if children are exposed to a wide range of pluralistic ideas, they will come to question the absolute verities and become corrupted in the process.

Let me respond to these fears by saying that all education has a moral and ethical dimension, and that there would not be any education worthy of the name if it did not. It is often overlooked that the schools try to cultivate both intellectual and moral behavior. Granted they teach intellectual skills, and that this is at the heart of the curriculum. They attempt to develop knowledge and proficiency in the various subject matters: English, mathematics, history, the natural and social sciences, art, music, literature, foreign languages, etc. But the schools also seek to develop good behavioral habits. This kind of moral training begins in kindergarten and the primary grades. Children are cautioned to be reasonably quiet, not to be rambunctious or to disrupt the classroom. They are taught manners, to raise their hands if they wish to ask a question, to be polite in responding to others, to be punctual, neat, not to cheat on examinations, etc. Instruction in the common decencies and polite manners of civilized behavior is implicit in the entire curriculum.

To state that parents and teachers are already actively involved in moral training is perhaps a truism, yet truisms, it is often forgotten, are, after all, true. The question is: Are there any guidelines to follow? As I have already suggested, there are two kinds of education in the ethical sphere: (1) the development of character, which is appropriately called *moral* education, though it also has an ethical dimension, insofar as it seeks to cultivate values, and (2) the development of intellectual skills and of critical ethical inquiry, which can clearly be called *ethical* education. Both dimensions are appropriate at home and in the schools, though one may be pursued in isolation and to the detriment of the other. It is essential that we begin with character education, but at some point we need to go beyond this in order to develop the ability for ethical deliberation.

Character Education

The character of a person refers to his or her general disposition and tendencies. *Character* defines the personality traits and habits that will guide a person's conduct or refers to the characteristics a person has, his personal attributes. We use the term in many senses. Novelists and dramatists seek to portray the unique idiosyncratic tastes and distinctive outlook and demeanor of persons through mannerisms and mental and moral qualities. The term *personality* refers to the sum of such character traits. This may include peculiar likes and dispositions, mannerisms in dress and conduct. People differ widely in their traits and tastes. If a person is odd or strange, we may say that he or she is a "character," a word of humor or even derision. We may thus label some persons as comical, others as hot-tempered; some may be hard-working and serious, others foolhardy and indiscreet; some are vain, others timorous; some easy to forgive, others seething with resentment. We note that some persons never seem to achieve anything; they may be secretive and unscrupulous. Others are open, friendly, trustworthy. Some are miserly, others generous.

There is a common moral usage for the term *character,* which may connote positive or negative qualities. If we say that a person has *good* character, we mean that he is reliable and has integrity. On the other hand, if we question a person's moral character, we imply that he is devious, dishonest, or has some other undesirable trait.

We applaud persons who "have character," meaning that they have self-discipline or self-restraint, and that they can control their passions and fancies. We say that they have *strength* of character. Another person may lack character; that is, may give in to every whim and caprice and be unable to ward off temptations. A brave and resolute character can confront danger with equanimity; a cowardly person is overcome by fear. An honest person can be counted on to deal fairly with others; a dishonest person is devious. When we use the term *character* we are not only referring to the specific traits of a person—his idiosyncratic attributes—but also to his general disposition or tendency to act in a certain way. A term that is commonly used is *habit,* and we say that people have good or bad habits. Some are neat, others sloppy; some loquacious, others dour; some punctual, others tardy. Here we are referring to the deep-seated general characteristics of the person. Indeed, if we know a person well, we generally can surmise how he will behave in future situations. What he will do is usually predictable, for his actions are "characteristic" of him.

People may, however, behave uncharacteristically at times, and there may even be a personality change after a period of crisis or achievement. Some people have been known to give up family and career and adopt an entirely new lifestyle. A loyal and dedicated employee may become disloyal to his employer. A repressed woman may suddenly get drunk and light up, to the surprise of everyone. Or a calm person may suddenly fly off the handle in an intemperate fit. Human behavior is sometimes unpredictable. A person does not always act as we expect; free choice and autonomy may lead to novel actions. Some claim that when they behave in a seemingly uncharacteristic way, they are showing their *true* character, which previously had been masked.

Traits and habits of character are not fixed indelibly in cement but interact with one another, and may be modified by living and learning. Whether one's general character is genetically determined or a product of environment is not easily ascertainable. Both genetic and environmental influences structure our behavior. How one's natural endowment is structured and expressed depends on stimuli within the environment. The behaviorist points to the fact that we build conditioned responses, and channel our behavioral drives along certain lines. This is due, no doubt, to the pain or pleasure that we have received from the social environment. A child soon finds that disruptive behavior is frowned upon by elders and that polite comportment is applauded. External sanctions or rewards—coming from parents, teachers, and peer groups— are internalized and motivate future behavior. The child builds up habits of expectation and acceptable behavioral responses. The earliest years of education and training are the most important in structuring good habits and moral virtues, and in guaranteeing moral decency and individual excellence.

How do we inculcate appropriate behavior? I submit that there are built-in tendencies within normal people, by which the moral decencies are naturally expressed. The basis of this is laid when the mother and father feed the child, keep it warm, and provide protective, loving hugs. Each day of affectionate care is a new chance for altruism to develop. As the child grows older and relates to others in the family—sisters, brothers, and relatives—and to friends and colleagues in the world beyond, an appreciation for the moral decencies can take hold.

Unfortunately, in some individuals, there may be little or no moral growth, or developing altruistic tendencies may be deflected. How and why this occurs is difficult to ascertain. No doubt unloving or abusive parents play a tragic role in abnormal development. There is evidence, however, that some psychotic personalities, who manifest amoral, psychopathic behavior, have some chemical or brain defect that may be partly genetic in origin. For normal moral personality to develop, at a minimum, the child needs to be nourished by moral empathy. The starting point here is to build and develop character, and to instill by positive reinforcement those general traits and dispositions we consider worthwhile. Let us discuss the various models of moral training that are used.

Level 1: The Authoritarian Obedience Model

Authoritarian parents believe in strict discipline. They insist that there are absolute rights and wrongs and that the duty of the child is to obey without question the received moral code. There is great fear that if the child makes any exception and is not punished, he or she may become wayward and delinquent. In strict fundamentalist and old-time English boarding schools, spanking is a method commonly used to punish infractions of the rules and enforce discipline. The main effort is to instill within the child the sense that he must obey the strict letter of the law. Presumably, fear of detection and punishment or, conversely, approval and reward for moral rectitude, insures compliance.

One can sympathize to a certain extent with parents who are fearful that if their children are allowed too much latitude they will turn out badly: be indolent, take drugs, engage in petty theft, have promiscuous sex, or turn to violence. Moreover, many parents feel deeply threatened if their children reject their values and choose to chart their own lives. Hence, the obedience model is a defense resorted to in order to protect parental authority.

This explains much of the rage vented by some parents and communities against the schools. Many conservatives are frightened by change and worried that their children will grow up to differ with them over fundamentals, particularly religious convictions. Reactionary parents resist exposing their children to the theory of evolution, comparative studies in the social sciences, much of modern literature, and moral education because they are fearful that their children will reject their hidebound moral values and adopt alternative lifestyles. This is particularly the case with many theists committed to what they regard to be the biblical virtues. Such parents, for example, are intensely opposed to sex education in the schools, since they think it will corrupt the young. For them, the main content of sex education can be summed up in one word: "Don't!" They believe their sons and daughters should abstain from sex until marriage, even though they may not marry until later in life, if ever.

They also rail against "values clarification," for they fear it may expose their children to members of the community with different ethnic and religious backgrounds and alternative conceptions of living. What is especially threatening is the idea that one can question the fixed verities, as any kind of critical inquiry tends to do. The notion of absolute rights and wrongs is "corrupted" by situation ethics. Indeed, the advice to think for yourself and learn to make your own decisions is viewed with horror, for they believe it provides license for children to do what they want.

One can appreciate the desire of parents who love their children to do the best for them. Yet it is clear that the authoritarian obedience model has hardly reached the level of mature moral development, for to follow a customary code of behavior because one is compelled to do so does not insure moral conduct. Outward compliance with inflexible moral rules because of fear of punishment in no way guarantees that a person's intentions are genuinely ethical. Moreover, this rigid model does not tell us how to cope with the many conflicts encountered where there may be differing moral principles and values in the community. Nor does it assist the individual who may be in a moral dilemma. When the rigid structures of an authoritarian personality are challenged, that person may be unable to to adopt appropriate coping mechanisms— or even to function at all. He may be so keen to follow the commandments that he is unable to deal with the nuances of deliberation and the complexity of moral choices. He may be so imbued with the need to respect authority, particularly if it is sanctified in an ecclesiastical or legal context, that he is unable to exercise judgment or choice.

Some obedience to moral rules is not without merit, and sometimes parents, teachers, and society have to enforce compliance with the fundamental norms of a civilized community. Surely society can use reward and punishment to induce certain kinds of conformity. This is especially the case with violent criminals, which society must protect itself against. These are individuals who are either genetically disposed or so hardened by experience that they are prone to engage in deviant social behavior. Here all the power of the law is necessary to guard the rights of innocent people within the community.

The authoritarian obedience method, however, is hardly sufficient in itself; for this kind of moral "education"—if that term can even be used—is equivalent to *indoctrination*. Moral character can hardly be developed, for the child simply accepts what is handed down, and customary morality is never transcended. We have seen the difficulties with such an intransigent approach to morality in Chapters One and Two. Such a narrow conception may be particularly damaging to a child's moral growth, for if he never goes beyond this level, he may be permanently handicapped, morally speaking. Such individuals, when they become adults, may display unfeeling behavior or resort to immoral deeds or even crime.

Level 2: Internalized Empathy and Self-Restraint

There is a second stage of moral growth that is essential to development; this is a positive approach to morality. By that I mean the need to develop within the young person an appreciation for the moral decencies. This can only happen when moral principles and rules (1) are *internalized*, (2) are fulfilled not simply out of fear but because of genuine feelings of *empathy*, and (3) are developed out of a realistic sense that one must master and *restrain* one's own passions.

Here the young person is encouraged to develop his own inner moral sensibilities, which are able to function on their own, without external censure or sanction as the primary stimulus. Cynics might argue that this form of moral conscience is simply the psychological equivalent of rules instilled by parental or social approbation and disapprobation and that the child has in effect internalized the commandments of external authority. But this is never adequate to insure mature moral conduct unless, in addition, there is the growth of an independent and autonomous moral sense. One does not have to be told by legislative fiat that something is right or wrong, good or bad; one is able to experience a sense of duty oneself. Here *moral* responsibility and a sense of obligation have become part of the personality. They are structured within the disposition so that a person genuinely appreciates the needs of others and can sympathize with them. He has a compassionate and beneficent regard, and does not wish to harm others knowingly.

It is surely the case that parents and teachers who use the authoritarian model as their first line of instruction want their children to develop the milk of human kindness.One can't believe that they would want their children to merely conform to the commandments or do the right thing for the wrong motives. The point is that there is no guarantee that early insistence on inflexible obedience will lead to an internalized moral sensibility. That is why moral education must at some stage move beyond obeying rules to conscious voluntary choice.

The same considerations apply to the development of internal self-restraint over one's appetites and desires. Here, matters are far more complicated. Presumably, the censorial superego does limit and restrain the hedonistic id of infantile sexuality. Both church and state seek to define appropriate behavior and to label as wicked or illegal any deviation from certain norms of sexual conduct. They also seek to regulate excessive drinking, gluttony, or the unbridled quest for power. But again, unless a person at some stage in life is able to appreciate the need for psychological balance and be concerned about his own health, he will be prey to every random passion that may overtake him. His inner life will be tyrannical, and he will be at war with himself, unable to discipline his desires, unaware of the economizing principle that enables him to save for tomorrow, unable to forgo short-range temptations in the light of long-range goals. His life will be discordant and unstable.

What is essential, both for inner restraint and altruistic empathy, is the importance of developed character. Thus I believe that both parents and teachers need to do what they can to structure good habits and develop virtuous character. How to do that is the great issue. Aristotle's profound insight in the *Nicomachean Ethics* was that those who wished to study ethics must first have developed some sense of right and wrong, and a virtuous character. I submit that our generalized habits and traits are environmentally developed by instruction and learning, even though there are genetic predispositions and tendencies within the species and the individual that make this possible. If this is the case, then we need to begin the development of character in the child's earliest years, and parents and teachers must assume a measure of responsibility for how the child will grow. It is permissible to instruct children by laying down some commands—do's and don'ts—based upon what we ourselves have learned, and we need to punish inappropriate behavior and reward appropriate behavior. But we need to go further and nourish within the child his own perception of moral realities: we need to live, work, and play together with others in the community. His moral sensibility is then not simply equivalent to the censorial social order but becomes truly his own.

I can assist and encourage the child to stand and to take his first steps, but it is he who must gain mastery of the skills of walking, running, climbing, etc. Similarly, I can teach him the basic vocabulary of a language and the rules of grammar, but it is his own cognitive talents that need to take hold and grasp meanings and see connections. We can only provide the materials and guidelines for moral growth; the child needs to transact with his parents and peers in the social process of learning and accommodation. He needs to develop his own moral quotient (M.Q.) by living with and learning from others.

Two essential ingredients are love and a sense of belonging to a community—especially through intimate face-to-face interaction—and the child must experience the feeling that those in his environment are not hostile, but love him, are concerned for his well-being, and have his best interests at heart.

He may not learn to respond empathetically to others, unless those about him demonstrate compassion for him. A child who experiences loneliness, feels unwanted, or is abused at the hands of others will find it more difficult to mature as a loving and empathetic person. But if he is properly cared for, the moral decencies can become established in a child's conduct. I would emphasize the superiority of positive reinforcement over carping criticism of a child's faults. Generalized dispositions and habits can be developed and conditioned if there is a constructive self-affirming attitude toward life.

Which principles and values should we seek to develop? Here we would refer first to the elementary moral decencies of integrity, trustworthiness, benevolence, and fairness, and to their various subclasses. Similarly we can turn to the excellences in one's personal life. We need to cultivate autonomy, self-discipline, self-respect, creativity, motivation, an affirmative outlook, etc.

If my thesis is correct, then only in an enriched moral environment can the young child and adolescent best become himself, flourish, and develop ethically. The first level is perhaps the starting point, for one needs some obedience to minimal rules, but this is never sufficient, for one must proceed to the second level of internalized empathy and self-restraint. One must encourage and cultivate self-development, not constantly admonish, certainly not punish healthy individuality or impose excessive repression.

It is clear that I differ with some earlier humanists, who believed that the only way to develop human potentialities was by providing the child with a completely *unstructured* environment, allowing him to make every decision for himself. I think that this approach is gravely mistaken. On the other hand, if adults are to learn to cope with freedom and flourish under it, they must be exposed to it while young. Thus we should not so fear for our children that we do not allow them to make their own choices. However, to provide a totally unstructured moral environment is foolhardy utopianism, because the young child is uncomfortable and confused by too many choices, the consequences of which he is not experienced enough to understand. Therefore, it is essential that training in certain general rules and the moral decencies be undertaken.

Level 3: Ethical Cognition

Essential to moral education is the development of the capacity for ethical cognition. Ethical understanding is not confined to the adult world; it is a skill, like other intellectual abilities, such as reading and mathematics, that needs to be nurtured in the child and adolescent. Not that the child is capable of reaching mature judgments by himself or autonomy in the ethical realm. Nonetheless, it is essential that the seeds of ethical conduct be deeply rooted in virtuous habits, as cultivated by a child's elders. Without these foundations, ethical inquiry is apt to be capricious and rudderless. It is only when there exists some internalized structures that authentic ethical cognition can take hold. Cognition itself, however, is able to play a role in structuring character in growing children, adolescents, and young adults. Unfortunately, those who insist upon the authoritarian model fail to appreciate the possible function of rationality in the development of moral sensibility. By this I mean that the processes of learning must of necessity include rationality.

For example, if parents say, "You must do this now," and if the child were to ask why, is the appropriate answer simply, "Because I command it"? This is hardly an ethical response, even though many parents resort to it. I do not advocate giving reasons in the earliest years, but as the child grows, the parent should, where appropriate, give explanations: "You must go to bed early tonight because you have to get up early in the morning to go to school; if you don't sleep enough you will be tired and won't have fun." "Eat your vegetables because they have vitamins that will make you strong." "Don't steal; you would not like someone to take your toys." "Don't hit your brother; how would you like him to hit you?" "Share your candy with your sister, and when she has some, she will share it with you."

Here the parent (1) gives *reasons* for appropriate conduct, (2) spells out *grounds* for such behavior, (3) refers to *consequences* (harmful consequences are to be avoided, good consequences achieved), and (4) appeals to *consistency* (don't make exceptions to rules that you want to apply to yourself.)

These are practical, everyday situations parents can use to cultivate critical ethical intelligence. There is a practical common sense at work, and the moral decencies are so deeply rooted in consciousness and so evidently part of human experience, that it is possible for parents to engage in ethical dialogue with their children. One doesn't need a college degree or any formal education to be aware of elementary ethical principles: don't lie, steal, cheat, break promises, etc.

Presumably, at the higher reaches of ethics, one attempts to develop some impartiality in one's conduct and some appreciation of the "ethical point of view" and of decent ethical conduct in regard to others. The Golden Rule is deeply etched in sensible conduct: We should do unto others as we would have them do unto us. In addition, we should not knowingly harm another person out of hatred, spite, jealousy, or revenge. We should seek to lend a helping hand to another person in distress. We should not allow exceptions for grievous immoral conduct.

In this learning process, the issues are not simply abstract or intellectual, since one is attempting to internalize feelings. Some sense of guilt, shame, or embarrassment about conduct that is inappropriate, unbecoming, or immoral should be conveyed to the young, as well as a positive sense of caring for the feelings of others. The best method here is to fuse beliefs and attitudes, thoughts and emotions, cognitions and empathies. There is clearly an emotive element, for character is not simply intellectual but has feeling in its content.

Nonetheless, almost by definition, ethical awareness involves some intellectual appreciation of reasoning. Although the parent and the society have their moral values and principles, these may mean nothing to the child until they become part of his internal conscience. Even the authoritarian person at some point needs to appeal to rationality. Often the reason given for obeying the moral decencies is because *God* declared them to be binding. We must grant that some individuals may be motivated to adopt a code of conduct because of the force of a religious system. But unless the moral attitude is truly felt and becomes binding in itself, as an inherent part of a person, and unless he acts not simply out of the fear or love of God, but because he has a genuine sense of right or wrong, it is not *ethical* as such. One is hardly ethical if one's behavior is that of an unconscious automaton who conforms to a code without appreciating the rationality of one's conduct.

What Should Be Taught?

The questions often asked are: "What should be taught by parents and teachers?" "Is there any common ground?" "Can we agree about basic values and core principles?" There are surely widespread differences within society about moral beliefs and values. People will argue about sexual freedom, abortion, euthanasia, capital punishment, war and peace—and there can be irreconcilable differences. But if my thesis is correct, then there is, quite separate from more recently developed ethical principles, a continuous bedrock of moral decencies, and these decencies should be taught.

We want our children to exemplify the highest moral principles in both deed and action. We want them to be truthful, to keep their promises, to be honest and sincere, to be loyal and dependable, to have good will, to not harm others, to be beneficent, to show gratitude, and to be just. This cuts across national cultures, and is part of the common heritage of humankind. True, there may be serious disputes about the application of these principles to concrete situations, and honest persons can differ about how to solve moral dilemmas, especially when there are conflicts. That is why we need to develop the humanist principle of tolerance, and why we must learn to live together and cooperate wherever possible, negotiating our differences. The world is pluralistic. There are different religious, cultural, social, and political institutions and diverse value systems. We should learn to live and let live. The values and norms of others are not immune to criticism, which we should be prepared to engage in forthrightly; we should seek to persuade others and be persuaded ourselves of the truth of an ethical claim. But we should always seek in principle to settle matters peacefully, not by violence or force; we should strive to find common ground; and we should be prepared to change our values and principles if need be.

As a humanist, I would add—at least for those who share my values—the desire to develop within children an appreciation for the excellences. I want my children and grandchildren to lead autonomous lives in which some independence in judgment can develop. I wish them to develop their own unique individualities, even though they may not agree with me. I can help to launch them on the sea of life, but they must steer their own courses by their own lights, even if these are independent of mine. I realize that this may offend many parents; still, each person must live his own life—others cannot live it for him. Do we want mere clones of ourselves who do our bidding, or creative persons who have fully developed their own talents and opportunities? To achieve their goals as mature persons, must they not develop some internalized self-discipline? Unless a person can order his life with some measure of harmony, his days will be scattered, at the beck and call of every random desire.

Should we not also want children and young people to learn to use their intelligence to guide their decisions? Is not practical wisdom important in living? Should children not develop some self-respect for their own talents and abilities, avoiding the torment of self-hate? Yes, and they should, if they can, lead a life of nobility that merits praise. Self-love, instead of demeaning guilt, can develop a healthy attitude toward living. Would we not also want young people to be creative and resourceful, capable of inventive discovery and innovation? If so, they will need to develop a career and contribute to society and their own growth. We hope they will be well motivated, of good will, affirmative in outlook—not negative, pessimistic, or nasty. Related to this is the obvious need for proper nutrition, exercise, and good health. Should they not also be able to enjoy life fully, including erotic experiences and high aesthetic appreciation? In sum, do we not wish that they be happy, creative, self-actualized persons who find life bountiful and overflowing with joy?

If we want this kind of children, we should avoid simply indoctrinating them or making them facsimiles of ourselves. A parent who loves his child recognizes that he is a unique individual, who should be allowed to define himself and flower. We can lovingly help him as best we can, but it is up to him to find his own way in seeking the good life. We hope that he will, at the same time, be morally sensitive to his parents' needs, assist us should we ever need help, and be considerate of our interests and desires. The process of respect should be mutual and reciprocal. The ethical excellences are the moral decencies incorporated into a person's life.

I believe it is a mistake for parents to instill a narrow religious belief system in their children, or prevent them from learning about the beliefs of other people. To baptize or confirm a baby into a faith— without his consent—and to seek to brainwash him is unfair. I am not denying that parents have the *right* to do so—a longstanding right recognized by civilized societies. Yet at the same time, we may ask: Why not allow a child to decide for himself what he wants to become when he grows up, the career he wishes to follow, whom he wishes to marry, and what religious beliefs he will adopt? I realize that this may be difficult for those who fervently believe that they have the absolute truth and that it would be a sin—and harmful to the child—to stray from the fold.

In my view, education should be open-ended: the child should receive the best in cultural enrichment; he should be exposed to the wide world of ideas and develop an awareness of alternative ethical systems. If my children reject my beliefs, then I may grieve, but it is their free choice. The lives of my sons and daughters are as important to them as mine is to me. They were not created in my image; each one has his or her own image to discover and display. That is the meaning of life—every person has the opportunity to create his own life-world. The best that I can hope for is that my children will, like me, find life to be a great and wondrous adventure, full of meaning and excitement. If all we have is life, then we must live it to the fullest and hope that our children will learn from our example and do the same—though their "fullest" need not be the same as their parents'. In the last analysis, the lust for life itself is the be-all and end-all of living, which youth must discover themselves.

The Need for Critical Ethical Inquiry

Basic to the ethics of humanism is the need to develop the capacity for critical ethical inquiry. This is true not only for individuals who have matured in their cognitive abilities but also for society and the world at large. We need to eat the forbidden fruit of the tree of knowledge of good and evil.

Unfortunately, moralities fixated at the authoritarian level—or even developed to the internalized level—are unable to cope with all the challenges of life. Only cognitive responses can deal with new situations, ones not covered by even the best of an internalized morality. For we constantly meet ambiguities for which the best response has to be reasoned out.

Although there are general guidelines that intelligent human beings who have eaten the forbidden fruit will take into account in their ethical deliberations, in the last analysis there is no substitute for independent critical inquiry. We hear very little about the need for practical wisdom—bequeathed by the ethical philosophers—yet today, it is perhaps the best guide we have for making effective judgments. What we ought to do can only be determined in the concrete situations encountered in life: earning a living, building a career, buying and furnishing a home, tending a garden, participating in relationships, debating questions of social policy, or negotiating with people of different philosophical and political outlooks. There is no substitute for using critical intelligence to solve our problems, though the enemies of humanism bemoan the lack of absolute rules to tell them what to do.

Given the rapid pace of change and the massive dislocation of the social and natural environment that ensues, the old proven verities, where applicable, should be used. Where they are not relevant, we are in need of new, perhaps even radical, departures in thought and action. The old moralities are often, in reference to the present context, inadequate, for they do not tell us what we ought to do in the face of new opportunities, and they merely throw up intransigent obstacles to change. (Not that change is always for the better, but it is ongoing in any case.) It is difficult to fathom how a postmodern urban and technological society can hope to base *all* its ethical principles and values on the codes of ancient nomadic and agricultural civilizations, going back two to four thousand years.

How can the Ten Commandments or the Sermon on the Mount help us to determine the ethics of biogenetic engineering, space travel, organ transplant, ecological preservation, the information explosion, or nuclear stockpiling? Not very well, for our forebears, though intelligent human beings with passions and aspirations no doubt similar to ours, had a limited knowledge of the universe and of man's place within it, based on the best scientific and metaphysical conceptions of their day— but surely not entirely applicable to ours. They were not experienced enough to discover a proper morality for all future societies; nor could they be expected to legislate a perfect morality for generations unborn— even though they may have believed that their transcendental systems of morality were divinely revealed. Nor indeed can we, much further advanced in science and technology, be so presumptuous as to believe that we can structure the ethical system of all future societies. Who can predict what our descendents will learn about the universe, what new powers they will unlock, and what future dangers may threaten humankind? In our own time, the age-old concept of a "just war" is giving way to a realization that any war may include nuclear weapons, that their use cannot be limited, and that vast destruction of human societies will ensue.

I reiterate, the single most important ethical imperative we can develop for ourselves and bequeath to the future is the need to be *critically intel-*

ligent. By this I do not simply mean scientific understanding or technical proficiency or the many other possible specialized applications of intelligence. I mean first and foremost *ethical rationality* and *moral wisdom,* which all too few people possess in sufficient quantity, and which they are all too often ready to abandon in their hunger for transcendental certainty and salvation.

This life and the world in which we live provides us and future generations with wondrous opportunities. But to fully enjoy and exult in them, we need to use our practical cognitive and ethical skills to insure that they can be realized. All of this means that in the last analysis, unless we can impart to our children—and indeed, develop for ourselves— the skills of ethical reasoning, we will continue to find life difficult and its problems and conflicts insoluble. The highest goal of learning, thus, should be the development of good judgment and ethical rationality. Determining how to teach this is not always easy. Some people seem naturally to have a kind of practical wisdom about living, others to be foolhardy and stupid. Still, it can be developed best by exposing growing children, and especially adolescents and young people, to honest discussion and dialogue about the great ethical issues of the day.

I would suggest that the clarification of our principles and values should be the starting point of critical ethical inquiry. The term *values clarification* has been used to refer to programs often taught in the schools.[1] But these have been savagely attacked because they do not teach the favorite absolutes of conservative critics, who fear that students may come to question and perhaps weaken received notions of right and wrong when exposed to alternative value systems in a pluralistic setting. Some aspects of this criticism may be warranted, but not all. For the beginning of ethical wisdom is indeed clarification. But what does this entail? In the first instance, it means clarification of our preexisting *de facto* values— the things we hold dear and cherish—and of our *prima facie* ethical principles, the general principles that should guide our conduct. We begin with values and principles embedded in the habits, dispositions, and states of character we have already developed; we do so not to overthrow them, but merely to consciously understand them.

Related to this cognitive process of clarification and examination are the duties and responsibilities intrinsic to the social interactions of which we are a part. To clarify these by defining and analyzing them is essential to any process of ethical inquiry. These can no longer be automatically assumed as customary habits or unexamined prejudices;

they are capable of comparative evaluation and redefinition. Here we have reached a higher level of ethical deliberation, for we have entered the realm of justification. And we seek to consciously appraise our principles and values, not merely assume them; to judge them for their adequacy in light of the evidence, the consequences of our acting upon them, and their consistency with values and principles deeply held by other individuals and groups within the community and world. It is at this stage of ethical deliberation that we are able to either reinstate the values and principles we cherish, retaining the valuable and enduring elements of the moral heritage of civilizations of the past, or perhaps, if need be, to modify and transform them by discovering and introducing new principles.

The intransigent defenders of the status quo and of the unmodifiable, absolute commandments are unable to contemplate the stretching or revising of their principles. But this may be necessary in life. This process of reflective evaluation can be a source of civilizing moderation in the mature personality; rather than leading to impulsive behavior, as some fear, it may help us to develop wiser choices or policies. Insofar as we can act in the light of an intelligent appraisal of the full context of action, our behavior is apt to be more balanced and considerate. That is a key goal of cognitive education; it can be liberating insofar as it frees us from the inadequate or outworn dogmas of the past and enables us to reach higher levels of ethical understanding. To illustrate the point: The improved status of women and racial minorities was achieved in opposition to prejudices based on different norms that passed for "morality."

The need for developing reflective ethical wisdom is seen not only by its relevance to an individual's personal choices, but in a deeper sense, by its role in society. There is today an urgent social agenda that needs to be achieved on a worldwide scale; for the pace of global transformation is so radical and what we thought were the stable institutions of the past are being altered so massively that only the best use of intelligence can ever hope to build new, cooperative structures. We live in a polyethnic world in which diverse cultures exist, expressing a wide range of values and principles. Of course, this was always true, but improved communication, transportation, and transnational organizations have turned mere existence into competition and conflict.

We need to find common ground between the diversity of systems and doctrines. Worldwide appreciation for human rights and the need to respect privacy is a positive movement toward the discovery of a general transcultural ethics. Since we all live on the same planet, is there not an imperative to develop a planetary *ethical community,* in which all individuals and cultures can participate? A planetary society is already forming rapidly, and new economic, technological, scientific, political, and social institutions are emerging. There is now the need to move on to a higher level of appreciation for the world community. I believe that this is the case, and if so, we must reconstruct our values and principles in light of this. There are those who seem to wish—by their implicit behavior and claims—to indoctrinate everyone into one faith: Christianity, Islamism, Hinduism, the ideology of totalitarian Marxism, or the newer paranormal cults of unreason. But if any one of these were to succeed, humankind might very well slip backward into a new Dark Age.

The great danger is that in being uprooted from the small communities in which we originally lived, we may become mass men and women, insensitive to the moral decencies, and that we may uncritically follow new promises of transcendental salvation as the Holy Grail, abandoning our confidence in critical ethical intelligence and science. In the new global community that is emerging, our sense of moral decency and responsibility must not be lost, and the domain of human rights and respect for freedom and privacy must not be compromised. Given the new planetary society that is developing, it is clear that the ancient faiths and moralities will not fully serve us. Can we marshall the vision and courage required to build a better world for all members of the human family? The essential ingredient in this new world of planetary humanism depends on the cultivation of ethical wisdom. Exiled from Eden, our highest ethical obligation is toward the world community, not only for our present world, but for future generations who shall inherit the earth.

Note

1. See especially Sidney B. Simon, *Values Clarification* (New York: Hart Publications, 1972), and Sidney B. Simon and Sally W. Olds, *Helping Your Child Learn Right from Wrong: A Guide to Values Clarification* (New York: Simon and Schuster, 1976).

Part III

Part III

7
Human
Rights

What Is a Human Right?

As we move on to the world stage, ethics takes on problems not encountered in our small communities. We ask: Are there *rights* that all human beings possess and that ought to be respected by every civilized society in the world community? Do they cross the boundaries of diverse nation-states and cultural regions and apply to all persons? If there *are* such rights, how do they square with ethical principles and the common moral decencies?

The term *right* has been widely appealed to in critical ethical inquiry, especially since Kant. I wish to deal here with a specialized meaning of the term *right*; it is the theory that all humans possess certain immunities and privileges that are inalienable and that cannot be abrogated. It is this sense of right that is often the most troublesome to achieve; yet the post-modern world is passionately moved by the recognition that human rights ought to be respected by all and enforced by governments. Indeed, an individual who believes that his rights have been violated has a justifiable claim against society.

Intrinsic to the idea of right is the further idea of a *claim:* A person (or group of persons) who has been denied something that is considered to be rightfully his (or theirs) asks for rectification of the injustice through adjudication. A right in this sense is inextricably related to a demand. Correlative to this is the implication that society or humanity at large has an obligation to respect this claim, and that it is binding on human conscience.

I am referring to ethical or moral rights or claims that an individual makes on others. There are also legal claims that give the protection and sanctions of law. Thus a person has the right to lawfully acquired property, and if he has a legal title to it, it cannot be confiscated without due process or just cause. Similarly, one has other rights clearly recognized by law—such as the rights of citizenship, of voting power, or of contract. Many of these are specific and depend on legislative enactment or judicial interpretation. Within a legal framework, rights, powers, privileges, and immunities are specifically enunciated, and one can request that one's rights be legally protected, and in civil courts one can sue for damages those who violate them.

Do there exist, outside a legal system, ethical rights that pertain to individuals as *persons,* ones we may say are inherently theirs? For example, may we not say, at minimum, that all persons are *equal,* in the sense that they are all *human*; that among the most basic of human rights is the recognition that each person has equal *dignity* and *value*; and that this ought to be respected by the world community? This right of recognition now has force in democratic societies, though it did not apply a century and a half ago in respect to blacks, who were treated as chattel and denied human rights.

We may ask: Are there *basic* inalienable human rights that apply to all men and women, young and old, no matter what their ethnic or racial background, economic or social status? Are these indefeasible, in the sense that they cannot be annulled without the expressed consent of the person?

It is surely not the case that if there *are* such rights they have been recognized everywhere historically. Indeed, civilization reveals an arduous struggle by the human race to establish such rights and to see to it that they are respected. There is no doctrine of human rights to be found in the Bible or the Koran. The concept of inherent human rights is a recent development. All that one reads about in religious literature are commandments handed down from God and our obligations and duties to obey Him. But there are no correlative claims that people have against God, no demand for accountability for the evils of the world, no redress for grievances against Him. All moral benefits are conferred on man by God on the basis of His idea of grace and mercy, but there is no suggestion that we will be treated fairly and our rights respected. Indeed, the Greek and Roman gods violated what we consider to be the minimal right of not exposing people to cruel and unusual punishment, and the Christian God apparently is willing to mete out eternal damnation to those who do not obey his commandments or lack faith in him. The same is true of Yahweh and Allah. Moreover, insofar as God is portrayed in some faiths as capricious in deciding whom he will and will not save, he hardly respects human rights. Biblical literature in particular does not condemn slavery. It kept women in conditions of servitude to their husbands and it sought to indoctrinate children into the faith, often violating their right to knowledge. If rights are God-given, as some latter-day apologists now maintain, why did it take so long for the religious consciousness to recognize them, and why did it fail to find these rights in biblical sources? They surely did not exist in the Garden of Eden, where Adam and Eve had no rights against an all-powerful God who expelled them without a hearing because they ate of the forbidden fruit.

Perhaps we should take an entirely different tack and argue with those who say that all rights are natural and inherent in human nature, though recognition depends on the development of reason. The doctrine of natural rights, so eloquently appealed to by Thomas Jefferson in the Declaration of Independence, maintains that certain truths are "self-evident," that "all men are created equal" and that "they are endowed by their Creator with certain inalienable rights," including "life, liberty, and the pursuit of happiness." Unfortunately, again, not all races or nations have found these propositions self-evident. They were extracted from rulers only after protracted conflict, and they were not extended to slaves in the United States until after a bloody civil war. If we remove God, natural law, or self-evidence, what happens to human rights? Do they disappear or flounder on shaky grounds? What are their epistemological foundations? Are there other sources of human rights?

The term *human rights* designates a two-sided transaction. It does not apply to persons in abstract isolation, but in a process of social interaction. On one side of the transaction is the demand or claim on the part of an individual (or group) who believes that he (or they) has been left out, is oppressed, disadvantaged, or dispossessed, and that his (or their) rights need to be respected. Such demands are rooted in the historical experiences of countless generations of men and women who have lived and died for their principles, and who have sought to gain acceptance of their rights. In this sense, a person says that he or she possesses inherent rights. The other side of the transaction is implicit:

there must be a responsive acceptance of the claim by those who hear it and believe that they have some obligation to meet the appeal and correct the injustice.

The drama of moral progress is the struggle, ever widening, of rights claims, from smaller to larger groups of people, from what at first may appear to be the unreasonable complaints of a recalcitrant or dissident minority, to a majority that eventually comes to agree with it. Without the sense that we *ought* to respect the right, it would have no foundation. It entails both a claim and a sense of obligation, a claimant and a respondent. Be it the dispossessed tenant farmer, the factory worker, the oppressed woman, the black person, the helpless or abandoned child, the handicapped individual, the homosexual, the sick, helpless, or the forlorn—there is the conviction that these human beings should be treated fairly and that their rights should be respected.

Thus, ontologically, human rights are characteristics that emerge in human transactions; they are not separate from them. Like ethical principles, they are prescriptive and normative. They are rules to guide individuals in their behavior toward one another. They grow out of constant processes of demand and acceptance, and thus are not empty or abstract concepts. They are not rights, properly construed, but *rightings,* a process. To demand a right would make no sense on a desert island, where a stranded seaman may live alone; his rights come into being when a boatload of other people arrives. Rights are potential properties of transactions, but they mean nothing independent of actual transactions; they are functional and relational. They are given force because they are rooted in the historical march of civilization on behalf of the ideals of liberty, equality, justice, and fairness, and in the institutions and associations that men and women have given form to. This does not make them any the less obligatory because they are nourished in and through the beliefs and practices, visions and ideals of human beings. The same thing is true of art, science, philosophy, religion: all are products of creative human invention. As we have seen earlier, because they are relative to human culture does not mean that they are subjective or capricious.

Human rights do not have or need a transcendental referent to be obligatory, universal, or general. To be sanctified by religion after the fact is simply to take one part of human experience and support it with another. Though one may deceive others about the ontological status of rights, their content is still thoroughly *human,* which does not make them any the less morally obligatory. They are still clothed and sustained by all of the intensity of feeling and ardor that ideals can arouse in human conduct.

If this is how human ideals, ethical principles, and human rights emerge, how are they to be tested? This is another matter, for as I have already suggested about other ethical norms, they are reinforced by the degree of fidelity and loyalty we attach to them. Also, and most appropriately, they are to be tested by their *consequences*. To say that there is a human right is simply to say (1) there are claims that we make as humans, and (2) if they are truly to be considered equitable and just, then we have an *a fortiori* obligation to respect and fulfill them. Why? Primarily, I think, because of the demonstrated negative effects of violating them. The test is consequential, for rights lay down effective rules for governing society. They have an empirical rationale, for they prescribe the most efficacious ways of living and working together, and they are transcultural, because as humans we share common problems and needs. They thus have both a biogenic and a sociogenic basis. But since civilization at long last is truly global, human rights have emerged as the moral conscience of humanity as a whole. The respect for a doctrine of human rights has a profound effect on human consciousness, and those societies (largely democratic) that recognize them are better able to allow the moral decencies to be expressed and to realize values, individual and social, diverse or similar. Human rights are so central as the buttress of civilized communities that they are cherished for their own sake—and not simply for what they lead to by way of benefits for the common welfare. Pragmatic and utilitarian considerations loom large in their justification, but they are also prized as intrinsically worthwhile.

Indeed, the common moral decencies developed during interpersonal interaction at some stage in human history are now expanded still further, and a new level of moral awareness emerges. The doctrine of human rights is a far more extensive latter-day elaboration of the basic principles of ethics. Today rights do not apply only to those recognized on juridical grounds within a defined legal system but also to all humanity in the world community. The recognition of general human rights is a result of a revisionary morality attempting to discover new principles. This involves a modification of customary morality by critical ethical inquiry and the creation of a new global ethic.

Are There Basic and Universal Rights?

Any number of rights are recognized as binding on legal grounds. These depend on the particular contracts and agreements entered into within a specific society. I have a legal right to plant flowers in my own garden, but not in my neighbor's garden. I have the right to teach my child a foreign language, but my neighbor does not have the right to impose *his* language upon my child. I can wash and wax my car as I see fit if there is no water shortage. Members of a labor union who have paid their dues have privileges within the union that nonunion members do not have. Students who are duly registered at a university can use the library, but others cannot. These rights are contingent on an individual's prior commitments, and they are a function of his role within specific institutions as recognized by law.

Are there any human rights so fundamental that they ought to be respected around the world even if they have not been enacted into law? The Magna Carta (1215), the American Declaration of Independence (1776), the French Declaration of the Rights of Man (1789), and the United Nations' Universal Declaration of Human Rights (1948) all attempted in their own time to declare certain rights to be universal, and to call for their legal and ethical recognition.

The acknowledgment of such rights is a function of the level of historical development and is relative to concrete social conditions. Some of these rights presuppose political stability, educational attainment, and some level of economic development. They are not to be viewed as abstract, empty, or formal rights. Perhaps there is no point in laying down a universal right if it is impossible to fulfill. Accordingly, the basic human rights that I will delineate are especially relevant to post-modern technological societies already at a high stage of development. Thus, to say that we ought to respect another person's rights implies that we can; at least it lays down ideals that civilized communities will seek to live by or attempt to achieve. A poor society may not be able to provide adequate health care for everyone, nor may it be able to guarantee a job or a minimal standard of living—though it may seek to do so at some stage in the progressive amelioration of the human condition.

One can appreciate the tendency to call these rights "universal" or even "absolute"—because they *are* so fundamental—yet in actuality they are no more than *general,* for the same reasons I have already spelled out in the earlier discussions of ethical principles and moral decencies.

They may conflict, they may not be applicable in all cases, they may be overridden in certain circumstances. Thus, they are *prima facie* in the sense that at some stage in human history they were discovered to be binding, though how and in what sense depends on the context. I must confess that I would prefer to call them *universal* because of the dramatic appeal and eloquence of that term. We surely do not wish to exclude anyone—to say that this, that, or some other sector of humanity is benighted, wicked, or inherently undeserving of equal care and consideration. Human rights *should* apply to all human beings. But still, rights are general and *prima facie,* for they are not absolutely binding in every situation, and may not be practically realizable. How and whether they apply depends on their being balanced with other considerations: needs, wants, values, excellences, principles, decencies, facts, conditions, and consequences. Nevertheless, we can ask: What would we consider the most basic rights, at least ideally, realizing that not every community is able to achieve them fully? I will catalogue what we may consider to be fundamental: ten classes of basic human rights and forty-one ancillary rights listed under these. The reader may wish to include others, but the following are the most compelling.

I. Right to Life

1. *Security and protection of one's person (freedom from fear).* Every human being has the right to have his life protected and his person and home secured against violence or threats of violence. Everyone should have the right to call for police aid against those who would seek to endanger his life or person. This includes physical injury, the threat of death, psychological intimidation, and harassment.

People cannot pursue their goals, express their values, or attain happiness unless there are reasonable assurances of protection. Individuals and their families, friends, and neighbors, at home, at work, or elsewhere, need to be free of fear or danger. Rules should be established, laws enacted, officials selected to insure that peaceful conditions prevail. This may involve the establishment of a police force and a juridical system explicitly charged with protecting the citizens of a designated area from assault, rape, robbery, and other violent acts, and with apprehending and convicting those who have committed crimes and are a danger to the public order.

2. *Defense from external aggression.* Individuals living within a defined area need to be protected from the marauding bands or invading forces of other tribes or nations by the establishment of security forces or defensive armies. Without conditions of peace, no one can live in safety or security.

3. *Freedom from endangerment by the state.* Many have used the arbitrary power of the state against citizens or aliens residing within it. This means arbitrary arrest, imprisonment, cruel and inhumane punishment, torture, or murder. Individuals need to be protected from repressive governments. The extent of the jurisdiction of governments over individuals needs to be clearly defined.

In principle, the death penalty should be abolished, save in extreme cases where there is an imminent threat to the peace and safety of the community. Where it is legally permitted, it should not be applied for political offenses, nor should it be imposed on people under the age of eighteen or over seventy, nor on pregnant women. The convicted should have the right to appeal, to apply for a pardon, or to have the sentence commuted. Capital punishment should not be applied while the sentence is being appealed.

II. Right to Personal Liberty

The right to personal liberty is extensive and society should forbear from excessive regulation of personal liberty. Every person should have the right to move about; to satisfy his personal wants, values, and needs; to pursue his career; to have freedom of thought and conscience; and to be permitted free expression in speech and publication. Every individual should be allowed to raise his family and associate freely with others. The chief constraint is that he does not harm others or prevent them from exercising their rights.

1. *Freedom of movement and residence.* Every law-abiding person born in a territory has the right to move about within it and to change residences. He should be free to leave his own country, to travel across frontiers safely, and to return. This right may be restricted only in extreme circumstances in a democratic society, such as when public order, safety, health, or the national security are at stake, or in order to protect the rights and freedoms of others.

2. *Freedom from involuntary servitude or slavery.* No person shall be bought or sold. No one should be held against his will or compelled

to perform forced labor. This does not apply to prisoners lawfully confined, services discharged as part of one's normal civic duties, or military service, although the right of conscientious objection should be respected.

3. *Freedom of thought and conscience.* Individuals have the inalienable right to hold whatever beliefs or values they wish without the state's extirpating or applying sanctions against them, as long as the practice of those beliefs does not violate laws. This applies to the full range of religious, philosophical, scientific, political, moral, and aesthetic ideas.

4. *Freedom of speech and expression.* Individuals have the right to freely preach and advocate, publish and make known, dramatize and artistically render their beliefs, ideas, and values. This expression should not be regulated, censored, or suppressed. Every effort must be made to defend this right against all attempts to abridge it.

This does not give us license to libel or defame others, and thus injure or destroy their reputations or careers. Although an injured party cannot demand prior censorship, he may sue for damages after the fact. Where individuals are unfairly defamed or libeled by offensive and untrue allegations appearing in some medium of communication, the aggrieved individuals should have the right to reply or correct the misstatements. The principle does not give pornographers the right to exploit children.

This right may not be fully applicable in times of war, where there is a clear and present danger to the safety of a democratic society, though it can be temporarily abridged only in extreme cases and as a last resort.

5. *Moral freedom.* Individuals should be allowed to express and satisfy their diverse values, moral ideals, and convictions, even though these may differ from commonly held or official attitudes, so long as they do not interfere with or harm the rights of others within the community. This applies to the multiplicity of tastes and proclivities in activities, dress, manners, and speech. Individuals should be allowed to pursue their visions of happiness, to adopt the style of life they prefer, and to enter into careers and professions of their own choosing, consonant with economic realities.

6. *Privacy.* The right to privacy entails the right to confidentiality, i.e., the assurance that personal information about an individual will not be divulged without his or her consent. Personal moral freedom means control over one's body and sexual orientation. Adults should

have the right to express their sexual preferences, so long as they do not seek to involve unwilling participants in their conduct. Privacy rights apply to various forms of sexual expression, including masturbation, adultery, and homosexuality. The state should not prohibit sodomy, prostitution, or pornography. It does, however, have a right to be concerned with the spread of disease and to seek to protect the welfare of minors.

Privacy also includes the right to reproductive freedom: to practice birth control, to have an abortion, to use artificial insemination, or surrogate parenting.

Similar rights apply to health care based on informed consent, voluntary euthanasia, death with dignity, suicide, the right to join voluntary associations, and own personal property. (For a fuller discussion of privacy, see Chapter Eight.)

III. Right to Health Care

1. *Adequate medical treatment.* Concomitant with the right to life is the right to receive adequate health care and treatment consonant with the economic resources of the community. This means that no individual will be denied lifesaving care or other forms of treatment if he is unable to pay for it himself. Special systems of insurance and Social Security should enable individuals to cope with catastrophic illnesses or accidents.

2. *Informed consent.* The kind of medical treatment a person will receive must depend on the patient's freely given consent. This assumes that the person is an adult and is mentally and physically competent to understand the options and the kinds of treatment proposed. It means that one has a right to refuse medication (unless he has a highly contagious disease) and not be hospitalized against his will.

3. *Voluntary euthanasia.* Adults who are suffering and are in a terminal state should have the right to refuse treatment. They should be allowed to die with dignity, and in some cases should be given the means to hasten death if they request it. This includes the right of active euthanasia or suicide.

IV. Freedom from Want

1. *Basic economic needs.* Where a community has sufficient economic wealth, it ought to provide the means to satisfy the basic minimal needs

of individuals who, through no fault of their own, are unable to work or to provide for their own needs. No one should be allowed to starve or to die from lack of shelter, adequate clothing, or medical care. The welfare principle, based on beneficence, extends these provisions to children, the handicapped, the elderly, and the disadvantaged in society. Neither the state nor society at large has an obligation to satisfy all the wants of all individuals. The best principle is for individuals to earn a living so that they can provide for themselves and their families.

2. *Right to work.* Although it is often difficult for modern industrial nations to provide jobs for everyone, people ought, at least in principle, to have an opportunity for gainful employment and the ability to support themselves. Every individual should be allowed to exercise, when possible, freedom of choice in regard to employment. There should be favorable conditions in the workplace and reasonable hours and wages. Remuneration ought to be sufficient to provide an adequate standard of living for the worker and his or her family. Compensation should be based, whenever possible, upon merit. The principle is as follows: from each according to his ability, to each according to his needs and merit. Those who contribute most to society may receive higher rewards on a differential scale, and society should distribute goods and services on the basis of both merit and need. It is often difficult to apply this principle in practice and there are serious loopholes, which taxation and welfare benefits and pensions attempt to correct.

There should be equal pay for equal work without discrimination on the basis of sex, race, ethnic or national origin, or any other distinctions. For those who are temporarily unable to work, an effort should be made to provide unemployment insurance and/or job retraining.

3. *Care for the elderly.* Individuals who are able to work and contribute to society should not be compelled to retire. Those who have reached the stage of retirement should receive some benefits in the form of old-age insurance, Social Security, and retirement plans so that they can receive adequate health care and satisfy their basic economic needs.

4. *Right to leisure and relaxation.* All individuals should have the right to rest and should not be compelled to work all the time. Even the Old Testament enjoins people from working on the Sabbath. In modern terms, there should be paid holidays and vacations and a limit to work hours. Society should provide opportunities for all people to pursue enjoyable activities, to play, and to relax.

V. Economic Rights

1. *Right to own property.* Individuals should be allowed to lawfully possess property. They may use, enjoy, and receive gain from it by engaging in commerce and trade and buying and selling goods. No one should be deprived of his property arbitrarily or without just compensation.

2. *Public property.* Society may expropriate property for reasons of the public good or safety, but only after following lawful procedures. A society or state can pursue cooperative economic activities. It may regulate, manage, or own enterprises, where it considers such activities to be in the public interest, where the private sector is unable to provide needed goods and services efficiently, and where it does so democratically.

3. *Right to organize.* Employees may join trade unions and bargain collectively with employers. They may refuse to work and may strike if the conditions and terms of their employment are not satisfactory. Workers should be consulted about matters concerning their vital interests and conditions of safety in the workplace.

4. *Protection from fraud.* Persons have a right not to be defrauded by untruthful or dishonest advertising or deceptive selling of goods and services. They have a right to sue for damages and to hold liable parties who perpetrate fraud. The state has the duty of enforcing legal contracts that have been broken.

VI. Intellectual and Cultural Freedom

1. *Free inquiry.* There should be an untrammeled right to engage in scientific, philosophical, and intellectual inquiry. Experimental inquiry is essential for the advancement of knowledge and should be permitted unless it involves human subjects who have not given their informed consent and are at risk. An exception is technological application that is dangerous to the public. There should be no political, ecclesiastical, or economic sanctions imposed on those who wish to inquire. There should not be any censorship of their published findings, however unpopular they are deemed to be. A similar principle of freedom applies to artistic creativity and discovery: artists, writers, and poets should be allowed to express themselves without censorship or repression.

2. *Right to learn.* All individuals within the society should have an opportunity to educate themselves and their children without

restrictions based upon religious, ethnic, or class considerations. The daughter of a poor person should have as much right to education as the son of a wealthy person. Although parents should have some say about the education of their children, they do not have a right to deprive them or others of exposure to ideas or values they oppose. Some qualification may be made for material deemed pornographic. Educational achievements may be based on intellectual merit and excellence, and not everyone can enter every field, profession, or institution of higher learning. Nonetheless, individuals should have equal opportunity to fulfill the highest potentialities of which they are capable and to compete on equal terms.

3. *Right to cultural enrichment.* All institutions that contribute to cultural enrichment should be available to all individuals who can use them. This refers to libraries, museums, public parks, and other recreational facilities, and to the arts and institutions that advance the sciences.

VII. Moral Equality

All human beings are equal in dignity and rights. As a rational moral agent capable of choice, each person is entitled to the same considerations as everyone else. This does not mean that they cannot be treated differently in their various capacities in society, nor that their roles, duties, or rewards should be the same.

Moral equality specifies:

1. that persons be afforded *equal opportunity* to fulfill their unique talents in accordance with merit;

2. that everyone shall have *equal access* to public services;

3. that *no discrimination* be made on the basis of race, color, sexual orientation, religion, nationality, language, creed, social background, origin, or property ownership.

VIII. Equal Protection of the Law

1. *Right to a fair trial.* Every person has the right to a fair and open hearing by an independent and impartial court legally established for that purpose, and should be presumed innocent until proven guilty.

The accused should be notified in detail of the nature of the charges against him. He should be allowed to defend himself personally, be assisted by legal counsel of his own choice, or have a counsel made available to him and paid for by the state.

He should be allowed to examine witnesses and present his own witnesses in order to establish the facts.

He cannot be compelled to bear witness against himself.

He cannot be coerced to confess or plead guilty.

He should have the right to appeal the verdict to a higher court.

If acquitted of a nonappealable judgment, he cannot be subjected to a new trial for the same charge.

2. *Right to judicial protection.* Every person has the right of recourse to a competent tribunal for protection against acts that violate his basic rights. His request for remedies cannot be used against him.

3. *Right to humane treatment.* Persons who are incarcerated by the state shall not be subjected to cruel, inhuman, or degrading punishment. They shall not be tortured or deprived of adequate clothing, medical care, food, or shelter.

Accused persons waiting trial shall be segregated from convicted criminals and have the right to a hearing on the setting of reasonable bail.

If convicted and imprisoned, the prisoner's treatment shall be humane, not vindictive, and the main purpose of his incarceration shall be to protect society if he is deemed dangerous, and to rehabilitate him for eventual return to society if his crime was not too heinous.

4. *Rule of the law.* The laws of a society shall be legislated by representatives of the people, executed by elected officials, and interpreted and applied following due process. Rules and regulations shall not be based on arbitrary dictate or fiat. There shall be a sufficient opportunity for redress by the people and remedies for unjust acts. The rule of law shall be applied both to the ruler and to the ruled without distinction.

IX. The Right to Democratic Participation in Government

1. *Right to vote.* The laws of society shall be based on the freely given consent of those governed. Every adult citizen should have the right to participate in the affairs of the state in which he lives.

There should be regular, free, and open elections to determine who the chief representatives of the people will be, and to ratify or reject the main policies proposed or previously enacted.

Suffrage shall be universal and equal, for all adults without any exclusion. The ballots shall be secret.

2. *Legal right of opposition.* Individuals within society shall have the right to oppose the policies of the government and to differ with the chief officials charged with enacting and carrying them out. They can freely and openly dissent from these policies by means of speech, publications, petition, assembly, and the vote.

They can organize with others to make their views known and seek to change public opinion. They will be immune from reprisal or prosecution for opposing the government.

3. *Civil liberties.* The liberties of citizens must be duly protected, including those of dissenting minorities. This includes freedom of thought and conscience, speech, expression, assembly, and other rights and liberties enumerated here.

4. *Right of assembly and association.* Individuals in a society can freely associate with others of their choosing in order to form clubs, friendship centers, political parties, teams, schools, churches, fraternal organizations, and the like, and to fulfill any purpose that they may share with others. They may peacefully assemble in any way they deem useful so long as they do not resort to violence or endanger the public safety.

5. *Separation of church and state.* The state shall not impose or establish a single theological or ideological doctrine as the official church or dogma of the state. Individuals are free to believe or not believe, and to hold any form of belief or unbelief they wish. The state shall be neutral and shall neither favor nor disfavor religious belief or the lack of it, but will defend liberty of thought and conscience for all.

X. Rights of Marriage, Family, and Children

1. *Right to marriage.* Adult individuals shall have the right to cohabit and to marry if they so wish. Marriage should be based upon the freely given consent of the engaged parties. It may be either legally recognized or based on common law. There shall be no bars to marriage on the basis of race, religion, ethnicity, or other conditions. A marriage relationship is commonly a heterosexual union of man and woman, but it may be freely entered into by adults of the same sex as well.

2. *Right to divorce.* Married individuals should have the right to dissolve matrimonial bonds at such time as they see fit, and to live separately. If there is a contract, then fair distribution of joint property

shall be arranged. If there are children, equitable custody, visitation, and support shall be established.

3. *Right to bear children.* Individuals have a right to procreate so long as they are competent and able to care for and support their offspring.

4. *Rights of motherhood and fatherhood.* Expectant mothers are entitled to special care and protection during pregnancy and for a reasonable period after the birth of each child. Expectant fathers are also entitled to some consideration during the same period.

5. *Parental rights.* Parents have a right to care for, raise, and educate their children as they see fit, so long as they do so without harming or abusing them.

6. *Rights of the child.* Children have rights that parents may not violate; and if they do, society may intervene to protect them. Children may not be physically or sexually abused by parents, or deprived of adequate nourishment, health care, clothing, or shelter.

Children may not be deprived of the right to learn. Although parents are responsible for their children's education, they cannot withhold education or refuse to allow them cultural enrichment, the right to read, to discover and know, to appreciate others' points of view, or to expand their horizons of understanding.

Animal Rights

Although this chapter chiefly concerns human rights, we should not overlook the rights of other species.

Do animals have rights? To argue that they do, we must recognize that other sentient beings have value, that they should not be transgressed upon, and that we should not inflict unnecessary suffering on them or use them capriciously, as in the wanton slaughter of whales or seals. This is a transactional concept: it involves the development of a conscious sense of duty by human beings (who serve as proxies for the animals) and who believe that there are limits to what should be done to other sentient beings. Presumably, if the human species were to encounter other forms of intelligent life in the universe, the question of rights would occur in a similar process, for us *vis-à-vis* them. We should not mercilessly crush a harmless spider or injure a fawn, else we would have no case to demand considerate treatment for humans against the threats to our safety were we ever to encounter extraterrestrials. We can argue on consistent ethical grounds to live and let live, but aside from the possible science-fiction scenario, one can still maintain on good grounds that animals have rights, and that our pets and other species we encounter in the wild ought to be accorded humane treatment.

The biblical mentality gives man dominion over the earth and all of the species, to use them as he wishes for his own purposes. I think there should be some limits placed on this predatory attitude. Although animals are not moral beings in the sense that they behave rationally or are aware of their moral duties, nonetheless we have responsibilities to them. They have some dignity and are entitled to some measure of respect, though this should be applied in reasonably prudential terms.

The moral conscience of humankind has always recognized our relationship to the animals that we live with, those that we domesticate as our pets or work-servants, and those we hunt, milk, or breed for food.

On this basis, certain elementary obligations need to be recognized: We should not mistreat animals, abuse, starve, beat, or torture them. We should not inflict cruel and unusual deaths or allow them to suffer needlessly. We should, where possible, attempt to keep endangered species from becoming extinct. We should not despoil the environment to the extent that animals are unable to live or breed. We can argue on ethical grounds that hunting is immoral if it is done simply for the pleasure of the sportsman. It may be justifiable to protect populations from wild predators or to thin out herds for their own good. A case can also be made to limit or prohibit the hunting of animals for ivory, leather, or fur, especially when other materials are available.

Vegetarians go further and oppose the eating of meat and fish. We need not take such a radical position, for, as omnivores, humans have historically been hunters and gatherers, and the production of meat has become such an integral part of the economy that the food supply of large portions of the world may be at stake.

Anti-vivisectionists would forbid scientific experimentation on animals, but this is an extreme position, for such research may be vital on utilitarian grounds for the health of the human species. Every effort should be made where possible, however, to avoid inflicting needless suffering on animals during experimentation.

Rights of Citizens of the World Community

The preceding classes of rights are *ethical,* but they need to be given legal recognition in order to be binding in human affairs. Most of these rights have evolved out of the cultural, economic, political, and social structures that have prevailed. Unlike the common moral decencies, they have not been universally recognized by all societies, but have been hard won. They are based on the development of cognitive insight and compassion.

The world today is divided into nation-states, each having jurisdiction within a defined territorial area. Unfortunately, under present conditions the rights of persons can be protected only by the sovereign state in which they reside. In some places rights are abused by the state. The effort to establish a viable body of world law and a federal system to defend human rights is far from complete. The League of Nations was, and the United Nations is, based on unions of sovereign states; rights could be protected only within the framework of the defined areas. Only some of the nation-states of the world are democratic, permit freedom, or seek to protect human rights. We have today reached the point where the ideal of a world community takes on special significance and force. This community is an ethical community, for it is based on the recognition that there are general human rights that apply to all individuals, no matter where they reside.

In the twentieth century, humankind has witnessed the most abhorrent violations of basic human rights. In the Nazi era, racists preached doctrines of racial superiority and inferiority, and practiced genocide on a vast scale. Fascism violated the most elementary moral decencies. Totalitarian communist regimes, particularly during the Stalinist era, similarly violated human rights. The defeat of the Czarist regime did not bring respect for civil liberties, fair trials, humane treatment, or democratic participation by Soviet citizens. Millions of people have been sacrificed in recent memory in the cauldrons of misguided idealism and hatred. Wars of terror and infamy have been conducted against helpless populations and innocent victims, all in order to achieve ideological goals. However, the violation of basic human rights—crimes against humanity—has not been the exclusive doing of a few monstrous regimes. Sadly, authoritarian and repressive regimes continue to exist, denying their citizens basic rights. Moreover, almost every nation has at some time resorted to barbarism—over its own nationals or foreign peoples—in order to extend its hegemony and exploitation. Present-day European democracies, including Britain, France, Spain, Portugal, Holland, and Belgium, maintained vast imperialist empires in the eighteenth, nineteenth, and twentieth centuries and cruelly exploited native populations. The European nations were also engaged in fratricidal warfare. In World War I, Europe's youth were sacrificed in senseless slaughter. The United States, land of the free, has not been immune, for it tolerated slavery until the mid-nineteenth century, and has engaged in wars that have offended the sensibilities of civilized people.

But one cannot naively accept the claims of those who maintain that wars of oppression and violations of human rights have come only at the hands of capitalist, imperialist, and colonialist regimes. Given the so-called cultural revolution of China, the Cambodian holocaust, Stalinist terror, and the persistent violation of democratic human rights within many communist countries, this claim is inaccurate. Similarly, it is not a question of secular tyrannies alone violating rights or creating gulags. In the name of God (but seeking gold or profits) tyrants have decimated populations in the past: the Spanish and Portugese conquistadors in Latin America, Christian exploiters in Africa, proponents of aparthied in South Africa, or the purveyors of terror in Muslim lands.

Unfortunately, the violations of human rights is still pandemic. What is necessary at this stage in human history is the recognition that such rights are transnational and that people, no matter where they live, should have a right to appeal to the conscience of humanity over and beyond national frontiers.

In the twentieth century, there have been wars of liberation and of national self-determination, which in one sense were progressive, for they freed ethnic minorities from domination by others. In this chapter we have been discussing individual human rights, but there is also something like the right of self-determination for minority populations. Ethnic minorities in the past have been oppressed, as in the horrible massacre by the Turks of the Armenian population during the World War I, or the British treatment of the Irish. Conflict between ethnic minorities continues today, though perhaps on a lesser scale: in Belgium between the French-speaking and Walloon-speaking populations, in Quebec between French- and English-speaking inhabitants, in Northern

Ireland between Catholics and Protestants, in Southeast Asia between the Cambodians and Vietnamese, in the Middle East between Shia and Sunni, and in Africa between various tribal groups. Thus the conflict among racial, ethnic, national, linguistic, and religious groups continues to smolder and fester.

Can we transcend these divisive animosities and overcome the chauvinistic loyalties that have divided humankind? Has humankind not reached a new stage in history? Although we surely need to appreciate the right of cultural diversity and pluralism, do we not have to go beyond narrow ethnicity and chauvinistic nationality? Do we not have a higher and more enduring ethical commitment to the world community? If we are to preserve and enhance human rights, must we not finally recognize the global context in which human rights are now placed?

8
Privacy

Public Versus Private

The right to privacy is deeply ingrained in the liberal democratic tradition, and is so basic to the entire concept of human rights and humanistic ethics that it deserves separate extended treatment. This right is based on a distinction between the public and private domains of behavior. The central idea is that a democratic society should allow an individual latitude concerning his own life.

This principle is vehemently opposed by totalitarians. It is also continually attacked by conservative religionists, who believe that God commands certain virtues that it is sinful to flout, and that the state or society has a right to impose a set of moral standards and to punish individuals who violate them. But not all religionists reject the right to privacy principle. For example, liberal Protestants, Catholics, and Jews respect the right of personal freedom. And many conservatives share with libertarians a genuine commitment to individual liberty—though some conservatives are contradictory, for they may oppose regulations by the government but at the same time allow other social institutions, such as the church, to impose a conception of the "moral order" on the broader society.

There is some confusion about the range of personal freedom, and hence, a constant battle between liberals and conservatives about when to limit it. Virtually everyone believes that an individual does not have the right to injure or harm others, and that he is accountable to the community if he does so. One cannot kill, maim, rape, or rob with impunity. A society has the right—indeed, the obligation—to establish a system of law to protect individuals who live within its territory from mayhem or injury. But in many societies, the same laws used to guard the public order may be highly repressive of personal liberty.

The laws of a society ultimately have an ethical purpose: to protect the members of a community from harm, to maintain a system of law and order so that tranquility will prevail, to provide wholesome conditions so that individuals can pursue their diverse purposes, to insure the general welfare, and to maximize the opportunities for happiness. Regulations run the full gamut, from police protection and the national defense, to economic, social, cultural, and educational well-being. Surely there or should be limits to what a society may seek to control by legislation. A totalitarian society leaves its citizens little room for free choice; a democratic society, on the contrary, wishes to allow individuality, initiative, diversity, and uniqueness to flourish.

An often-asked question is: Should society legislate morality? The answer to that is that it does so all the time. To prohibit murder or robbery is to express our moral disgust at certain kinds of inappropriate behavior. Punishing those who commit fraud or providing civil mechanisms for enforcing contracts is done to insure that the community's standards of moral decency are upheld. The public has an obligation to enact legislation that protects everyone and assures the common good. A society ideally will enact its laws by democratic means, after a careful deliberative process, and it will repeal those that it considers noxious or unwise. In a democracy, laws ultimately reside in the freely given consent of the governed, as determined by majorities and due process.

Are there ethical limits that should be placed on public legislation? Are there areas in a democracy in which the public has no right to intrude? Those who maintain that the government should *not* legislate morality are referring to private morality; they are also opposing public opinion that does not respect idiosyncratic styles of living and seeks to regulate or suppress them. We have already enumerated a list of basic human rights that should be protected and implemented by civilized democratic societies. Among these rights are those related to a person's private life. Thus we recognize that there is a domain of privacy that should not be invaded.

What is this domain? Is there a demarcation line that can be drawn on *a priori* grounds between the public and the private? Is there a simple criterion for determining permissible and impermissible state authority? John Stuart Mill's[1] ethical principle that individuals should be allowed to do whatever they want so long as they do not harm others provides *adultery, prostitution*

V I .   vice vise

some help, but it is too general and cannot be used as an absolute criterion. Moreover, the term *harm* is vague, for any number of private actions have been deemed "harmful" to the community, and hence subject to prosecution. People have insisted that adultery, pornography, sodomy, and any other number of acts do "harm" to the social order and should be prohibited by law. At times it seems that virtually anything one does has some impact on others. If one drinks liquor excessively, he will harm his family, those in the workplace, or perhaps someone on the road. If he smokes, he is likely to get lung cancer, and this will be a strain on public health services.

Mill thought that an individual had a right to "harm" himself if he so wished, and that society had no right to prevent him from doing so if his conduct followed from his own free choice. But there are others who think that Mill's general statement is so broad that exceptions might justifiably be made to it. Even Mill limits his principle, for an individual does not have a right to sell himself into slavery. Should Mill's principle apply to psychotics or to someone who wishes to commit suicide? Are there other exceptions? If so, perhaps the domain of privacy can be so whittled away that virtually nothing remains.

The anarchist is opposed to all laws he considers to be oppressive; he wants individuals to be allowed virtual *carte blanche* to do as they wish. For the libertarian, powerful governments are the main source of violence against individuals, and the greater need is to protect individuals from paternalistic and arbitrary state power. The libertarian says we should err on the side of privacy, allowing virtually unlimited latitude, rather than on the side of oppressive state government. He believes, further, that if freed from restraints of government, individuals will be kind, just, sincere, and honest. This view seems much too utopian. It would be a great risk to the public order to allow a system of law and police protection to disappear. The use of private armies and protection agencies based on contracts in the place of centralized sovereignty (as Robert Nozick suggests[2]) can degenerate into gang warfare—similar to the terrible situation that developed in Lebanon when the state's central power was too weak to enforce the law and a bloody civil war ensued. Although one needs a system of law to insure the common good, there doubtless should be limits placed on what can be regulated.

The Zone of Privacy Respected

Let us begin afresh by stating that the principle of privacy, like the doctrine of human rights, can be justifiably appealed to in order to limit social and state jurisdiction. The respect for the privacy of persons is a *prima facie* general rule; the appeal to it enables us in part to define the proper sphere of social regulation. It is not, however, an inflexible rule; the edges of application are sometimes ambiguous and open to challenge and redefinition. How the principle of privacy should be applied depends on critical ethical inquiry within a particular situation. We need to balance decencies, values, rights, excellencies, and responsibilities in determining its appropriate use. The principle is applicable in the light of what critical inquiry would find to be reasonable.

Let us state a tentative working definition of the ethical principle:

Society should respect the right of an individual to control his or her personal life. The zones of privacy that society should not intrude upon without good reasons are a person's body, possessions, beliefs, values, actions, and associations, insofar as these pertain to his or her own private sphere of interest and conduct.

There are, however, certain limitations. It is obvious that this rule refers to *adults,* not children, though parents and others will want to respect the personal dignity of children and adolescents and attempt to develop some maturity and autonomy. It is also clear that the rule applies to *voluntary* conduct, that is, conduct that follows from intentional choices, not to actions performed under duress or coercion. Moreover, it applies only to those individuals whose decisions are based upon some degree of knowledge and understanding and not to those with impaired rationality. The meaning of reflective competence in decision-making will be clarified later in this chapter regarding questions of medical ethics, where impaired competence may emerge. Here the criterion for choice involves the capacity for *informed consent.*

Although the principle applies first and foremost to an individual, it also allows two or more adults to enter into a consensual relationship in order to satisfy common interests and needs. This means that it applies to marriage relationships, families (where the abuse of children is not at issue), friends, lovers, and colleagues. It should also be apparent that consensual behavior that has an overt public dimension, injures other individuals, violates public order, or undermines the welfare of others does come under the domain of regulation.

The principle is based on the recognition that every human being is a *moral person,* and as such, is entitled to liberty within the private sphere. Others in the community may not necessarily agree with his beliefs, values, and actions, but they should tolerate his right to express them, so long as he does not violate the interests of others in the public domain.

Private Rights Delineated

The following areas lie within the zone of privacy and should be protected from societal or state intrusion: the inward domain of conscience, confidentiality, control over one's body, sexual preference, reproductive freedom, health care, right to die, voluntary associations, and personal property. The order in which these topics are discussed does not imply a value ranking.

I. Inward Domain of Conscience

A person has inalienable rights within the inward sphere of conscience. He has the right to think, believe, or value as he chooses, without any state or societal effort to censor, forbid, or extirpate his inner convictions, however mistaken the community may think he is. We may, of course, disagree profoundly with the views a person holds, and we may consider him to be ignorant, stupid, or wicked, or consider his beliefs to be downright false or pernicious. We may indeed seek to persuade him to the contrary, by presenting arguments, showing his inconsistencies, and pointing out the unfortunate consequences of his beliefs. But we do not have a right to brand him a heretic or infidel and thereby seek to deny him the right to his convictions. Totalitarian despots and ideological and theistic dogmatists have attempted to impose tests of orthodoxy or loyalty, but this expresses the most destructive form of tyranny over the mind of man. There is a right to inquire, to read, to learn, and to know: The life of the mind should be immune to social repression.

II. Confidentiality

The public, including the media, does not have a right to pry into or to seek to disclose information and knowledge about an individual's private life that pertains to himself alone and has no relevance to a public issue. There is a difference between public personalities and private individuals, and sometimes knowledge about the private life of a John F. Kennedy, Josef Stalin, or Margaret Thatcher, for example, will shed light on his or her public career. One might ask that some degree of respect for the privacy of such a public personality be observed, but this may be difficult because of intense public controversy. Nonetheless, even here some information should be privileged and ought not to be revealed without consent. Teachers, doctors, lawyers, or psychiatrists should not release information about their students, patients, or clients without their consent. An individual's private behavior may be relevant if he holds a public office, but even here there is an area of privacy that should be respected.

In modern society, where databanks are increasingly available, it is all the more important that governments, insurance agencies, employers, and schools protect the privacy of individuals so that they not be endangered, compromised, or embarrassed by the release of information. The media especially need to maintain high journalistic standards and avoid irresponsible gossip.

III. Control Over One's Body

One would think that everyone would accept the inviolability of a person's body and agree that it should never be invaded by compulsion or prohibition, yet societies are prone to dictate what a person should or should not do concerning his or her personal physical being. Privacy means that individuals should be allowed to eat and drink, and copulate in private as they see fit, so long as they do not harm others, without public exposure, condemnation, or ridicule. Given the wide diversity of human tastes, there are profound differences about what is good, bad, right, and wrong. There are, as I have argued, standards of virtue or excellence concerning certain character traits. Moderation, temperance, and prudence no doubt ought to be the guides.

Obviously, there are some forms of public display that the community may consider indecent, and that may so arouse public disgust that it may seek to prohibit them. Thus society may object to defecating, urinating, copulating or the display of nudity in public. But surely society does not have the right to enter a person's home in order to regulate his or her conduct.

A society should be concerned with the health of its citizens. It should provide information about good nutrition, the need for exercise, the dangers of alcohol, cigarettes, cholesterol, or noxious drugs. But does it have the right to prohibit these products by law? It should do what it can to persuade people to adopt lifestyles that are conducive to good health, but should not compel them to do so. Society does not exist for its own sake, as an end in itself, but for the good of the individuals who live in it; it is for the individual himself to determine what is good or bad for him. "He who wears the shoe best knows whether it pinches"—not the manufacturer or the state.

Social policies can be inconsistent and hence ridiculous: the state bans marijuana, cocaine, and heroin, but not alcohol or cigarettes. No doubt the justification for forbidding cocaine and heroin is that they are addictive, that individuals who use them have their liberty of choice impaired, and that they can lead to actions that injure others. But the same consideration applies to alcohol. Alcoholics are addicts whose judgment is often seriously undermined, and they are responsible for injuring other people. Alcohol and cigarettes are the most widely used addictive substances, and the danger to health and the death toll they cause are far greater than those caused by marijuana, heroin, and cocaine combined.

What may society justifiably ban? What ought it to permit? The extreme libertarian points out the contradictions in present policies, and wants an open and free marketplace. John Stuart Mill was opposed to policies that made it difficult for lay people to buy prescription drugs. I have no absolute criterion here, and I am not advocating the legalization of or traffic in addictive drugs, but only the decriminalization of harmless ones. If the goal of society is to preserve the health of its citizens, then many other products can be prohibited. By the same line of reasoning, why not ban chocolate and coffee, both of which can become habit-forming and are bad for the health if used excessively! Why not insist that everyone engage in vigorous physical exercise every day, and why not require participation in open-air gymnastics? As an avid jogger, I am a devotee of exercise as a way to reduce stress, avoid illness, and improve the cardiovascular system. Yet some people detest exercise. ("Every time I get the urge to exercise," some say, "I lie down until it passes.") It would surely be tyrannical for the state to force its citizens to exercise, even though despotic governments from Plato's time through the Maoists have attempted to require it. There is, of course, great fear that children will begin to use addictive substances before they are mature enough to reach a judicious decision; the state has the right to regulate this matter and prosecute dealers who jeopardize the health and welfare of the young. But whether it should seek to impose similar standards in respect to adults is questionable.

A free society will allow individuals to make their own choices about the care of their bodies. I believe that health is one of the principle excellences of a person, but it ought to be the responsibility of each individual, not the state. One can make a good case for the need for extensive programs of public health education, but implementation of such information should be a matter of choice.

IV. Sexual Preference

Included in the realm of privacy is the expression of one's sexual proclivities. This is the most intimate aspect of a person's behavior and ought to be left within the domain of private control. The state has no right to enter the bedrooms of its citizens.

1. *Masturbation.* The most private and innocuous sexual act is masturbation, which can be done in any private place. Why should society condemn this practice? I am not talking about legal prohibition— always and everywhere almost impossible to enforce—but moral condemnation. Much of the phobia against masturbation has a religious source. The Old Testament story about onanism is that the wasting of semen, either by masturbation or interrupted coitus, is sinful. Judah told his son Onan to sleep with the wife of his dead brother. According to the law, he had an obligation to inseminate his brother's widow. But Onan did not wish to sire a child as his brother's proxy, and so, "When he went in unto . . . his brother's wife, he spilled it on the ground, lest that he should give seed to his brother" (Gen. 38:9). "And the thing which he did," the Old Testament declares, "displeased the Lord: wherefore he slew him also." (Gen. 38:10-11). Ever since, religious fundamentalists and orthodox Roman Catholics and Jews have condemned masturbation as morally offensive. A fear of great antiquity

is that the loss of semen causes a loss of strength; this view was widely diffused throughout the world and is still found in Africa, Asia, and Europe. Of course, this is not applicable to women, but women's sexuality has always been more tightly controlled than men's. Many Roman Catholic theologians rated masturbation a greater sin than fornication.

For whatever reasons, strictures against masturbation have persisted. I remember that my parents were fearful that I would masturbate as a young boy, and so the family doctor presented me with a book which I read and later shared with my schoolchums. We all worried, for it warned us about the dangers of masturbation: it was said to cause venereal disease, lead to insanity, and cause warts on the hands and pimples on the forehead. Yet sexologists have found masturbation common to many species and a natural act in the psychosexual development of the individual. Many individuals, even into adulthood and old age, find it to be a gratifying source of pleasure, a way of satisfying private fantasies, and a means of providing psychic and physical release from pent-up tensions or the frustration of not having a satisfactory sexual partner. Studies have shown that even Catholic priests and nuns resort to this practice, finding the constraints of celibacy and chastity difficult.

2. *Consensual sexual relations.* Inasmuch as most sexual activity involves other persons, the question that can be raised is whether some forms of sexual expression are wicked and should be prohibited by law. I would argue that all forms must be left to private choice, although it must be understood that this suggestion applies *only* to consenting adults and not to children, and that adults do not have the right to involve sexually those below the age of consent. Children who are abused sexually in any manner and by any person, including parents, are entitled to public protection. The age of consent is debatable, and I will not seek to resolve that question here. But it does not begin at twenty-one, and may even begin somewhat earlier than eighteen, for some individuals mature more quickly than others. Aside from this restriction, privacy is defined as allowing consenting adults the freedom of their sexual preferences.

3. *Adultery.* Adultery is in the zone of private conduct, and the state has no right to regulate or punish people who commit adulterous acts. We may consider such acts to be immoral on *prima facie* grounds, especially where there is a viable marriage based on sincerity and trust, but where the marriage has broken down or sexual needs are not satisfied,

some individuals may feel that adultery is justifiable—or at least that is a person's private business. In all cases, it is for the individuals who enter into such relationships to decide whether or not they wish to have an affair, and it is not the business of the state to intervene. The same considerations apply to other forms of sexual relationships outside of marriage, including premarital sexual relationships, relationships between divorced people, and other kinds of cohabitation. Again, these are private, not public, matters, except where minors are involved.

4. *Sodomy*. Does the state have a right to determine which modes of sexual conduct are morally appropriate and legally permissible? Should policemen enter private bedrooms to scrutinize sexual behavior and punish deviations from vaginal intercourse? For traditionalists, the only permissible sexual conduct is within the marriage contract, and the only kind of conjugal intercourse is the missionary position. Anything else has been considered a form of perversion. The religious traditions of repression have played a major role in developing guilt-laden attitudes toward the erotic: concupiscence was condemned as degenerate, and any deviation from the "norm" was sick.

There are enormous subtleties and complexities in sexual arousal. Erotic fantasy plays an important role in stimulating sexual orgasm. According to sexologist John Money, there are "paraphilic love-maps," which many people need to fantasize or even act out to reach climax.[3] The term *philia* means love, and *para*, beyond the usual. A paraphilic love-map may not fully unfold within the personality until after many years. It may appear in wet dreams or during repeated acts of masturbation, and become an essential stimulant for orgasm to occur. Paraphilia can involve oral or anal sex, fetishism, voyeurism, transvestitism, masochism, sadism, and a wide range of other fantasies. Individuals who are unable to reach erotic satisfaction without their fantasies often seek out partners who will accommodate them. For the state to prohibit their sexual preferences would deny individuality and uniqueness in human sexual response, which may be as variegated as tastes in food, drink, or clothing. Given the wide deviance from what has historically been considered the norm, it is difficult to define precisely what is "natural" sexual conduct. Presumably, the only basis for state intervention is where venereal or other sexually transmitted diseases may be prevalent and the public needs protection, or where violence or injury is involved.

5. *Homosexuality*. Homosexuality has been widely practiced in all

cultures, and is even found in other species. It has usually been hidden from public view because of severe social disapproval and the resulting castigation and punishment. Clearly, the species could not survive if homosexuality became the norm, though some have claimed that it does serve a socio-biological function in the survival of the species. A great number of creative individuals have apparently practiced or approved of it, including Plato, Michelangelo, Leonardo da Vinci, Tchaikovsky, Walt Whitman, Gertrude Stein, Virginia Woolf, and André Gide.

There is a strong homophobic resentment within society, and many individuals find the idea of homosexuality disgusting. A basic issue is whether homosexuality is due to environmental influences or is genetic in origin. There is great fear that if the former is the case, young boys and girls may be influenced or "recruited" to adopt a homosexual lifestyle. Many parents are fearful of the gay-liberation movement, because they believe that if too much favorable publicity is given to homosexual lifestyles, young people will be attracted and abandon heterosexuality. Since teachers and other role models undoubtedly influence the young, they say, sexual deviance ought to be prohibited, or else society will become corrupted and decline in morality. There are strong religious prohibitions against homosexuality, and the Roman Catholic church has condemned it with great ferocity. This is all the more a problem for the church, since many priests are homosexual.

The Bible is explicit in condemning homosexuality. Jehovah destroys the cities of Sodom and Gomorrah by fire and brimstone as retribution for their sins. In one story, some of the men of Sodom surround Lot's house and demand that his male guests be delivered to them for sexual purposes. Lot offers his two virgin daughters instead, in order to protect the males. Evidently homosexuality was well-known to the ancient Hebrews and it was explicitly forbidden in Leviticus: "Thou shalt not lie with mankind, as with womankind: it is an abomination" (18:22). Later, in Leviticus, the punishment of death is commanded for this crime: "If a man also lie with mankind as he lieth with a woman, both of them have committed an abomination: they shall surely be put to death; their blood shall be upon them"(20:13).

Christian scripture likewise abhors homosexuality. Paul writes: "Be not deceived: neither fornicators, nor idolaters, nor adulterers, nor effeminate, nor abusers of themselves with mankind, nor thieves, nor covetous, nor drunkards, nor revilers, nor extortioners, shall inherit the

Kingdom of God" (I Cor. 6:9-10). Again, Paul admonishes: "And likewise also the men, leaving the natural use of the woman, burned in their lust toward one another; men with men working that which is unseemly, and receiving in themselves that recompense of their error which was met."(Rom. 1:27). It is clear that homosexuals, like thieves and murderers, will be exiled to eternal damnation, and that the only cure for their wickedness is faith in Christ.[4]

Some evidence indicates that homosexuality may be genetic in origin—at least for a significant portion of the population. If this is true, homosexual orientation is not simply due to preference and cannot be easily eliminated by therapy or other means. In any case, even if there are contributing environmental factors, a person's sexual orientation is established early in life and cannot, after a point, be easily changed. There are estimates that four to ten percent of the population is homosexual. Whether or not this disposition is genetic and a homosexual has little control over his sexual nature, he can structure his lifestyle to avoid excessive promiscuity, thus exercising some discretion and restraint. Many psychologists consider homosexuality to be a difference in orientation rather than a disease, but not morally condemnable, in any case.

A significant minority of the population is apparently bisexual; that is, able to respond sexually to both sexes. Whether bisexuality is genetic in origin or simply a preference is difficult to ascertain. There is some evidence for the former. Same-sex bonding and affectional relationships seem to provide considerable psychic satisfaction for those who can find suitable partners.

Should one's sexual orientation be a personal matter, and should consenting adults be permitted to express their proclivities in private? A humane social policy would permit sexual autonomy, so long as it involves adults and does not impair the health of the community. This would allow consensual homosexual acts in private, and would permit the establishment of clubs and bars for socializing.

The main concern is with the spread of disease. The sexual revolution began in part because of the availability of safe and effective contraception—so that pregnancies were no longer feared—and antibiotics, which were able to reduce the incidence of gonorrhea and syphilis. But the rapid spread of AIDS raises justifiable concern about public health. If the spread of a disease goes unchecked and it becomes pandemic, then society has a right to regulate behavior that transmits the disease and to promote public education about safe sexual practices. Infection by the AIDS virus is not due to God's wrath, nor is it a punishment for a sinful lifestyle, no more than cancer or other deadly diseases are punishment for individuals who contract them. The threat of AIDS has moved the male homosexual lifestyle away from indiscriminate one-night stands toward monogamous relationships built on the more enduring basis of companionship.

Homosexuals should not be condemned as sinful and wicked or be considered to have no redeeming virtues as human beings. It is not true that they are moral libertines, contributing to the decay of the social fiber. Like others in the community, homosexuals are for the most part honorable persons, capable of ethical excellence and aware of the moral decencies. Aside from their sexual proclivities, they are able to function in society as productive, creative, and responsible citizens. As such, they deserve tolerance, and their right to privacy is as compelling as the rights of others in the family of humankind.

6. *Prostitution.* The issue of sexual immorality is of special concern to the public in regard to prostitution. For although one might argue that prostitution should be a private matter between two or more consenting adults, it becomes a public matter when a prostitute engages in commerce on the streets or in other public places, or contributes to the spread of disease. In such cases there may be harm to others.

Prostitution should be of little concern to the state as long as it does not involve minors, slavery, or violence. If two individuals wish to engage in a sex act, that is their business, assuming that the transaction is entered into in private and without an overt affront to public decency and order. In France and other countries, special houses (bordellos or massage parlors) are maintained for prostitution. It becomes a public matter only when individuals who engage in such practices resort to crime such as robbery or blackmail, and/or where they inflict injury upon unwary customers. Some countries require that prostitutes be periodically examined for diseases and also that they be provided with condoms. We have to guard against militant calls for vice squads to crack down on prostitution. Naturally, health is a public concern, but one should permit sexual freedom, unless or until there is an overriding urgent and widespread danger to public health. Once that has been restored, legal supervision or restraint ought to be relaxed.

7. *Pornography.* Another area of much contention is pornography.

Should the state censor materials that some people in the community consider obscene or which appeal primarily to prurient interests? In some cases the criterion may be too narrow, and reasonable people may differ about standards of taste and decency.

We should surely distinguish between the public and private availability of allegedly pornographic materials. One cannot insist that any and all public expressions of sexual behavior be permitted without regulation, for some public displays might not only offend the sensibilities of individuals within the community but also disrupt the public order. A voluptuous woman dancing stark naked on Fifth Avenue might offend some people or cause a traffic jam, and the community has a right to prohibit it. Similar behavior within a person's house (with the shades or shutters drawn) should, however, be beyond the reach of the law. Why should pornography not be permitted in theaters or clubs open to adults, who have been informed as to what kind of performance is going on inside and who are willing to pay for it?

A strong defense can be made against any effort to impose censorship on written materials and artistic expression. People should have the right to read or view what they wish without Big Brother imposing sanctions. It is difficult to know where to draw the line in defining *obscenity*. What is offensive to one person's sensibilities may be stimulating, pleasant, or informative to another's. Some may find *Hustler* magazine to be disgusting, others, *Playboy* and *Penthouse*. Some have objected to *Lolita, Ulysses,* and *Madame Bovary*. What about Michelangelo's David, standing nude in Florence, or the nudes on the ceiling of the Sistine Chapel in the Vatican? What about the *Dialogues* of Plato, which defend homosexuality, or the Bible, which has many highly pornographic sections in it? In Genesis we read that the daughters of Lot got him drunk and then slept with him so as to give him sons. This act of incest is not condemned. Similarly there are many passages in the Old Testament depicting polygamy and concubinage—which many people find offensive. Should the Bible be censored?

Sexuality is a topic of deep and abiding human interest. Even if a book, magazine, song, video, or film appeals primarily to prurient interests and has little redeeming social, moral, literary, aesthetic, political, or intellectual value, this still is not a justification for prohibiting it. Some individuals may find sexual pornography interesting. Why should they not be permitted to stimulate their prurient interests—if they do so in private? Those who are turned off by pornography are not forced to see or hear it. But why should *their* tastes dictate what other people may find enjoyable? In one sense, the most obscene literature is that depicting wanton acts of murder or gruesome torture. The same person who rails against pornography may accept with equanimity a Rambo who butchers hundreds of enemy soldiers or a cowboy who randomly murders Indians. If one begins banning books, films, and plays because of sexual pornography, why not those that present violent themes as well? Why not extend this censorship to false religious myths constantly being foisted by religious charlatans on an unsuspecting public? Why not ban atheism or blasphemy? Why single out sexuality for special condemnation?

Clearly, this does not apply to young children, and the family and the state have an obligation to shield them from pornography. However, it would be ludicrous to impose the standards for a twelve-year-old child on the entire adult population. An underlying premise of many censors is the view that most varieties of sexual expression are wicked and sinful. Humanists, on the contrary, believe that since eroticism can contribute to human happiness, the state ought not to ban literary or artistic expressions of it.

In recent years, the battleground has become complicated, because some feminists have allied themselves with the forces that demand censorship. Such women maintain that pornography is degrading, and one can appreciate their concern and abhorrence. Their objection applies to pornographic literature and films that treat women as mere *objects* to satisfy male lust and/or that depict violence against them. Various forms of this can certainly be considered vulgar and disturbing. But what about the "Rape of the Sabine Women," hanging in the Metropolitan Museum of Art, or the Old Testament story of the slaying of the Midianite women and children who were not virgins? Many people find the nude body not degrading, but interesting, whether it is the Venus de Milo or the voluptuous nudes of Rubens. All of this involves taste. The problem is that once the law begins imposing someone's moral "standards" on literature, the arts, and the media, someone else's rights to read or entertain himself freely are violated.

The censor says that he wants to ban only "hard-core," not "soft-core" pornography. But who is to judge what is "hard-core"? Why not leave it to authors and editors, producers and viewers, to determine whether they wish to publish, produce, read, or watch something, without imposing narrow standards of morality on everyone?

Some have objected to the fact that certain magazines or films have depicted young children or adolescents in degrading sexual encounters. Those who use children to produce such material have violated child-protection laws and should be prosecuted, for sexual freedom applies only to consenting adults. Similar considerations apply to snuff movies, which allegedly depict real murders. These acts are criminal and cannot be tolerated. It is one thing, however, to prosecute pornographers who engage in criminal activities, and it is another to ban literature after its publication.

A special question should be raised about pornography on television, for unlike movies, where one can consciously choose to pay to attend a performance in a theater, television is available to anyone who flicks a dial. A case can be made to limiting hard-core pornography to cable television alone, where a person presumably pays for the service. Similarly, the state should not prohibit the sale or purchase of pornographic video cassettes. Unfortunately, in most countries, the mass media are a vast wasteland, inundated by hucksters selling everything from pantyhose to beer, from pretzels to religious salvation. Presumably, the best safeguard in a free society is to elevate the level of taste and appreciation for consumers, authors, editors, and producers alike, for we all have a responsibility to cultivate high standards of morality in the public domain.

V. Reproductive Freedom

1. *Birth control.* This section would not deserve separate treatment were it not for the existence of powerful theological forces that seek to deny women and men control over their own sexual reproduction. The Roman Catholic church in particular has a strict moral code that prohibits contraception, abortion, sterilization, artificial insemination, *in vivo* and *in vitro* fertilization, and other methods of intervention in the reproductive process. The natural law allegedly limits sexual intercourse to procreation and all other forms of sexuality are held to be illicit. But rational human beings can decide whether and when they will reproduce. Men and women engage in sexual intercourse not simply to conceive but also for the psychic satisfaction and erotic pleasure they derive from sex.

This means that couples have the right to use contraceptive devices if they so desire. Since the rhythm method is often unreliable, condoms, pills, jellies, and diaphragms may be used. Persons engaging in sex should be able to be counseled on how best to prevent unwanted pregnancies. Included in this is the right to choose sterlization.

2. *Abortion.* The right to abortion is a right subsumed under other rights: the right to privacy and the right to control one's body. Historically, males have dominated females economically, socially, and sexually, and have sought to determine when and if women should bear children. But the fetus grows within the woman's body, not the man's, and society has no ethical right to demand that she continue any pregnancy she does not wish to bring to them.

Whether to have an abortion is a serious ethical issue; one can argue that it ought not be resorted to by the woman without careful reflective inquiry, and not without consulting the father, if he is known. It should not be used as a primary method of birth control, but only as a last resort, if contraceptive methods have failed. It should be a responsible decision, made after due consideration of all factors. But if a woman decides, after due deliberation, to have an abortion, it should be her right to do so, and neither the state nor society should compel her to desist. I do not believe that the indiscriminate resort to abortion on demand can be justified on ethical grounds. Indeed, one can argue that under certain conditions, it is wrong for a woman to have an abortion, particularly if the pregnancy began as the result of a conscious decision by a woman and her husband.

Nonetheless, based on the principle of control of one's body, it is the woman herself who should have the final and legal right to make the decision. There are many situations in which an abortion is warranted—if the woman was raped, if the fetus is severely handicapped or likely to have a degenerative disease, if the life or health of the mother is at stake, if the woman is unmarried, or if she is unable to properly care for the infant. Society does not have the right to dictate to her the conditions under which abortion is an option.

There is justifiable concern as to whether abortions should be performed late in the pregnancy, when the fetus is viable and can live outside the womb. I agree that, save in extraordinary situations, an abortion ought to be performed before the second trimester, and if possible before the fourth month. It is difficult to know when an embryo or fetus becomes a person, and when human life begins. Surely the embryo (conception to third month) is not a person, as the Roman

Catholic church has begun to insist fairly recently. Neither is the fetus (fourth month to birth) a human person entitled to the same protections and rights as a child that has been born. Still, to perform an abortion late in the pregnancy does not appear to me to be wise.

The point to bear in mind is that absolutist principles on either side of the dispute are not helpful: Neither abortion on demand nor absolute prohibition, but rather a balanced policy seems the judicious course to take. The United States Supreme Court, in *Roe* vs. *Wade,* has said that the moment when human life begins is a metaphysical and theological issue, and that on the basis of the principle of privacy, we ought to allow each woman to decide whether to have an abortion. That seems to me the most sensible policy to follow. Those women who are opposed to abortion are not compelled to have one, but can follow the dictates of their own consciences. But the same right to conscience should be afforded those women who do not regard abortion to be murder. The principle of tolerance is especially relevant to a pluralistic and democratic society that respects the right of individual autonomy in moral choice.

Should teenagers have the same rights as adults in this area? One hears a great deal about the increase in teenage pregnancy and of the large numbers of children born out of wedlock. This has probably occurred in part because in former days women of child-bearing age married earlier. Young people, who now reach puberty at the ages of twelve, thirteen, or fourteen, are not any more sexually interested today than were their grandparents—they are only marrying later. It would be far better in my judgment if young people abstain from sexual intercourse until they are mature, when they are better able to develop a relationship with a member of the opposite sex. But girls in their teens who are sexually active have the right to receive contraceptive information and after due consultation with their parents and counselors, where this is possible, should be permitted to have an abortion. They too have a right to control their own bodies.

3. *Artificial insemination.* The Roman Catholic church has condemned a wide range of biomedical techniques that enable infertile couples to have children: artificial insemination, *in vitro* and *in vivo* fertilization, and surrogate motherhood. The church's opposition is based upon what it considers to be "God's immutable and inviolable laws." Presumably, conception should only occur by means of the conjugal act of intercourse, and procreation can only be "actualized in marriage

through the specific and exclusive acts of husband and wife."5 Thus having the husband masturbate in order to produce sperm and permitting scientists or doctors to fertilize an egg within the womb (*in vivo*) or in a petri dish (*in vitro*) would be illicit. Similarly, a surrogate mother who agrees to have her ovum fertilized by a medical procedure and who carries the child to term would be condemned.

The church has objected to the use of "unnatural artificial techniques," and yet the pope sports false teeth and glasses, which surely are artificial devices, and priests and bishops may wear pacemakers. They do not object to these, they respond, since the devices improve a natural process, whereas contraceptive devices impede a natural function from taking place. If "impeding a natural function" is to be used as a criterion, then one should never drink wine, for it may cloud cognitive functions. Space travelers should be precluded from encircling the earth in satellites or floating weightless in space, for the natural laws of gravity are being defied. Moreover, *in vivo* and *in vitro* fertilizations are not impediments, but improvements of natural processes and functions.

If the only method of procreation permissible is by having the male's sperm inseminate the female's ovum during a conjugal act of intercourse, then why did God impregnate the Virgin Mary and defy His own natural laws? Also, is not God the master abortionist, destroying innocent fetuses—since one-third of all pregnancies end up as miscarriages!

Reproductive freedom also entails the right to genetic counseling. It is now possible to ascertain a great deal about the embryo, including its sex and whether it has any genetic defects. Couples who receive genetic counseling—and find themselves at risk—are able to determine whether they wish to procreate, and if a pregnancy ensues, whether they wish to have an abortion. All forms of experimental fetal research and the abortion of a defective fetus would be prosecuted by right-to-lifers. Moreover, the Vatican has announced that it will attempt to persuade civil legislators in various countries of the world to enforce the natural and divine law as interpreted by the pope. All of this egregiously violates the principle of privacy.

VI. Health Care

1. *Informed consent.* Every adult of sound mind has the right to decide what should be done with his or her body. This applies with special

meaning to the kind of medical treatment or health care that he or she will accept. Patients should not be treated without their consent; they should not be compelled to undergo courses of treatment they object to. Consent for treatment or research must be voluntarily given by mentally competent, rational, and properly informed adults. This principle assumes that the person is mature enough to decide, and that he is conscious and has command of his faculties. It also means that the decision will be an informed one, based on a presentation by a physician of the essential facts of the illness. This should include a diagnosis of the symptoms, an analysis of the possible risks and complications of the proposed course of treatment and of alternative treatment methods, and the likelihood of failure or success. Since much of medicine is an art based upon educated guesses, in some cases there are no certainties about what will ensue. Nevertheless, it is the patient who should make the final choice, after a process of consultation.

In the past, paternalism was taken as the appropriate model to be used in the medical field. The doctor knew what was best for his patients, and he determined the course of therapy, perhaps in consultation with other specialists. This was the authoritarian model. The doctor's qualification to decide for the patient was presumed on the basis of his training and knowledge: the patient was a passive and dependent subject. The principle of informed consent assumes that the patient is an autonomous being, and that his relationship to doctors, clinics, or hospitals is a contractual one. Anything done to him must be based upon his assent. The best process is one of mutual participation: the physician proposes, but it is the patient who in the last instant must agree to go ahead.

Every general rule has its exceptions. This principle applies where there is time to decide; in an emergency, where the patient may be unconscious and there is no time to wait for him to regain consciousness, doctors and nurses should consult the nearest family member, although in a life-threatening situation, an exception might have to be made even to this.

Informed consent makes sense only if the patient is capable of understanding what is at stake, and if his or her choice is not made during extreme pain or emotional distress. It would be best if the decision were a reflective one, based on freely given consent. This assumes that the patient is willing and able to make his or her own choice. In some cases, the patient may wish not to know the full details and may wish to leave the decision to the doctor, whom he believes "knows best."

Should the doctor be honest and truthful with the patient in all cases? One cannot make absolute assertions here. All other things considered equal, this *prima facie* principle ought to guide his conduct, but in some cases patients may not be able to handle an adverse prognosis. Would the patient be harmed psychologically if the full truth were conveyed? Would it cause extreme depression and despair? Where the doctor knows the patient and the family, he may decide to use discretionary judgment, revealing only what he thinks the patient can assimilate and accept. The general rule is that he should be truthful, but must balance this duty with other factors.

2. *Involuntary commitment.* Should a patient ever be committed to a hospital against his will? Should he be forced to take medication? In principle, no. But there may be exceptions, particularly in regard to mental patients, whose judgment may be so impaired that they are unable to make a competent decision. If an emotionally disturbed or psychotic individual refuses treatment, yet threatens harm to others or himself, he may be committed temporarily for observation and possible treatment, but only until such time as some balance is restored. There is a danger that involuntary commitment will be used by a repressive society to punish nonconforming individuals and to incarcerate them without due process. Society ought to tolerate idiosyncratic, dissenting and/or nonconforming behavior without labeling it "crazy."

Some individuals, however, may be so sick that they may are unable to decide for themselves whether they need treatment, and they may resist it in spite of the best efforts of their doctor and relatives to provide needed care. The rights of mental patients need to be protected against arbitrary confinement or forced therapy. Thomas Szasz, one of the leaders of the movement against involuntary commitment, has rightly pointed out that mental hospitals in the past often functioned as jails and that patients were grossly denied their rights.[6] Lobotomies, shock treatments, and other questionable forms of therapy were routinely performed on helpless patients, who were unable to protect their bodies and who were deprived of dignity. Psychoanalysts and psychiatrists are not to be taken as infallible priests whose judgment cannot be questioned.

One must not be an absolutist: some patients are unable to care for themselves, yet resist any and all medication or assistance. In such cases, upon the advice of two or more psychiatrists or physicians and with due legal protection by the courts, such patients might temporarily be confined for their own good or society's protection, but they must be released after a period of time. It would be helpful if society had some ways of caring for such individuals short of institutionalization. There are numerous tragic cases of parents or relatives who are unable to get any help for severely schizophrenic or psychotic persons.

Informed consent does not apply to young children, to severely retarded persons, or to patients who are comatose or senile. Here their relatives and/or legal guardians should assist in the process of evaluating possible courses of therapy.

Informed consent presupposes some level of medical education. The ideal is to disseminate a high level of scientific information to the populace so that it will be made aware of the fact that it is ultimately responsible for its own health care. Medical treatment should be the mutual responsibility of both doctor and patient.

VII. Right to Die

1. *Voluntary euthanasia.* Informed consent is all the more vital today, given the great advances in medical technology that enable doctors to keep patients alive who might otherwise have died. Questions often raised are: When ought doctors to stop treatment? What if a patient no longer wishes to live? Do doctors have a duty to force treatment on him against his will? Should they allow the patient to die and even hasten his death if he so requests it? The term *euthanasia* literally means "good death." Do we have an obligation to help people to die, thus releasing them from their suffering?

Euthanasia, I submit, is permissible, and perhaps even ethically obligatory, but only when (a) the patient is dying from a disease or accident, and his case is terminal; (b) there is intolerable pain and suffering; (c) the patient is rational, competent, and informed of his condition, and (d) his choice is voluntary.

Passive euthanasia simply means that extraordinary and heroic means will not be used to keep a patient alive if he does not wish them employed. It also means that no further treatment, except to reduce the pain, will be offered; even intravenous and tubal feedings will be removed. No effort will be made to resuscitate a person if his heart or lungs stop functioning. If the patient wishes to be discharged from the hospital in order to die at home, no attempt will be made to keep him institutionalized. Voluntary euthanasia is an ethical principle now widely accepted by the civilized community. Recognition of this right was achieved only after arduous battle. But there is still great resistance from absolutists, who insist that only God can decide when a person can die. Some even proclaim that there is some virtue in suffering, as Christ was in agony on the cross. In response, we may argue that those who wish to suffer until the bitter end may do so, but those who wish to die with some dignity and a minimum of suffering should be accorded that right.

Thus we have a duty to accede to the expressed desire of a person who opts for passive euthanasia, and not prolong his agony. The principle of beneficence is relevant here. We ought to be kind, sympathetic, and compassionate, and where there is great pain or distress, do what we can to lessen it. There are numerous horror stories of patients who were repeatedly resuscitated against their expressed will and made to endure weeks or months of prolonged agony by a persistent medical profession that believes its primary duty is to keep a patient alive. We all recognize that we have a moral obligation to prevent cruelty to animals, and to mercifully put them out of their misery if they are injured or dying. Should we do less for our fellows who implore us to alleviate their distress and allow them to die?

In numerous instances, patients who are being treated against their will are inflicted with cruel and unusual punishment. One famous case is that of Donald C., who, due to an explosion, was seriously burned and blinded, and his limbs reduced to stumps. He was forced into a Hubbard bath every day despite his vehement opposition, and suffered excruciating pain. Donald was able to survive his ordeal, but he has protested ever since about the violation of his integrity as a human being.[7] Another famous case is of a physician who was stricken with terminal cancer, suffering debilitating pain. Knowing the prognosis for his case, he requested that he not be treated further. But the hospital staff was afraid to follow his wishes, and resuscitated him several times. He angrily and despairingly pleaded to be allowed to die, which he eventually did, in spite of continuing heroic efforts to save him.[8]

The task of the doctor is to apply his technical skills as long as he can; the moral issue of whether patients should be allowed to die is not the doctor's choice to make. Indeed, if the patient's case is hopeless, the doctor has a *prima facie* duty to respect the patient's wish. He can violate the patient's decision only if he can provide some countervailing ethical reason.

Another ethical principle emerges to guide choice: nonmalfeasance. A doctor is not supposed to harm a patient, yet keeping a patient alive against his or her expressed desire is a form of harm. Living is not always better than being allowed to die; and by forcing a dying person to live and endure pain, a doctor is injuring him. The underlying principle, of course, is the right to control one's own body.

Active euthanasia comes into play if a patient goes further and requests that his death be hastened. Should one accede to his wishes and help him to die? Is it ever right to speed up the process? In some tragic situations, individuals have felt an ethical obligation to assist the loved one who cries for help. This is particularly true if he or she is a member of the family. The absolutist considers this an act of murder, and if one sits by and allows the patient to kill himself, one is accessory to a suicide, which he equally condemns.

Yet the moral dilemma we face is urgent: If the prognosis of death is certain and if the quality of life is so impaired because of intense suffering, then why should individuals be compelled to live? If one accepts passive voluntary euthanasia on ethical grounds, why not active euthanasia as well? If one does not resuscitate or force-feed, can one administer ever-larger doses of morphine so as to hasten death? Should those near the person actively intervene to terminate his life? It depends on what is involved. Perhaps another person must purchase the medication necessary for the act, but it would be preferable if the person who wants to die administers it to himself. "Ask not that I inflict the wound that will slay thee."

But what if the person I love is unable to lift his hand to drink the potion or inject the drug into his vein? What then? I have no answers to help make that awful decision. Some may not wish to be party to another person's death, but others have been so distraught by the loved one's plea for succor that they have succumbed to their wishes. One man, whose wife was suffering from an advanced case of Alzheimer's disease, shot her. Another young man whose brother was completely paralyzed due to a motorcycle accident, was unable to resist the pleas of his brother, and did the same. There is the case of Derrick Humphrey and his wife, Jean, who knew she was dying of cancer and asked Derrick to bring her poison, which she then drank.[9] In the Netherlands, there are health-care practitioners and doctors who, at the patient's request, assist dying people to end their lives.

Every dilemma is unique, every individual different. Some individuals may choose to fight against the darkening of the night, and never to submit to death willingly, but instead, to savor each breath until the last moment. Others, feeling it is hopeless and wishing to lessen their own anxiety and that of their relatives, may wish to hasten the end and ask the help of their loved ones.

There are, of course, considerable dangers that society must be aware of. And there is the "slippery slope" argument. First, we must not impede the dedicated efforts of the medical profession to find new ways to save and enhance life; to give in and accept defeat may undermine the tenacity of the medical profession, which engages in research and finds cures. We are, of course, talking only about hopeless cases, so far as we can determine that they are hopeless. Nonetheless, there is still something disturbing about hospitals becoming places for persons to go to die rather than to survive, and there is a fear, not without some merit, that doctors will be viewed as executioners if they are willing to administer the death potion.

It would perhaps be better to leave these questions to private discussions among a patient, his family, and the doctors, and not make every instance a public matter. Doctors have in the past exercised their judgment, and there have been innumerable cases of silent euthanasia, active and passive, without public scrutiny. This is difficult today because of hysterical surveillance by disciples of the right-to-life movement, and because doctors are fearful of malpractice suits or legal action by the state.

Euthanasia runs the risk of being abused. There is always the danger that someone will be tempted to hasten the death of Aunt Millie without her consent, for her inheritance. Moreover, there is the problem that individuals may evaluate their health conditions incorrectly and conclude prematurely that they have an incurable illness. Some individuals have a low threshold for pain and may prefer to die rather than continue to suffer, even though the prognosis for recovery may be good. Therefore, society ought to move cautiously about encouraging euthanasia on demand.

Nonetheless, I submit that the right to euthanasia ought to be respected—with safeguards. Above all, it must be based on informed consent and not done impetuously or under duress. The decision should be a reflective one reached over a period of time. Matters are complicated when the individual has had a sudden stroke or is in a coma, and we are unable to ascertain his wishes. My wife's father, a vigorous Frenchman of seventy-seven, in apparent good health, was felled by a sudden stroke and almost completely paralyzed. He was unable to control his bowels or to speak. He lingered in such a state for four months. A CAT scan indicated that so much brain damage had occurred that his chances of recovery were nil. In Roman Catholic southern France, one cannot even lightly utter the word *euthanasia*. And so a proud and self-reliant man suffered until the bitter end, with little dignity and almost no quality of life. In his case, one could not ask him what should be done: Did he wish to live or die? Should he be resuscitated? (He was, several times.) Should his feeding tubes be removed? (They were apparently very painful.) One solution is to draft a living will, before an illness strikes, to deal with such eventualities. Another is for a person to make his intentions known to those about him, who could serve as his proxy.

One complication is the fact that in some cases one cannot know whether the patient will die or pull through. A new cure may be discovered, or the patient may summon sufficient resources to recover and live many more years of an enjoyable life, with or without a handicap after a process of rehabilitation. Mistakes have been made in the past and no doubt will be made in the future. A good case in point concerns the distinguished American philosopher Sidney Hook, who suffered a debilitating heart attack and stroke. He concluded that his time was up, and began to insist that his wife and children pull the plug. This decision was based on a long-standing ethical belief in euthanasia. But his family refused to accede to his wishes. He remained adamant and they kept denying his request. Hook survived that crisis, and has gone on to live several more years of a productive life, for which those who know him are grateful. Yet he insisted in an article written several years after the episode that his request should not have been denied, and that if the same situation should arise again, he should be allowed to die. The exception, he says, should not be allowed to prove the rule, and he maintains that the decision should have been his.[10] Yet in such situations, other people are called upon to help. The questions here are: What is the ethical case for suicide for medical reasons? Are other people obligated to assist? Should they seek to prevent a patient from taking his own life?

2. *Suicide.* The right to suicide is extremely controversial, particularly when it is contemplated by young people. Religious moralists insist that only God can determine whether we live or die. This argument is specious, for if only God can decide, then we should not attempt to stave off death; medical science would collapse, since doctors are interfering with God's will. Nor could anyone ever adopt the hero's role in battles for ideals, for to do so is often to risk a suicidal course. Japan has dramatized *hara-kiri,* and military men like Mishima have extolled it as among the highest virtues. Philosophers from Socrates to Schopenhauer have argued for suicide's permissibility in one form or another, on the basis of reflective choice.

In Socrates' last days, awaiting the carrying out of his death sentence at the hands of the Athenians, he discoursed on whether he should flee Athens, as his supporters and disciples urged, or stay and submit to what he viewed as an unjust sentence. Socrates' disciples pleaded with him to escape and live in exile, which he declined to do. Forced to drink the hemlock, he freely chose his own death, in one sense, for he refused to be civilly disobedient, to break the laws of Athens. He had no fear of death. No evil can befall a righteous man, he said, and he expressed intimations of immortality.[11] Other philosophers have also concluded that at some point it would be better to die than to live: a free, fully mature, and rational person thus can make a case for his own suicide.

I must confess that, personally, I think suicide is an act of utter folly. If all that we have is life and if we have no illusion of immortality, then we should live it fully, to the best of our ability. Life is too precious, bountiful, and worthwhile to be squandered prematurely. There is always the prospect of a brighter tomorrow, with new opportunities for creative adventure, achievement, and enjoyment. Thus, I think that giving in to the desire to commit suicide is tragic, and I can see almost no justification for it. It is particularly senseless when it is committed by young people. In such cases, we ask: Where have we failed them? Why did we not realize they were in distress? Similarly, how strange for someone in midlife, at the height of his powers, to take his own life! A friend of mine, Piet Hein Hoebens, a brilliant young editor and influential Dutch journalist who was interested in parapsychology and had written several important papers, committed suicide. All of his friends and colleagues were stunned, particularly since he was only in his thirties.

We learned later that he had for many years been suffering from depression, and had intimated to his wife on several occasions that some day he would end it all. When he finally did, those in his immediate circle were rendered speechless, feeling helpless over his act of desperation.

I can see almost no justification for such acts. We have a *prima facie* ethical obligation to stay alive, not only for ourselves, but for those around us; suicide betrays and injures those who love us. I am not an absolutist here, because some may find their personal situations so intolerable and so without redeeming meaning or hope that they may decide to terminate their lives. Obviously it is not something that I would do. But it is, after all, a personal decision, in which someone may weigh his values and obligations and conclude that he had better depart. Still, in my personal catalogue of virtues and vices, I consider suicide to be the gravest sin one can commit against oneself. Yet who can plumb the depths of human despair, and the motives that lead to self-destruction? Undoubtedly, some forms of depression are chemical in origin; some underlying psychotic disorders may be gnawing deep within the person's bowels; and he may be unable to control his choices. But for those who can, I can find no glorious or courageous sentiments in their deeds.

But the question remains: Should it be illegal for someone to try to commit suicide? I suppose that the answer is yes, insofar as he may harm others in the process. For example, if someone stands on the World Trade Tower and threatens to jump, potentially injuring pedestrians below, should we try to stop him? Yes; by psychiatric and other forms of counseling, we should seek to persuade him not to leap. Should we pump out the stomach of a person who has taken poison? There is no easy answer, but I would again say *yes*. We do not always know his motives and perhaps we can, by our compassionate concern, help bring him back to the world; perhaps he will some day be grateful to us for saving him.

If a person wishes to commit suicide and succeeds, there is nothing we can do about it. But some emotional distress may be only temporary and many failed attempts are cries for help. We should if we can try to nurture the grieving soul, and the suicidal person may go on to lead a significant and productive life.

The major justification for suicide—in my view—is in regard to passive or active euthanasia. But that act is carried out when a person is already dying, is suffering intolerable pain, and the quality of life is diminished. Under such conditions, suicide can be viewed as a reasonable act justifiable on ethical grounds.

Another case for suicide has been made that we must consider. I have in mind situations of utter hopelessness, where people are cornered, perhaps tortured unbearably, and believe that they are awaiting death. I am thinking of the many tragic cases of suicide during World War II, where victims were driven to desperation by the Nazis or Japanese, and at the point of entering the torture room or gas chamber, decided to hasten death in order to end their suffering or prevent the enemy from enforcing final control over their lives. I suppose that under such conditions, a reflective person might conclude that it would be far better to exercise an option, even if it is only to be the instrument of his own death.

3. *Infanticide.* The question of euthanasia is sometimes raised in regard to infants, even though they are not able to decide for themselves. What do we do when a severely handicapped, genetically defective, or severely retarded child is born? Is it ever permissible to terminate its life? Is infanticide justifiable? Many societies in the past have practiced it. The ancient Greeks, for example, exposed unwanted infants on a mountainside to die. I do not think that infanticide is justifiable on ethical grounds, unless the infant is severely physically handicapped, *and* is also dying. For genetically defective infants, where this can be ascertained beforehand, the best course is to abort them well before birth. But this knowledge may not always be available.

In my view, retardation is not a sufficient ground for infanticide. We have an obligation and duty to preserve and enhance innocent human life, and to try to teach these unfortunate persons through love and education to reach whatever potential they have. They have rights as human beings, equal dignity and value. They are no less entitled to moral consideration than normal children.

In some cases, however, an infant may have a debilitating disease or defect (such as spina bifida) and the prognosis is that he will die if corrective surgery or prolonged intensive care is not given. If corrective surgery or intensive care can take the infant to some level of functioning so that he can have some quality of life, then this course of action is preferred, and we even have an obligation to see that action is taken. It is only when the infant is grossly malformed and unable to function without machinery and would die extremely young anyway that we might permit it to die as quickly as possible. The proper course is the withholding of treatment, allowing nature to take its course. To keep the child alive would only prolong its agony. The ethical principles applied here are *beneficence* (we act from a sense of kindness to prevent further pain and suffering) and *nonmalfeasance* (we do not wish to inflict harm upon the baby). Each terrible life-and-death decision should be left to the parents in consultation with the doctors involved in the particular case; keeping all infants alive should not become a matter of blanket public policy, as the right-to-life groups insist.

VIII. Voluntary Associations

Individuals have a right to enter into relationships with other individuals on many levels in society. This is a voluntary act by which a person consciously decides to associate and congregate with other like-minded individuals. The relationships may range all the way from the small family unit to a club, fraternal organization, school, political party, or corporation. When such associations are large-scale and have an effect on the public and involve or influence the individuals in the community, they can be regulated or scrutinized. Such associations are not immune to the criminal laws, and if they perform a public or quasi-public function, they do not have the right to exclude other individuals on the basis of race, creed, religious orientation, or national origin.

IX. Personal Property

The realm of private conduct includes the right to own private property and to use one's personal possessions as one wishes, so long as one does not interfere with or intrude on the rights of others. Included under the heading of personal property are clothing, furniture, vehicles, homes, private businesses, and professional offices. The right to property is limited to the rules governing its use. The property must be lawfully obtained by purchase or inheritance, and lawfully disposed of. Society can place limitations on how the property is acquired (fraud, for example, is illegal). Moreover, it may tax wealth and earnings, inheritance, and in some cases, limit the kinds of communal ventures one can enter into. I am confining my discussion to private property, not corporate, which involves a public dimension, though it is sometimes difficult to distinguish the two areas. In the name of the common good, society has a right to regulate property ownership and use, particularly where other individuals are employed or involved in the process of production, distribution, or consumption. The dispute between capitalist and socialist morality will not concern us. Some socialists have sought to restrict private property, but even here it should be clear that the state ought not to deprive an individual of his personal property without due process.

Democratic societies recognize and respect the rights of individuals to conduct their own lives, satisfy their own values, and pursue their own ends and goals in order to achieve a good life. They wish to encourage the maximization of freedom of individual choice, consonant with public order and the common good. The right to privacy is an essential premise, and ultimately, the best society is one which seeks to cultivate autonomy or free choice. Such a society presupposes, however, that individuals within it will conduct themselves as responsible moral agents, that they will behave decently, and that they will tolerate and respect the rights of others. There is no guarantee that this will ensue, because ethical behavior does not develop in a vacuum. The enemies of a free society are rapacious individuals, insensitive to the needs of others, focused only on gratification and pleasure, committed to self-power and self-aggrandizement at the expense of others. It is vital, therefore, that a humane society do what it can to nurture virtue and decency in its citizens, so that they can live responsible lives.

Notes

1. John Stuart Mill, *On Liberty.*

2. Robert Nozick, *State, Anarchy, Government* (Cambridge: Harvard University Press, 1974).

3. John Money, *The Destroying Angel* (Buffalo, N.Y.: Prometheus Books, 1985), Chapter 17.

4. Gerald Larue, *Sex and the Bible* (Buffalo, N.Y.: Prometheus Books, 1983), Chapter 22.

5. "Instruction on Respect for Human Life in Its Origin and on the Dignity of Procreation: Replies to Certain Questions of the Day," Cardinal Joseph Ratzinger and Archbishop Alberto Bovone (The Vatican) February 22, 1987.

6. Thomas Szasz, *The Therapeutic State* (Buffalo, N.Y.: Prometheus Books, 1984), and also Thomas Szasz, *The Theology of Medicine* (New York: Harper and Row, 1977).

7. C. Levine and R. M. Veatch, *Cases in Bioethics: The Hastings Center Report* (Hastings-on-Hudson, N.Y., 1982).

8. Ibid.

9. Derrick Humphrey and Ann Wickett, *Jean's Way* (London: Quartet Books).

10. Sidney Hook. "In Defense of Voluntary Euthanasia," *New York Times,* March 1, 1987.

11. Plato, *Crito, Phaedo.*

Part IV

Part IV

9
The Tree
of Life

The Meaning of Life

I have throughout this book sought to defend the ethics of humanism from its detractors. There is a large body of moral wisdom and experience intrinsic to the race that we share in common. There are also new ethical principles and values that emerge in critical inquiry and can be justified on rational grounds. The common moral decencies, standards of excellence, responsibilities, the development of character, and basic human rights (including the right to privacy) provide objective standards for ethical choice. Humanistic ethics thus offers a viable alternative to transcendental systems of morality.

The critics of humanism, however, may say that we have not responded to the *ultimate* existential question posed by theists and skeptics alike. Merely to say, for example, that a person has responsibilities in life, and that if he doesn't fulfill them he is ethically underdeveloped, or that there are general human rights applicable to all societies in the world community, does not answer the ethical skeptic's quest for a *deeper* justification for ethical conduct. We are thus forced to dig into the very bedrock of our assumptions about human reality. There is no turning away from the skeptic's demands, for he wishes to keep probing, doubting that we can discover the foundations of the ethical life. He is not simply asking for a justification of the entire structure of ethical responsibilities, but is basically seeking a solution to the question of the "meaning of life."

To be told by the humanist that if one eats of the fruit of the tree of knowledge of good and evil one will find empathetic ethical knowledge is well and good. But is there not something more? What is the meaning and purpose of life itself over and beyond our obligations and duties to others? The theist has overlooked another tree in the center of the Garden of Eden: *the tree of life.* If we eat of the forbidden fruit of that tree, will we discover the ultimate secrets of life?

In Genesis, God became angry with Adam for eating of the tree of knowledge of good and evil, and drove him from Eden. God complains: "Behold, the man has become as one of us, to know good and evil" (Gen. 3:22). Fearful that Adam will go further in achieving power and perhaps begin competing with Him on His own terms, God states, "And now, lest he put forth his hand and take also of the tree of life and live forever," and drives man out of Eden, placing cherubims and flaming swords to block every path in order to keep man from entering the way of the tree of life and eating of its fruit.

What is the tree of life? There are few references to it in the Old Testament. In Proverbs, we encounter the statement: "Happy is the man that findeth wisdom and geteth understanding" (3:13). Continuing, a little later we read, "She is a tree of life to them that lay hold upon her: and happy is every one that retaineth her" (Prov. 3:18). This seems like sage advice for a humanist interested in using critical ethical intelligence. Still later we read that the righteous person shall flourish but the wicked sinner will not. Indeed, "the fruit of the righteous is a tree of life" (Prov. 11:30). This again supports moral behavior as a source of enrichment.

In Revelations, the last book of the New Testament, the metaphor of the tree of life reappears, but there is a radical shift in its meaning. Here the tree of life is related to the immortality of the soul, which becomes central to the entire Christian doctrine of salvation; but this can only be achieved through Christ. The author of Revelations claims that whosoever accepts the Gospel will be allowed "to eat of the tree of life, which is in the midst of the paradise of God" (2:7). In the last chapter of Revelations, we are told that in the heavenly city is the tree of life, which bears twelve kinds of fruit; the leaves of the tree are "for the healing of the nations" (22: 2). Only those who follow God's commandments have a right to the tree of life and may enter the gates of the city (22:14).

For the theist, the ultimate meaning of life is thus found in the role one assumes in the divine plan. Each person acts out his or her part in this drama, and can achieve eternal salvation only in terms of it. This mythological tale of the fall from God's grace and of redemption through Jesus Christ is confused with reality. It is the transcendental temptation corrupting the soul, yearning to find solace for the torment of death and finding it in a new form of eternal life beyond this one. There is no evidence that the soul is immortal. Scientific and philosophical criticism have exposed the story for what it is: a grand illusion fed by wish-fulfillment. Yet entire religious systems of belief have been fixated on a tale of fictional salvation. The humanist is skeptical of this claim: "Why live life based on a fantasy?" he asks.

In the last analysis it is the theist who can find no ultimate meaning in this life and who denigrates it. For him life has no meaning per se. This life here and now is hopeless, barren, and forlorn; it is full of tragedy and despair. The theist can only find meaning by leaving this life for a transcendental world beyond the grave. The human world as he finds it is empty of "ultimate purpose" and hence meaningless. Theism thus is an attempt to escape from the human condition; it is a pathetic deceit. To the theist, death is not real; it is not final and tragedy is not irreparable. There is always hope of some saving grace. Living in this world, unable to cope with its problems, dilemmas, and conflicts, the theist leaps beyond it into another world, more akin to his fancy—though he has not come up with a clear notion of what the soul does in eternal paradise.

I think there is something basically dissonant about the transcendental temptation expressed in theistic poetry. The unseen God, the "I am" that Moses encounters on Mount Sinai, Jesus on the cross crucified and resurrected out of the empty cave, and Gabriel visiting Mohammed as a messenger of Allah and delivering the Koran are all fanciful contrivances spun out of the web of human imagination. Belief in these tales provides a release from reality. Believers who claim historical revelation do so without sufficient evidence and on the basis of two psychological impulses: willful belief and hope in an eternal tomorrow. No doubt generation after generation of men and women have accepted the articles of the creed unquestionably: it has a powerful tradition and institutionalized clergy to support it, and there has been, historically, strong opposition to any heresy or dissent from this view. Vast efforts have been expended to perpetuate this myth and to allay any doubts of its validity. But it is, in the last analysis, the credulity of believers who reject the reality of death and accept a belief in life after life, that makes this possible.

Such religious faith is pathological. The fact that generations of men and women have praised pious credulity and have condemned skepticism about these tales is a further symptom of an underlying malady that gnaws from within the heart. The theist who asks the question, "What is the meaning of life?" and insists that without some divine purpose life would be meaningless is not only masking his own insecurity but also displaying an infantile reaction; he has little faith in his own unaided powers of reason and fragile confidence in his ability to solve the problems of life on his own. Insofar as man is dependent upon God for his very being, his life has no significance in itself. This is all the more true if this life is simply a testing ground or a waiting room for the afterlife, a way-station to hell or paradise.

This does not mean that the religious believer is entirely without enthusiasm for the plans and projects he undertakes, is devoid of passion, motivation, or the lust for living, or is unwilling to solve the problems of living. Religious people, too, have expanded frontiers and conquered and founded empires, whether in the name of God or mammon. The life-impulse is too vital to easily suppress, and theists too need to cope as best they can with the challenges they encounter. Yet this impulse is allegedly incidental to their larger serious purpose within the divine scheme, and there always lurks in the background the illusion of immortality and the promise of something else—which thwarts them from eating fully of the fruit of the tree of life here and now.

If God is dead and there is no afterlife, does man have the courage to persist? If he rejects belief in a divine providence, is he forlorn, standing alone in the wilderness, lost, without significance or hope? Is he naked before death, and will he be consumed by the anxiety that he will disappear into nothingness? Can God alone, the God of faith and prayer, restore him whole and give him the courage to face adversity and tragedy? Or can he summon his own resources and sustain himself to live fully and *become* what he wills? The theist denies that he can, for if there is no God, then life would have no ultimate goal from the standpoint of eternity. Is human life a mere chance fluctuation in the ocean of galactic time, a brief flicker of light between two oblivions—the big bang and the big crunch? Is it thereby absurd, without rhyme or reason? If God is not the ground of the moral life, is he a vital postulate of the meaningful life? If he were removed finally, would all collapse in darkness and the void? And would all human values, ideals, hopes, and aspirations then disappear? Is belief in the first cause and final judgment necessary as a cognitive and psychological support? Is that why the myths of theism have survived, ever tempting humans in the vain illusion that the tree of life can give us immortality?

Living in the Universe Without God

Modern science has dethroned the God of classical religion and challenged the idea that the universe has a fixed order of ends. In the sixteenth century, natural science dispensed with teleology in explaining the material universe: there was no warrant to read in purposes in order to account for natural phenomena. Mass and energy followed predictable laws; material phenomena did not have ends to fulfill. In the nineteenth century, the theory of evolution displaced the traditional explanations for life: there were no fixed species or entelechies, but a gradual evolution by means of chance mutation, selective reproduction, adaptation, and survival. Under the logical critiques of the philosophers, the classical proofs for the existence of God collapsed. If God existed outside the natural universe as its transcendent ground, we could know very little, if anything, about Him or His plan for the human species. Belief in God was thereby shown to be an article of faith; it did not rest on proof. Scholarly criticism of the Bible and Koran has demonstrated that these books are not the finger of God etching its way through human history, but the product of human contrivance.

Atheists and agnostics deny that the traditional theistic God exists. The skeptic simply states that there is not sufficient evidence for the existence of a transcendent diety, and that the idea that He created the universe to fulfill His plan is without any reasonable foundation.

If this is the case, what follows for the human species? The earth, which is a minor satellite of the sun, speeds through space, caught up in the Milky Way, which is one galaxy of stars among billions of other galaxies. There *may* be other forms of life, perhaps even intelligent life, in other parts of the universe; that remains to be discovered and verified. But to think that everything on this minor planet and in the total universe was created for man is to inflate our egos. Is it not an unwarranted anthropocentric imposition on reality? Even if we seek to explain that the big bang in physics was due to some cosmological principle of intelligence, this does not entitle us to invest such an impersonal force with any of the moral qualities possessed by human beings. Nor does it allow us to devise a purposeful human existence purely by reference to this principle. It is an anthropomorphic expression of conceit to believe that God created man in His own image. On the contrary, the reverse is true: We created God in our image to fulfill our dreams and hopes of eternity. The anthropic principle expresses human pride inflated to the nth degree. Our hymnals and prayerbooks fervently express the hope that God the Father exists and that we are part of His scheme. All of this devotion is for naught, for the God of orthodox theism is no longer believable to the scientific humanist.

If the classical God of theism is dead for religious skeptics who have pondered the question, then what is in store for us? Where does human purpose come from? Could life have any meaning under such conditions?

Let me say that the question as traditionally framed is ambiguous. *Meaning,* as I interpret it, is a *relational* concept. Something does not have "meaning" in itself in some isolated or abstract sense, or in the universe at large. Meaning, like virtue, is related to some form of sentient life, which is able to connect, interpret, and relate things. To say that something has meaning implies that it makes sense or is significant to some conscious being. An organism learns from past experience that certain parts of its experience are related to others. Sudden thunder and lightning are signs of an impending storm. They have meaning for an organism that may run for shelter. A growling dog is a sign of danger, a purring cat conveys comfort. These events can be interpreted for what may follow, for their connections to natural events and their eventualities. In the human context, it is not simply natural signs that are interpreted, but symbols also take on subtle nuances within the processes of linguistic communication.

Various levels of meaning may be inferred from their functional relationships. The axioms, postulates, and theorems of mathematics have clearly specified meanings within a logical system. The metaphors of poets express another kind of meaning. It is difficult to sustain the argument that meanings subsist independently as reified essences in some transcendental realm. Meanings function within contexts of mentation and communication. They make little sense abstracted from them. What would the universe be like if conscious living beings were not present? This is a difficult question to fathom, for to say that something has meaning implies that it means something—in terms of response and understanding—to someone.

The secular humanist asks: If the deity vacates the universe, would things still have meaning? Yes, of course, but only in regard to living species, their interests, or responses. Natural events in the universe have no meaning in isolation, or in themselves, but only for us (or other species). We may ask: What is the meaning of a sunset, a meandering river, a volcanic eruption, or a supernova that explodes far out in the Magellanic archipelago? These events are all natural physical phenomena that can be explained by reference to discerned regularities and material causes. They simply happen. A sunset does not occur so that the human species can enjoy its beauty, nor does the volcano erupt to inspire fear. The sunset is caused by the energy we see emitted from the sun as the earth turns away from it on its axis; a volcano erupts and spews out hot gases and lava because of stresses within the core of the earth. Whether we find a river "lazy" or a supernova "magnificent" depends upon our point of view. It is we who react to natural phenomena. We may of course read into them whatever we wish. They have the potential to be seen by sentient beings, and to be found beautiful or awesome, lonely or frightening. But it is a conscious being who can creatively express for himself and others the meanings he perceives in natural events.

We often ask: What is the meaning of human life *itself* in the universe at large? But again, this question has no sense separate from the living beings (including other species) who function and experience life. Meanings are what we find in life and/or what we choose to invest life with. Life has meaning primarily for the sentient beings who live; it is relative to their needs, interests, longings, sufferings, and delights.

Theists, who claim to derive meaning from God, are simply reading into nature their own conceptions of a deity. Since religion is a product of human imagination, woven from the materials of human passion— fears, forebodings, anxieties, hopes, yearnings, and dreams—God has meaning in the universe only insofar as we attribute to Him the meanings we hope for. We wish He would answer our prayers, ease our pain and suffering, and save us from death. If we were to dispense with an idea of God, meaning would not collapse, because meaning is a human invention. Humans have been ingenious in inventing an infinite variety of belief systems that enable us to cope with the problems encountered in living. The human brain is adroit in spinning out tales to console and inspire. Nature is nature: but we add to and embroider upon it. Culture is the web of the intricate meanings that we have spun.

Creating Our Own Meanings

Life has no meaning per se; it does, however, present us with innumerable opportunities, which we can either squander and retreat from in fear or seize with exuberance. The meaning of life is not to be found in a secret formula discovered by ancient prophets or priests, who withdraw from it in quiet contemplation and release. It can be discovered by anyone and everyone who can untap an inborn zest for living. It is found within living itself, as it reaches out to create new conditions of experience. Eating of the fruit of the tree of life gives us the bountiful enthusiasm for living. The "ultimate" value for the humanist is the conviction that life can be found good in and of itself. Each moment has a kind of preciousness and attractiveness. The so-called secret of life is thus an open secret that can be deciphered by everyone. It is found in the experiences of living: in the joy of a fine banquet, the strenuous exertion of hard work, the poignant melodies of a symphony, the satisfaction of an altruistic deed, the excitement of an orgasm, the elegance of a mathematical proof, the invigorating adventure of a mountain climb, the pleasure of quiet relaxation, the lusty singing of an anthem, the vigorous cheering of a sports contest, the reading of a delicate sonnet, the joys of parenthood, the pleasures of friendship, the quiet satisfaction in serving our fellow human beings—in all of these activities and more.

Perhaps it is because the dour and fearful religionist concentrates all "meaning" on God and on his hope for a future life that he cannot fully enjoy these experiences, and hence, in a vicious circle, has to look outside his own life for meaning.

It is in the present moment of experience as it is brought to fruition, as well as in the memory of past experiences and the expectation of future ones, that the richness of life is exemplified and realized. The meaning of life is that it can be found to be good and beautiful and exciting on its own terms for ourselves, our loved ones, and other sentient beings. It is found in the pleasures of creative activities, wisdom, and righteousness. One doesn't need more than that and hopefully one will not settle for less.

The meaning of life is tied up intimately with our plans and projects, the goals we set for ourselves, our dreams, and the fruition of them. We create our own conscious meanings; we invest the cultural and natural worlds with our own interpretations. We discover, impose upon, and add to nature. Meaning is found in the lives of the ancient Egyptians, in their culture—labeled "religion"—built around Isis and Osiris and the pyramids, or in the ruminations of the ancient prophets of the Old Testament. It is exemplified by the Athenian philosopher standing in the Acropolis deliberating about the fate of the city-state. It is seen in the structure of the medieval town, built upon a rural economy, feudalism, and a Christian cultural backdrop. It is experienced by the Samurai warrior in the context of Japanese culture, in the hopes and dreams of the Incas of Peru, by the native Watusi tribes in Africa, and in the exotic Hindu and Muslim cultures of India and southern Asia. And it is exemplified anew in modern post-industrial urban civilizations of the present-day world, which give us new cultural materials and new opportunities for adventure.

All of this illustrates the fact that human beings have found their meanings within the context of an historical cultural experience, and in how they are able to live and participate within it. Life had meaning to them; only the content differed; the form and function were similar. Life, when fully lived under a variety of cultural conditions, can be euphoric and optimistic; it can have intrinsic merit and excellence for its own sake, and it can be a joy to experience and a wonder to behold.

The Tragic Sense

The theist, however, is a profound pessimist; none of this, he remonstrates, is enough. Life, real life, by itself, is finally empty and devoid of purpose or meaning. A detached, melancholy fatalist, or a nay-saying critic, unable to fully participate in or savor the fullness of life, may reject the possibility of achieving happiness here and now. He may find sex, adventure, or art unsatisfying in and of itself. He is interested in spiritual values and his ultimate transcendental fate, which, when compared with the material and natural values of this life, pale into insignificance.

There is a basic indictment that the despairing pessimist levels against life. He is crushed by evil in the world and by what he considers to be original sin. For him the evils of life outbalance the goods. He focuses on the worst outcomes of our strivings and yearnings.

Let us examine the main lines of the pessimist's indictment:

1. *The vale of tears argument.* Life is full of suffering, pain, and anxiety. It is not a source of laughter and joy, but of sorrow, tragedy, duplicity, cruelty, diseases, injustice, and evil. There is failure and disappointment. There are accidents, tragedies, and defeats. There is ongoing conflict and strife, war and violence, enmity and hatred.

2. *Human beings are impotent.* Some things are within our power to achieve, but most of the important events that befall us lie beyond our ability to prevent: a sudden disease, an unforeseen accident, or an unexpected anomaly. Life is ambiguous, full of contingent events. No one can fully predict the future or prepare for calamity. What will be will be; the tides of fate and injustice are such that they will overwhelm us. There is little we can do against them but submit and suffer. We can only apprehend with passivity the vastness of the universe, and, perhaps, by prayer and supplication, be rescued from the worst tragedies that may befall us.

3. *The myth of Sisyphus.* Life is full of endless repetition and hard work, and yet our gains never last. Sisyphus was condemned to push a large rock up the mountain but was never able to complete his task, for when he reached the top, the stone rolled back, forceing him to repeat the labor endlessly. The litany is that we work hard and toil, but there will be no final success or solution, no rest for our tired spirits and aching souls.

4. *Schopenhauer's dilemma.* We fluctuate between restlessness and boredom. We are goaded by desires, we strive to achieve our ends; in the process we are uneasy. But when we do satisfy them, we are quickly satiated and ennui sets in. There is never any surcease from the mad process, but a constant state of flux between two unfortunate extremes. Only nirvana or nothingness can release us from the pounding of desire and the torment of dissatisfaction.

5. *The impermanence of things.* We discover that nothing is permanent or absolute; all things that come into being also pass away. The beautiful sapling grows into the splendid oak tree, but it eventually dies. The young stallion becomes the decrepit old horse. The lovely young girl becomes the aged matron; the handsome youth, the senile and dottering fool. The child on the beach playfully builds a palace of sand, but the ocean waves soon swamp it and its distinctive form is flattened. All institutions and constitutions eventually are consumed

by time. The majestic architectural remains of the great civilizations of the past are today nothing but faded reminders of their once great grandeur—they have no life in themselves. The inexorable destiny of all human institutions is decay. In the long run, all the vibrant ideals that men and women have lived for will eventually disappear, for, from the eye of eternity, whatever we now do will dissipate and be forgotten.

6. *The finality of death.* In the last accounting, the most awesome reality facing us is our own finitude and eventual demise. The existential *angst* that each and every person faces is the fact that he and his loved ones will some day be buried (or cremated) and will disintegrate. From the standpoint of death, everything appears meaningless. For what end all the yearnings and strivings, all of the hoping and cheering? Everything that we have ever done in life will erode away and be destroyed. Everything will be reduced to its simplest parts and returned to the eternal flux. From ashes to ashes, from dust to dust—we too will be submerged in the endless sea of time.

The theist finds these realities unbearable, and so he postulates a God who will free him from the defects—the evil and tragedy—he encounters. He extends all of his desires and dreams to another life in which there is no restlessness, no boredom, no impotence, and no wickedness, but rather, ultimate permanence, goodness, and eternal life. Realistically viewed, however, his own belief system is in itself an idle dream to be replaced by others, and it will crumble along with the other barriers erected to hold back the ravages of time. If all things are impermanent, so too are the religious monuments men have erected.

The theist's world is only a dream world; it is a feeble escape into a future that will never come. He is unable to lead this life fully, and hence has wasted part of it. Consumed by a sense of sin, guilt, or worry about a tomorrow that may never come, did he, in the last analysis, betray the promise inherent in his life because he believed in a myth? Would he have been better off without the solace of his illusions?

Given the propensity of humans to spin salvational tales of consolation, we can seriously raise the question of whether we can live without them. If we were to abandon our illusions, would we be better able to learn to cope with failure, defeat, impermanence, and death, and stand up to the real world? Can we humans summon the psychological resources and the courage to live on our own and face the universe realistically?

The humanist's rejoinder to the pessimist is optimism: *Life is, or can be, worth living,* he affirms.

The real question to be raised is whether life is worth living on its own terms, without any illusions of immortality. Unfortunately, that question cannot be resolved entirely by reason. There are rational arguments that one can present to the forlorn spirit who is crushed by events and unable to cope with them. Religion is a method of adjusting by escaping into reverie and unreality. Ultimately, being able to live as a humanist may only be a question of courage and motivation, and if motivation is gravely impaired or absent, there may be little we can do to engender it. The ultimate courage is to be and to *become* in spite of existential reality, and to overcome adversity and exult in our ability to do so.

The Bountiful Joys

One can respond to the pessimist's catalogue of the evils of life by presenting an opposing statement of its manifold possibilities and joys.

1. *The fullness of life.* The vale of tears is balanced by the summit of joys, the sorrows of life by its achievements, the depths of despair by the peaks of success. If life has tragic dimensions, it also has intrinsically worthwhile experiences. Though we may suffer grief at some moments, at other times we experience humor and laughter, enjoyment and delight. Although the priests remind us of the failures and defeats of human existence, humorists delight in fun, and we can savor and find pleasurable moments of experience. There is room in life for tears; but rather than submit to our fate, we can create a better life by exerting intelligence and effort, and by reducing or eliminating ignorance, hunger, deprivation, disease, and conflict. Many of the ills of life can thus be remedied and ameliorated; the goods can outweigh and outdistance the evils, the tears can be balanced by joys.

2. *Human power.* We need a proper sense of our own powers. Although there *are* some things that are beyond our ability to eradicate or control—like death, if not taxes—the history of civilization illustrates that fortitude and intelligence used wisely enable us to overcome adversities. Earlier civilizations may have been unduly pessimistic about sin, corruption, and natural catastrophes. But science and technology enable us to understand the causes of phenomena and to find appropriate remedies for them. To the primitive mind, there first appears to be

no rhyme or reason to things. A flood washes away crops; a village starves. Perhaps we'd better sacrifice a child or a lamb to appease a god's anger—such is primitive "reasoning." And those who so "reason" submit to their fate in the hope that the gods will rescue them. For things he cannot control, a man feels need to develop some notion of a divine order as way to lessen his anxiety.

But we should recognize that although we may suffer misfortune, there is always the possibility of good fortune. Today's sorrow may give way to tomorrow's luck. The drama of human civilization also reveals the potentialities for untapping new discoveries and powers. It is by means of creative work that we can overcome adversity; we have the powers that will enable us to change things for the better. We need to gather our resources after defeat and strive anew. Human will *can* ameliorate adversity. The future depends on perseverence, ingenuity, and the indomitable human spirit.

3. *The satisfaction of striving.* The myth of Sisyphus has exaggerated the dilemma, because there can be significant enjoyment and enrichment in working to reach our goals. Performing a task repeatedly need not be painful drudgery, but a source of immense satisfaction—as athletes discover in endless hours of practicing for a sports contest. Indeed, perhaps it is the quest itself that is the chief source of life's enrichment. The lover pursues the beloved, the entrepreneur builds a new industry, the novelist spends years on his magnum opus. It is within the creative acts themselves that we find the stimulation. It is not what we achieve so much as the activities undertaken in achieving it. The means expended to attain our ends cannot be divorced from the ends themselves. We should not condemn all labor as a crushing burden. Indeed, having nothing to do in the Garden of Eden or paradise may be equivalent to a state of hell.

4. *Expectation and realization.* Schopenhauer's dilemma can of course be rebutted. His attitude expresses the reactions of a jaded sensibility. What about the exuberant attitude, which finds the opposite qualities in life? There are great and exciting expectations and desires that stimulate us to action, and there are great thrills in experiencing and striving for them. When we finally achieve our ends there are the joys of consummation, the immense gratification in quenching our thirst, satisfying our hunger, and releasing our passions. Moreover, once we have attained our goals, new and interesting ones always emerge. Thus

we stand between the pleasures of expectation and the delights of realization.

5. *Novelty.* In answer to the argument of impermanence, one may respond that although it is true that nothing lasts, the flux of change has some redeeming value.

The many uses of history. First, the efforts of earlier civilizations are not entirely forgotten; they remain in human memory, in the artifacts, works of art, books, and monuments that have survived. They have become part of world culture, and we appreciate and profit from them. Some good that we do may survive us, and future generations perhaps will be indebted to us for what we have bequeathed to them. Using ethnology and archeology, we are able to partially uncover and reconstruct past civilizations. We can put them in broader perspective as part of world history, from the cave drawings of prehistoric men and women in France, Africa, and Australia, down to the present moment. The past thus becomes meaningful in the present, as each culture assimilates, appreciates, and reinterprets its past heritage for itself.

Still, the impermanence of things is an indelible part of reality. One can see this in astronomy, where the cosmic scene is a spectacle of the birth and death of stars and galaxies, all moving at tremendous speeds in an ever-expanding universe. Perhaps everything that has ever been can potentially be rediscovered in someone's present.

The appreciation of novelty. Second, there is always something new under the sun. We can see this in the world of manufactured objects, where we await with great anticipation the latest brand or model; yesterday's product is already outmoded, tomorrow's may be perfected. This is no doubt an illusion, yet last season's fashions, books, or styles give way to those of the upcoming season. The splendid walnut tree eventually perishes, but there are new trees to replace it. Caesar may die and all may mourn him, but Augustus will reign. There is the excitement of something new—which may at first shock us by its audacity. Granted there is grandeur in the classical styles, but these will be replaced by different modes of expression, themselves perhaps destined to become classics and to survive their detractors. Thus there is some virtue to impermanence. Uniqueness, individuality, and novelty all have some place in a pluralistic universe and can be savored for their own sake while they last. Nothing lasts forever, moans the melancholic. Yes, I reply, but how lovely are the new sprouts emerging to take their place!

6. *The tree of life.* Last of all, we are reminded, are senility, death

and nothingness, which await every human being. That is a brute fact, and there is no escaping it. We can stave off death and prolong life by modern medicine, and in the future the human species may find new ways of extending life far beyond threescore and ten by proper nutrition, exercise, and medical therapy. We can hope that there will be breakthroughs for future generations that will increase longevity significantly, so that men and women may live and enjoy life for many decades more in reasonably good health. We are reminded of death by the pessimists, of life by the optimists. Given the fact of death, our main focus should be on life—not to pine about its termination, but to take every moment to be precious.

Life Is Worth Living!

My argument may fall on deaf ears. Some individuals have been so turned off by life's challenges and responsibilities that they claim to find it distasteful, debilitating, and depressing. They are so weighed down by burdens that their only response is negativity. They are dismayed by and even angry at the exuberant person. They resent mirth or laughter; they are always serious. Some may, in moments of desperation, even contemplate suicide.

How do we respond to such individuals, who do not find life worth living? I suppose that at some point logic fails, and we cannot prove anything to them by argument; for the zest for living is instinctive and noncognitive. If it is absent, there may be some underlying physiological or psychosomatic malady gnawing at the marrow. The exacerbated tragic sense has many causes, and who can say with certainty what deep-seated cause has led to a distorted sense of reality? Extreme depression may be physiological, even genetic, in origin. But its origin may also be found in the frustration of one's basic needs. It may have its roots in homeostatic imbalance, the repression of the sexual libido, the lack of love, friendship, or community, the failure of self-respect, the inability to find some creative work or a beloved cause to strive for, or the lack of wisdom. Presumably, if these needs were satisfied, a person could grow and develop, and might find some creative basis for a meaningful and enriched life. If a man doesn't find his present life worth living, then perhaps he ought to put himself in a situation where he might.

Countless individuals have sung praises to the tree of life in the past and will continue to do so in the future. The fruit of the tree of life is wholesome and nourishing, and in eating it we find that its secret is that *life is intrinsically good.* This is the basic touchstone for the ethics of humanism. Each and every person needs to create the conditions that will enable him to live richly and joyously. This, in the last analysis, is the purpose of all moral and ethical rules and regulations. They are good and right not simply in themselves but also for their consequences—for what they make possible: wholesome, creative, happy lives. The common moral decencies and responsibilities need to be respected as essential to the very framework of life in the community. But the test of an ethical system is also whether it enables individuals to live exuberantly. Generation upon generation of human beings in the past have found life rewarding, and generation upon generation no doubt will continue to do so in the future. We need not escape to nirvana or seek salvation elsewhere—which is actually an escape to *nowhere.* The acts of creative living, including the sharing of life with others, is the *summum bonum* of the human condition. That is the response the humanist gives to the theist. There is nothing ultimate or absolute beyond the living of life fully: *it is its own reward.*

Postscript on Barbarism: The Dark Side of the Moon

Perhaps my thesis is too optimistic. Perhaps I have a distorted sense of the positive reaches of humanist ethics or of the intrinsic potentiality of human beings for achieving the good. The pessimist will no doubt counter my thesis with a full litany of the perfidious horrors of human history and of the tendency in certain eras for human beings to resort to the most unspeakable moral crimes. All of this allegedly points to the failure of purely humanistic or secular moralities in the face of evil. An extreme illustration of human wickedness is attempted genocide: the Roman massacre of the Carthaginians, the barbarian invasions of Rome, the bloody Crusades, the Inquisition, the Turkish slaughter of the Armenians in World War I, Stalin's liquidation of millions in the gulag, the Nazi extermination of the Jews, and the forced marches inflicted by the Khmer Rouge in Cambodia.

I do not hold a doctrine of original sin. I do not believe that human beings are born depraved. Nor do I hold the contrary naive view that all human beings are by nature good, that they naturally seek good, and that sin is simply due to ignorance. Human beings are born neither good nor evil, but are capable of both. Although we are capable of a deep-seated moral sensibility, a wild beast also seems to lurk within, able to pounce when uncaged and commit immoral deeds. Perhaps both impulses exist side by side within the human breast. How do we ascertain which will be expressed? Does it depend upon conditions in the environment, on whether positive and ameliorative tendencies will present themselves? Or should we give a genetic account of evil? Do we need to apply strong social sanctions to repress the evil tendencies within?

The most profound depths of human depravity have been revealed in modern times: The Nazi era is one such testimony to human evil. Was this an aberration of history or does it tell us something about human nature that we have chosen to overlook?

My own personal experience of the crimes of Hitler and his followers sears my memory as I recall the events of World War II. I can testify to the horror of the Holocaust. I was an American GI, barely eighteen years old, serving in the Ninth and Third Armies that liberated Europe and helped defeat Nazi Germany. I arrived at Dachau and Buchenwald days after the liberation of those concentration camps. When I first visited Dachau, I stood in the pit where the ashes and bones of thousands of victims were strewn. I saw the high piles of clothing and shoes that had been seized from the victims. Later I visited Buchenwald and still later was with the army that took Pilsen in Czechoslovakia, virtually the last major city to be freed of the yoke of the Wehrmacht. I spoke to "displaced persons," as they were euphemistically called, victims of the Nazi scourge, who had suffered the torments of the extermination camps, and who with muted whispers recounted the tales of horror: men, women, and children herded into cattle cars, starved and beaten, driven into gas chambers, and then reduced to ashes.

One elderly Czech woman whom I met in the Sudetenland told me about her son, who she said had been a communist and was imprisoned by the Gestapo four years earlier, and whom she had not heard from since. She asked me, now that the war was nearing its end, whether he was still alive. I did not have the heart to tell her that he was most probably dead. Another man, a Jew we called Lieberman, had only an undershirt and trousers when I met him. He began working as an orderly for our unit in Munich. He had been an inmate in nearby Dachau, where he worked for four years in the crematorium. Dachau was not specifically a death fcamp like Auschwitz, which was explicitly charged with exterminating "undesirables." Nonetheless, starvation, typhus, torture, and beatings were common, and the death toll was high at Dachau. He related to me the horror of the Nazi labor camps. What was it that enabled human beings to reduce other humans to a class of subhumans and to treat them worse than animals, brutally and without any dignity? How can we explain the silent complicity of countless millions who made this possible?

I was in an Army unit that was responsible for rounding up and imprisoning a group of S.S. officers. They were polite and considerate in their relations with us—of course, they were the remnants of a once-proud army. I had a conversation with a highranking S.S. officer, whom I got to know and who told me he was related to the famous Messerschmidt aircraft family. I told him that I could understand the incarceration of men as prisoners of war and perhaps even their forced labor as part of the German war effort, but how could he explain, let alone justify, the deliberate extermination of innocent women, children, and elderly persons? He looked at me and replied, "It was necessary, for one never knows what will come from a Jewish womb." I stood horrified. Here was a man who, to all outward appearances, was civilized and cultured. Appealing to racist doctrines of Aryan superiority and Jewish inferiority, he thought he was able to justify genocide. Was he an aberration, or is there something despicable and evil deep within the bowels of human nature that can be aroused by an unrestrained tyrant like Hitler?

At that time there were millions of foreign laborers who had been imported into Germany and were working on the farms and in the factories. The allies called them "slave laborers." Our army liberated thousands in the Münster area. What distressed me was that once freed, they began to pillage the countryside, and rape and murder civilians; and so we had to round them up and put them in detention camps. Large numbers did not wish to return to the Soviet Union, for life was better for them in Nazi Germany. I was dismayed at the tales they told me of Stalin's labor camps, the terror and repression their friends or relatives had suffered, and their intense fear of returning. Many, we later discovered, were forcibly repatriated to the Soviet Union by the Allied forces and imprisoned or executed upon arrival.

How explain such barbarism? Can only a theistic system of morality prevent it?

Three ingredients were present in the Nazi and Stalinist gulags.

First, an ideological fanaticism, which permitted entire groups of people to be labeled the enemy—Jews and Gypsies by the Nazis; capitalists or kulaks by the Marxist-Stalinists. This so perverted logic and moral restraint that any kind of savagery could be justified. Hatred and resentment thus smouldered, and other humans were fiendishly reduced to nakedness and destroyed by their tormentors. The Jewish question could only be solved by genocide, said the Nazis; class enemies of the revolution had to be liquidated, said the Stalinists. Second, these were totalitarian societies in which all power was concentrated in the hands of a small, dictatorial group. There was no legal right of opposition, no democratic criticism permitted to restrain their unlimited power. The democratic principle of tolerance was abandoned to the fury of self-righteous, demonic fanatics. Third, the infamous doctrine accepted was that one could use any means—including terror and genocide—to achieve one's ends. This led to the degradation of the common moral decencies, ethical principles, and human rights. Moral development was denied and an ethic of command and obedience was enforced. One's obligation was to follow orders, said the Nazi Adolf Eichmann, who saw to it that the trains arrived on time at the death camps. Similarly, the comrades of the Party had to follow the orders of the sacred church of Marxist-Leninism without any expression of disloyalty. There was no place for dissent.

Is there a monster deep within human nature that gives birth to such heinous crimes? I prefer to believe that *such horrors are aberrant and contrary to our deeper moral sensibilities.* (I hope that I will not be accused of excessive humanistic idealism.) The Nazis tried to hide their foul crimes and to exterminate in secret. Stalinists sought to cover up their terrible deeds, as the Moscow show trials of the late 1930s indicate, as if they knew that they were flouting the elementary moral decencies essential to any civilized community. They were madmen overflowing with misplaced visions, not harbingers of a new age of morality; they were despots consumed by hatred and corrupted by a failure of ethical wisdom. I do not think that an ethic based only on a theistic god can restrain the beast within—especially as we ponder the brutal wars inspired by religious zealots, who have soaked the soil with the blood of human beings who were also, presumably, created by their God. Unfortunately, under certain social conditions satanic behavior is given full rein, and the impulses for moral virtue are vanquished.

These sad facts are all the more reason why a humanistic ethic needs to be developed—one based not on theism or ideology but on a genuine concern for other human beings and a willingness to tolerate diversity and differences. Humanistic ethics is deeply committed to ethical principles and values, and it abhors any flouting of the common moral decencies. At its heart is the recognition that human rights apply to *all* men and women. It is only in such an enriched ethical environment that we can hope to realize the fullness of life for everyone. Under trying conditions, we must remember that the other side of the moon is bathed with sunlight.

In Summary

I may now sum up my argument. At least two main sources of morality have developed historically: transcendental theistic systems based on the commandments of faith and established by custom; and normative principles and values grounded in critical ethical inquiry.

Theistic systems of morality are unable to cope adequately with the conflicts of the modern world. They attempt to hold men and women in bondage to the limited moral visions spawned in the infancy of the race. They advise or imply retreat into a cocoon in an elusive quest for salvation. The old verities are not fully applicable to the new realities of a world in which there is rapid technological, economic, social, cultural, and political change.

New sources of ethical wisdom can be discovered, but only by eating of the fruit of the tree of knowledge of good and evil. Since being cast out of Eden, human beings have the exciting option of becoming responsible ethical persons, helping to solve the challenges of the future by the use of critical intelligence.

The ethics of humanism draws deeply from the well of philosophical wisdom—of Greece and Rome, the Renaissance, the Enlightenment—and modern scientific learning. Critical ethical inquiry provides meaningful guidelines for ethical choice; we need to draw upon the best of the past—the common moral decencies that are the collective heritage of civilization, as well as standards of excellence that autonomous and rational persons exemplify. Humanism recognizes that individuals have responsibilities to themselves and to others in society, that we need to develop character, internalize compassion and empathy in our children, and to bring forth their capacity for ethical cognition. In the last analysis it is only by developing new principles relevant to the new age that reason will best serve us.

The ethical conceptions of tomorrow must be truly planetary in perspective. We must transcend the limits of the narrow loyalties and parochial chauvinisms of the past, and recognize that basic human rights are universal in scope, for all persons are part of a community of humankind.

We need not submit to pessimism or despair. We can live full and significant lives here and now. Eating of the fruit of the tree of life, we discover that intrinsic meanings emerge in the creative processes of living. Whether a person is able to enhance the good life depends upon him and what he does. Each person is responsible in large measure for his or her own destiny. Each person can untap the bountiful joys of life. This is true for everyone; we must learn to live, love, and work together in shared ethical communities. And it is true especially for those who have developed not only a sense of their own personal worth but also of the personal worth and dignity of every other human being in the world community.

Index